Tennessee Williams

Tennessee Williams relaxing in his Key West Studio

T e n n e s s e e   W i l l i a m s

Everyone Else Is
an Audience

Ronald Hayman

Yale University Press
New Haven and London

Set in Janson Text by SX Composing Ltd., Essex
Printed in Great Britain by Biddles Ltd., Guildford and Kings Lynn

Library of Congress Cataloging-in-Publication Data
Hayman, Ronald, 1932–
    Tennessee Williams : everyone else is an audience / Ronald Hayman.
        p.   cm.
    Includes bibliographical references (p.) and index.
    ISBN 0–300–05414–9 (alk. paper)
    1. Williams, Tennessee, 1911–1983.   2. Dramatists, American—20th century—Bibliography.   I. Title.
PS3545.I5365Z67   1993
812'.54—dc20   93–2544
                                                          CIP

A catalogue record for this book is available from the British Library.

The paper in this book meets the guidelines for permanence and durability of the Committee on Production Guidelines for Book Longevity of the Council on Library Resources.

10 9 8 7 6 5 4 3 2 1

C o n t e n t s

Acknowledgments

After accepting the commission from Yale University Press to write this book, I was invited by the BBC to make a radio program about Tennessee Williams and New Orleans with the producer Piers Plowright. Before and after arriving there with the sound engineer Roger Dowling to make a series of recordings, we received a great deal of friendly help from Bob Fleshman, Lucy Core, Jean Bultman, Kenneth Holditch, Julia Burka, George Schmitt, and many other people we interviewed, including Becky Allen, Ray Benoit, Rebecca Lentz, Dan Moseley, Walter Myles, and Bruce Raeburn. The program was called "A Bus Named Desire."

I went on to do research in the archives at Columbia University in New York and the Humanities Research Center at the University of Texas in Austin. I am grateful to the librarians and archivists and to the other people who helped me while I was in the United States: James Kilroy, Jane Smith, Sarah and David Chalfant, and Erika Goldman.

I must also thank Bernard Braden and Leo McGuire, who shared their memories of Tennessee Williams and the original London production of *Streetcar* with me; Catharine Carver, who read through a draft of the book, making invaluable annotations; and Robert Baldock and Susan Laity of Yale University Press, who made many helpful suggestions.

Photo Credits

The following individuals and institutions kindly supplied photographs for inclusion in the book: Associated Press, London, on pages 195, 202, 223; British Film Institute Stills, Posters, and Designs, London, 114, 130, 132, 134, 148, 149, 150, 152, 153, 159, 162, 175, 178, 179, 184, 189, 190, 191; Gillian Drake, Provincetown, Mass., 118; The Goodman Theatre, Chicago, 235, 236; Photography Collection, Harry Ransom Humanities Research Center, The University of Texas at Austin, frontispiece, 2, 3, 4, 7, 11, 15, 19, 21, 25, 27, 29, 31, 38, 39, 40, 43, 51, 59, 65, 71, 131, 144, 155, 156; The Historic New Orleans Collection, Museum/Research Center, 54, 55, 79, 103, 109, 111, 214, 238, Accession Numbers 1981.324.3.110, VC Sq6L, VC Sq63, 1979.89.7408, VC Sq42, 1976.36.18, VC Sq103, 1983.56.2; The Hulton Deutsch Collection, London, 62, 125, 126, 128; Museum of the City of New York, The Byron Collection, 105; Museum of the City of New York, The Theater Collection, 96, 115; The New York Public Library for the Performing Arts, 29, 157; Popperfoto, London, 188; Tennessee Williams Papers, Rare Book and Manuscript Library, Columbia University, 13; From the collections of the Texas/Dallas History and Archives Division, Dallas Public Library, 107; University of Iowa Archives, 44, 45, 49, 50.

Prologue:
Blue Devils

"Flee, Flee This Sad Hotel" was Tennessee Williams's original title for the memoirs he published in 1975, when he was sixty-four. He took the phrase from Anne Sexton's poem "Flee on Your Donkey," which starts:

Because there was no other place
to flee to
I came back to the scene of the disordered senses.

Here she is picking up Rimbaud's phrase "disordering of all the senses," and the sad hotel is a mental hospital. She has been interned in it before, and, returning, she has to surrender her car keys and her cash, keeping only her cigarettes. She reflects on the repetitiveness of her problems and on her isolation:

Everyone has left me
except my muse,
that good nurse.[1]

The poem both describes and exemplifies her way of translating experiences and mental processes into poetry. She no longer expects to recover—treatment can educate but not cure her. The doctors had promised her a different world, but nothing has changed. That is why she must flee the sad hotel; otherwise she will die there, still trapped in "the fool's disease."

She committed suicide at the age of forty-six; Tennessee Williams survived till he was almost seventy-two, and he was less deliberate than Rimbaud in using drugs to disorder his senses, but the words *flee*, *sad*, and *hotel* would all have been appropriate. Constantly restless, he could rarely settle anywhere for more than a few months, and he lived, as he says in the memoirs, "a life full of rented rooms." He concedes: "One should not refer to one's life as a sad hotel when it has often been a merry tavern. . . . It is quite dishonest to pretend one is eager to vacate it." On the other hand, his spells of happiness were comparatively brief, and he often believed himself to be on the verge of madness. "My nerves are tied in knots today," he wrote in July 1943, "I have plunged into one of my periodic neuroses, I call them 'blue devils,' and it is like having wild-cats under my skin. They are a Williams family trait, I suppose. Destroyed my sister's mind and made my father a raging drunkard. In me they take the form of interior storms that show remarkably little from the outside but which create a deep chasm between myself and all other people, even deeper than the relatively ordinary ones of homosexuality and being an artist."[2]

Most of the time 35 percent of his energy, he said, went into "the perpetual struggle against lunacy (neurasthenia, hypochondria, anxiety feelings, Etc.)," 50 percent was absorbed in working and worrying about work, while the remaining 15 percent was devoted to "a very true and very tender love for those who have been and are close to me as friends and as lover." But at times of pressure he was likely, he said, to put 89 percent into work, leaving only 10 percent for the fight against lunacy and 1 percent for friends and lover.[3]

Though he was sometimes generous to friends, he set a low value on his talent for friendship. In April 1945 he told the *New York Times*: "The real fact . . . is that no one means a great deal to me, anyway. I'm gregarious and like to be around people, but almost anybody will do. I'm rather selfish in picking my friends anyway; that is I prefer people who can help me in some way or another, and most of my friendships are accidental."[4]

At the end of *A Streetcar Named Desire*, as Blanche takes the doctor's arm, unaware that he is escorting her to an asylum, she says: "I have always depended on the kindness of strangers." When Williams wrote this line, he was thinking of himself: "Actually it was true, I always had, and without being often disappointed. In fact, I would guess that chance acquaintances or strangers have usually been kinder to me than friends—which does not speak too well for me. To know me is not to love me. At best, it is to tolerate me."[5]

In fact, a lot of people became fond of him. In company he was sometimes extrovert and amusing, sometimes withdrawn and silent. "Leaning back on a barstool," wrote Kenneth Tynan, "one of a crowd, he can simulate ease with a barely perceptible effort. Mostly he is silent, sucking on a hygienic cigarette holder full of absorbent crystals, with a vague smile painted on his face, while his mind swats flies in outer space. He says nothing that is not candid and little that is not trite. A mental deafness seems to permeate him, so that he will laugh spasmodically in the wrong places, tell you the time if you ask him the date, or suddenly reopen conversations left for dead three days before."[6] One of his closest friends, Donald Windham, depicts a man who rarely pays much attention to other people's needs or reactions. "When playing cards with you, he would suddenly feel hungry, get up, open a can of sardines in oil, and begin to eat them with his fingers as he continued the game. Smoking a cigarette, he would smile into space and knock the ashes vaguely in the direction of your shirt pocket. . . . He would claim never to have met, much less to have conversed with, the people you and he had spent hours talking to the night before."[7]

Williams found it as hard to grow roots into a relationship as into a place. One of his lovers, Frank Merlo, stayed with him for fourteen years: Merlo was happy to travel with him as he moved restlessly from place to place. "Already world famous in 1953," writes Elia Kazan,

Tennessee lived like a fugitive from justice, always changing his whereabouts, ever moving. He traveled along the archipelago of culture islands that were congenial to him, places where he might feel, for a time, at liberty to be unobserved and totally himself. . . . The centers of civilization that he found agreeable were, of course, those populated by his own kind: artists, romantics, freaks of one kind or another, castoffs, those rejected by respectable society. . . . The presence of his name and often his photograph on the front page of a newspaper in each new encampment did not quiet his unhappy conviction that he was not liked, not wanted there. . . . He still expected to be betrayed socially and personally, even by his closest friends and, as he grew older, by his lovers. But above all and most painfully, by his "public."[8]

A man who is always expecting to be betrayed is often a man who rationally or irrationally believes himself to be a betrayer. Like most of Williams's problems, this one had roots in his boyhood. His father, Cornelius Coffin Williams, who came from an upper-class Tennessee family, degenerated into a hard-drinking, hard-hitting commercial traveler. In his series of ill-judged efforts to make his highly strung son more masculine, he called him "Miss Nancy." The boy was given the same names as Cornelius's father, Thomas Lanier Williams, but when he was twenty-eight he started to call himself Tennessee. Cornelius had come from pioneer Tennessee stock, but at the same time as fastening on his father's Southern background, Williams was trying to divorce himself from his family and his boyhood identity.

His mother, Edwina Estelle Dakin, was the beautiful daughter of an Episcopal minister, and it was she who held the family together during Cornelius's vicious outbursts of drunken aggression and his prolonged absences from home. But Tom's closest relationship was with his sister, Rose, his senior by a year. Laura Wingham in *The Glass Menagerie* is modeled on Rose, who collected glass animals. They come in the play to represent her fragility and "all the softest emotions that belong to recollections of things past. . . . The area-way where the cats were torn to pieces was one thing—my sister's white curtains and tiny menagerie of glass animals were another. Somewhere between them was the world that we lived in."

He and Rose were both at what he later called "the most sensitive age of childhood" when the family moved to Missouri from a comfortable home with the children's grandparents in Mississippi. In St. Louis, the children felt different from the children they met at school and in the streets. Violence in the streets was less dangerous for Rose, Tom, and their younger brother, Dakin, than violence in the home. But Edwina was mentally tough, although she was often intimidated, and she hit back at her husband verbally. Later, after her unforgiving son had launched a series of literary assaults inviting her to recognize herself in the overbearing mother-figures he created, she defended herself by publishing in 1963 her own version of his life story, *Remember Me to Tom*.

It was Rose who sustained the worst damage. She had already been hospitalized several times for mental disorders when, in the autumn of 1937, she underwent a prefrontal lobotomy. Rose, who never recovered, spent the rest of her life in institutions. Tom never forgave their mother. He also blamed himself. In *The Glass Menagerie* he gives the name Tom to Laura's brother, a man described as "a poet with a job in a warehouse. His nature is not remorseless, but to escape from a trap he has to act without pity."

Williams never shook off the sense that he should have saved his sister from the operation. Three years later he met the nineteen-year-old Donald Windham, who testified: "His entire manner of behavior at that time was the result of his having such a backlog of emotional material stored inside him, so much accumulated 'by-product of existence' pressing on his heart, that he dared not receive any more, only release the complex images and insights he was packed with. . . . The emotional material stored in him was concealed. . . . His art sprang from his repressed self-knowledge and the resulting ingenuity his sense of self-preservation used in presenting these too-upsetting-to-face revelations to him in an acceptable way."[9] This helps to explain why most of his sexual liaisons at that time were brief and why he could never enter wholeheartedly into an ordinary friendship. He was better at communicating with strangers—either during a one-night affair or by writing plays. He was always glad to be interviewed, though in most interviews he tended to overplay the part of Tennessee Williams, giving too much of what he thought was expected.

In the introduction to *Cat on a Hot Tin Roof* he wrote: "A morbid shyness once prevented me from having much direct communication with people. . . . I still find it somehow easier to 'level with' crowds of strangers in the hushed twilight of orchestra and balcony sections of theatres than with individuals across a table from me. Their being strangers somehow makes them more familiar and more approachable, easier to talk to. . . . I want to go on talking to you as freely and intimately about what we live and die for as if I knew you better than anyone else whom you know." He exposed a great deal of himself in his plays, though he used his characters as masks, and in his best work it always seems as if what is on offer is intimacy with them, not him. But, as Kazan wrote, "Everything in his life is in his plays, and everything in his plays is in his life. He was so naked in his plays."[10]

Like Jean Genet, he created male characters corresponding to the figures in his sexual fantasies. As he said, "I cannot write any sort of story unless there is at least one character in it for whom I have physical desire."[11] He endowed his favorite male characters with the same qualities that had excited him in men he had known. In *Orpheus Descending* Val Xavier is about thirty, with "a kind of wild beauty about him." Stanley Kowalski in *A Streetcar Named Desire* is "strongly, compactly built. Animal joy in his being is implicit in all his movements and attitudes. Since earliest manhood the center of his life has been pleasure with women, the giving and taking of it, not with weak indulgence, dependently, but with the power and pride of a richly feathered male bird among hens." In *Cat on a Hot Tin Roof* Brick Pollit is an alcoholic but "still slim and firm as a boy. . . . He has the additional charm of that cool air of detachment that people have who have given up the struggle." Reverend Shannon in *The Night of the Iguana* has come close to giving up. About thirty-five, a man women find irresistible, he "has cracked up before and is going to crack up again, perhaps repeatedly." Chance Wayne in *Sweet Bird of Youth* is "exceptionally good-looking," though his "ravaged young face" makes him look slightly older than he is, but "his body shows no decline . . . it's the kind of a body that white silk pajamas are, or ought to be, made for."

Williams's susceptibility to masculine allure helped him to create characters that would arouse physical desire in the audience, and he provided such actors as Marlon Brando, Paul Newman, and Richard Burton with some of their most glamorous roles. But Williams was even more successful in creating characters for beautiful actresses. Vivien Leigh, Elizabeth Taylor, Margaret Leighton, Vanessa Redgrave, Geraldine Page, Barbara Bel Geddes, Deborah Kerr, Ava Gardner, and Carroll Baker were among the beneficiaries. Though Williams had scarcely ever felt sexual desire for women, he could empathize with them and make friends with them. Sexually unthreatening to them, he could bring the feminine side of his personality into play in his dealings with them, while in his dealings with men he often enjoyed talking as if they—and he—were women. "As for venturing into the Palisades after sundown," he wrote in a letter from Hollywood to a homosexual friend, "surely you don't suppose a girl of my character and experience would do anything so imprudent! . . . I have my books, I have my little Victrola and what with evening psalms and prayer and meditation, I find that the hours pass quickly."[12]

Another homosexual friend was addressed as "My Dear Daughter" or "my sainted Mother." The comedy in these letters pivots on conflating the religious with the profanely homosexual. He writes about a shrine in the steam room—which was a good place for picking up young men—and refers to the Order of St. Vaseline. Without trying to give himself lessons in the art of empathizing, he was relaxing into the habit of identification with the female viewpoint and developing the imaginative muscles that would later be used in empathizing with female victims of male lust such as Blanche and later still with lustful women rich enough to buy the men they fancied. Flaubert may never have said "Madame Bovary, c'est moi!" but

Williams explicitly claimed that he was Blanche or the Princess Kosmono-polis in *Sweet Bird of Youth*.

The ability to empathize became inseparable from a need to dramatize. Williams did not feel fully in possession of his experiences until he had writ-ten about them. And he compulsively rewrote them until he was satisfied. According to Gore Vidal, "He worked every morning on whatever was at hand. If there was no play to be finished or new dialogue to be sent round to the theater, he would open a drawer and take out the draft of a story already written and begin to rewrite it. I once caught him in the act of revising a short story that had just been published. 'Why,' I asked, 'rewrite what's already in print?' He looked at me, vaguely; then said, 'Well, obviously it's not finished.' And went back to his typing."[13]

He spent so many strenuous hours at his typewriter that he gave the im-pression of being self-disciplined, but the need to write was so urgent that it was more like self-indulgence. He had an addictive personality, and work the main narcotic in his early life. Donald Windham records that "a great deal of the time in those unsuccessful days he was literally punch-drunk from writing. No one I have encountered any place, at any time, in any field of endeavor, labored as intently as he did; and the desire to prevent his walk-ing straight into the wall when he got up from his typewriter, the longing to remind him of some of the meals he was forgetting, was irresistible. He asked no favors, except through his unresisting ineptitude; and his presence bestowed unexpected drama and richness on everyday events."[14]

He wrote compulsively, and the compulsiveness created a perspective in which writing ranked as real work while talking did not, even when the onstage realization of a play would be founded on discussions with pro-ducer, director, and designer. Kazan's production of *A Streetcar Named Desire* made Williams famous, but before the play went into rehearsal, at meetings held in the house of the producer, Irene Selznick, Kazan would sooner or later notice "a shifty quiver in our author's eyes, and it would turn out that he had another date closely following the one with us; I can't re-member that we ever had an open-ended get-together."[15] Tennessee Williams was a man permanently on the run.

Many of his characters are also on the run. More autobiographical than they seem, the plays are full of outcasts, misfits, and fugitives. In *Summer and Smoke* Alma Winemiller speaks about "my little company of the faded and frightened and difficult and odd and lonely"; the company's founding member was the author, and many of his alter egos are frustrated women with a vaguely artistic sensitivity but without a sufficiently robust willpower to achieve success or even to stand up for themselves. Alma is one such woman, Blanche another. Blanche is one of several sympathetic characters who are institutionalized as dangerous to society. In *Suddenly Last Summer* Catharine Holly has been committed to an asylum, while in other plays Williams identifies with characters whose physical maladies serve as metaphors for mental imbalance. Laura in *The Glass Menagerie* is lame; Isabel Haverstick in *Period of Adjustment* has a "nervous stomach." Men are not immune either. In *Cat on a Hot Tin Roof* Big Daddy's terminal illness signals his incurable alienation. The healthy characters who feel secure are usually also insensitive or brutal.

If Laura, Blanche, Alma, and Catharine are typical Williams heroines, the typical heroes are no less frightened, difficult, odd, and lonely. They tend to be less faded but more aware of fading, though they do not notice until they have begun to lose their youth that it was their only possession of value. Examples are Chance in *Sweet Bird of Youth*, Val in *Orpheus Descending*, and Sebastian Venable in *Suddenly Last Summer*, though he is dead before the action starts. All three are beautiful, highly sexed, and greedy for sensual experiences, and all three are victimized in such spectacular ways as to eclipse any victimizing they have done. Chance has infected his first girlfriend with venereal disease; but he does not deserve to be castrated. Val impregnates a married woman and is attacked with a blowtorch. Sebastian has been ruthless and sexually voracious; his punishment is to have the flesh torn from his body and eaten.

The exorbitant violence sometimes camouflages sentimentality, melodrama, and confusion of moral values. Not-so-innocent characters are awarded more sympathy than they deserve, while rough rednecks, right-wing politicians, and narrow-minded conformists are given no redeeming features. In the late 1950s, when Williams consulted a psychoanalyst who was familiar with his work and recognized "the psychic wounds expressed in it," one of the doctor's first questions was: "Why are you so full of hate, anger, and envy?" Admitting to the anger and envy, Williams denied the hate. Certainly he does not hate Stanley Kowalski, but the bad guys—Boss Finley in *Sweet Bird of Youth*, Jabe Torrance in *Orpheus Descending*, Violet Venable in *Suddenly Last Summer*—are treated melodramatically, with none of the compassion shown by Shakespeare or Chekhov. Whether as private as a lobotomy or as public as a lynching, the violence unleashed is monstrous enough to make the characters look subhuman.

Treating such themes as lynching, political chicanery, rape, incest, nymphomania, homosexuality, promiscuity, drug addiction, alcoholism, castration, impotence, and cannibalism, the plays shocked audiences unaccustomed to seeing such subjects dragged into the limelight, but the writing was at first motivated mainly by a need to absorb shocks. In an article that was published in the *New York Times* before *Sweet Bird of Youth* opened in March 1959, Williams commented on the violence in his work. His first four plays had all been violent, and the first to be staged professionally, *Battle of Angels*, was, he says, "about as violent as you can get on the stage." In the next nineteen years, only five of his plays had been devoid of violence: *The Glass Menagerie*, *You Touched Me*, *Summer and Smoke*, *The Rose Tattoo*, and *Period of Adjustment*. "What surprises me is the degree to which both critics and audience have accepted this barrage of violence."[16]

To justify it he cites "the Aristotelian idea that violence is purged by its poetic representation on a stage." This does not correspond to what Aristotle wrote. Williams claims the brutality in his plays has a moral justification. "I have always felt a release from the sense of meaninglessness and death when a work of tragic intention has seemed to me to have achieved that intention."[17] It was characteristic that he did not bother to check what Aristotle said, which was that emotions (not violence) could be purged by tragedy, which arouses pity and fear.

Without explicitly asserting that his plays have a tragic dimension, Williams implies this, and during 1957 he claimed to have "followed the developing tension and anger and violence of the world and time that I live in through my own steadily increasing tension as a writer and person." What gives his best plays their resonance is his ability to suggest social and cultural disintegration through personal breakdown. Later, more conscious of his power, he became not only self-conscious about the effects he created but more calculating and more repetitious. Themes stated powerfully and poetically in the early plays are reiterated sentimentally and rhetorically.

In later life he forced himself away from the burrow of beaverlike seclusion where he could have felt safe. By turning his privacy inside out, he had found rich theatrical material, but not enough for the quantity of plays he went on to write. Escaping from isolation by multiplying himself into a series of fictional identities and wiring his plots with electricity generated from his neurotic tension, he was modeling his theater on his life and on the childhood that had made him into a neurotic who ran away from private confrontations by making his life into a nonstop performance. In 1972, while he was appearing as an actor in *Small Craft Warnings*, he told an interviewer that he would do anything to get attention.

His flamboyant life-style was part of the drama in which he dressed up his everyday self. To camouflage his diffidence he wore white suits or tropical shirts and short trousers. The drinking and drug-taking, the panache and bravado were all part of the barricade he erected. Unfortunately for the biographer, his compulsive self-dramatization involved him in interweaving fiction with truth not only in stories and plays but also in autobiographical statements he offered as factual.

His career was launched on a lie. He pretended when he was twenty-eight to be three years younger so that his age would not disqualify him from entering a play-writing competition for writers up to the age of twenty-five. He looked younger than he was, and some of his best friends failed to find out the truth until years later.

This lie was arguably necessary. Certainly it helped him to achieve success earlier than he could have done otherwise. The lies he told in interviews were not necessary in this sense, though he must have felt driven by some form of necessity. Habituated as he was to recycling the facts of his life in his fiction, he felt that fiction was indispensable to make the facts more appealing. A great deal of his life had been almost intolerable when he lived it; why should his audience tolerate it?

Talking with apparent openness about his sexual experiences in a 1973 interview with *Playboy*, he camouflaged nearly all his confessions. Sexually, he says, he was a late developer. He was attracted to girls until he was twenty-eight, but had only had one brief affair. He had flirted with boys, but had never made love to any of them. He says his "first real encounter was in New Orleans at a New Year's Eve party during World War Two."[18] As we shall see, this was untrue.

The habit of lying may have been connected to his insatiable craving for the innocence he associated with early childhood. He felt he should have been able to avoid sacrificing this innocence, and his puritanical guilt drove him to relentless self-punishment. As Gore Vidal sums it up, "He was—and is—guilt-ridden, and although he tells us that he believes in no afterlife, he is still too much the puritan not to believe in sin. At some deep level

Tennessee truly believes that the homosexualist is wrong and the heterosex-
ualist is right. Given this all-pervading sense of guilt, he is drawn in both life
and work to the idea of expiation, of death."[19]

Williams's intake of drink and drugs was viciously self-destructive; most
damaging of all were his intravenous injections of amphetamines. Though
he survived until 1983, his life had begun to disintegrate twenty years
earlier. Deeply depressed by the failure of his later work, though making
millions of dollars, mainly from film rights and foreign productions of his
early plays, Williams could afford to indulge his appetites for casual sex and
self-destruction.

His self-destructiveness was inseparable from his hypochondria. The
addiction to drugs grew out of exorbitant dependence on prescribed
remedies. His childhood illness was undoubtedly genuine—for two years he
could not use his legs—and his convalescence must have been retarded by
the ignorance of the doctor and the credulity of his mother. The illness,
which started when he was five, was diagnosed first as diphtheria and later as
Bright's disease. His mother followed the doctor's instructions to keep his
throat packed in ice, changing it as it melted. His tonsils had become en-
larged, and one day, looking down his throat and failing to see them, she
called the doctor, who told her the boy had swallowed them. She was naive
enough to believe this for the rest of her life.[20]

Paralyzing his legs, the disease may also have stunted his growth—he was
to remain very short—and the protracted period of inactivity had perma-
nent effects on his mental development. Certainly he became a
hypochondriac, and believed from the age of twenty-four onward that his
heart was defective. According to him, he had his first heart attack in St.
Louis during March 1935, just after finishing a story called "The Accent of a
Coming Foot." In a note to the story, he wrote:

I found that my heart was pounding and skipping beats. . . . Everyone was asleep in
the apartment but me. I rushed down the back fire escape and I went wildly along the
midnight street, quickening my pace as my pulse quickened. I must have rushed for
miles, all the way from the suburb to Union Boulevard deep into St. Louis. It was
March: the trees along the street were beginning to bud. With characteristic
romanticism, I kept looking up at those green bits of life emerging again and somehow it was this that quieted my panic.[21]

In the story a woman, walking, had felt that every step had been "like a re-lentless crank winding up inside of her some cruelly sharp steel spring whose release would certainly whirl her to pieces." Legitimately projecting his own sensations into the character's, Williams seems to continue the same process of interweaving fact and fiction when he writes the note. In it, he says that later in the week he consulted a doctor who told him he had a defective heart. On 24 March, shortly after seeing the doctor, and two days before his twenty-fourth birthday, he suffered another crisis of tachycardia, accompanied by a stiffening of his fingers and a loss of sensation in his hands. According to his brother, "It was a terrible crisis of nerves, a fierce anxiety attack which he thought forever after was a real heart seizure." But a checkup in the hospital revealed that it was not.[22] It seems likely that his heart was quite healthy. We can never be sure whether he was giving accurate accounts of what doctors said, and later in his life he frequently managed to convince himself that he was dying. But he lived to the age of seventy-two.

1

Where You Hang Your Hopes

Edwina Dakin and Cornelius Coffin Williams met in Columbus, Mississippi, during 1906, after he had seen her rehearsing a trio from Gilbert and Sullivan's *The Mikado* for a charity production of musical excerpts. An old town on the Tombigbee River, Columbus is "so dignified and reserved that there was a saying, only slightly exaggerated, that you had to live there a whole year before a neighbor would smile at you on the street."[1]

Edwina's father, Walter Edward Dakin, was pastor of St. Paul's Episcopal Church in Columbus. After studying theology in Sewanee, he had worked as a schoolteacher and, not long after he married, had taken up an appointment in Tennessee as head of a private girls' school where his wife taught music. The daughter of German immigrants, she had spent several years in a Catholic boarding school. Soon after becoming headmaster, he decided to go into the church, and he was ordained in 1895. He was inclined to take advantage of his good-natured wife, who from then on, had to bear the main brunt of their poverty. While he spent lavishly on clerical vestments, she wore dresses made by cutting up old clothes, took lodgers, and did all the housework and laundry. His extravagance rested on her parsimony.

According to the younger of his two grandsons, Rev. Walter Dakin was "a very selfish person, very self-important and very much a social snob. He would not associate with Baptists, for example, or with Methodists, or with

*Cornelius Coffin Williams at Bellbuckle
Military Academy*

The Rectory in Columbus, Mississippi

people whose churches had no bishops. He was so lordly that when people got to know him they often called him the Bish—'here comes the Bish!'"[2] He made a more favorable impression on his older grandson. Tennessee Williams characterized him as "a kind man. He was soft spoken and gentle. Somehow he created about the whole house an atmosphere of sweetness and light."[3]

The Dakins' only child, Edwina, won a scholarship to Harcourt Place Seminary in Gambier, Ohio, where most of her classmates came from richer families than hers. Her ambition was to star in musical comedy, but she had to be content with amateur dramatics and singing in the church choir. There was no shortage of young men who wanted to take her out, and one of these, a local lawyer, introduced her to a man from Memphis who was in Columbus to plead a case in court for the telephone company, though he had left the law school of the University of Tennessee without completing his degree. He had volunteered at the end of his first year to fight in the Spanish-American War. Serving as an officer, he contracted typhoid fever and lost most of his hair, but Edwina found him attractive without it.

Cornelius's mother was descended from the early settlers of Nantucket Island. His great-uncle was a poet, Tristram Coffin. His father, Thomas

A Southern belle: Edwina Dakin at the time of her marriage

Lanier Williams, had served as railway commissioner for the state and had run three times for governor of Tennessee without being elected. Cornelius's tubercular mother had died at the age of twenty-eight, and his "rough and tough character" derived, according to his older son, from having grown up "mostly without the emollient influence of a mother." Cornelius was sent as a boy to Bellbuckle Military Academy, where he was always breaking rules and serving time in the guardhouse.[4]

After meeting Edwina, Cornelius, who was five years her senior, took her out dancing a few times before he left Columbus. When she succumbed simultaneously to typhoid fever and malaria, he sent a bouquet of roses every day. She turned down his proposal of marriage several times, but he obstinately sent an engagement ring through the mail. "Many men have said I love you," she wrote in her diary on 1 June 1907, "but only three said Will you marry me. I will marry one next Monday. Finis. Goodbye."

After being married by her father in St. Paul's Church, they honeymooned in Gulfport, Mississippi, where Cornelius had just been appointed manager of three telephone exchanges.

During her first pregnancy, which started about twenty months after the wedding, Edwina ran away from Cornelius, returning to her parents in Columbus. Nothing if not persistent, he visited her regularly, staying at the rectory each month for a few days. When their daughter was born on 17 November 1909, they named her Rose Isabel—Rose after her mother and Isabel after his.

Losing his job with the telephone company, Cornelius settled for work as a traveling salesman, dealing in men's clothes and later in shoes. By the end of 1910 he was drinking and spending money on card games and brothels. His marriage had deteriorated seriously by the time the second child, a boy, was born on 26 March 1911, but he was named after his paternal grandfather, Thomas Lanier Williams.

The young mother and her two children saw little of Cornelius. "One summer," she writes, "when we vacationed in Tennessee, I did not see my husband at all. Occasionally, he would pick me up at the rectory and we would drive off in his car for the weekend. I remember the ancient Ford, in which he carried his shoe samples, spinning around in one circle of mud after another in this macadamless world of Mississippi mud roads."[5]

At the end of 1913, Walter Dakin secured a more prestigious job in Nashville, and for two years the rectory was the children's home. They were brought up mainly by a black servant, Ozzie, who also did the cooking. "She never lost patience with us," Tom remembered, "when we teased her in a childish way. Not even when we imitated the children next door and called her, with unwitting cruelty, a big black nigger!"[6] The relationship between brother and sister was so close that Ozzie called them "the couple." Rose was "an ideal playmate. . . . She had an incredible imagination. We were so close to each other, we had no need of others."[7]

The children were frightened of their father, who arrived irregularly on weekend visits.

Then the spell of perfect peace was broken. A loud voice was heard, and heavy footsteps. Doors were slammed. Furniture was kicked and banged . . .

Often the voice of my father was jovial or boisterous. But sometimes it was harsh. And sometimes it sounded like thunder.

He was a big man. Beside the slight, gentle figure of my grandfather, he looked awfully big. And it was not a benign bigness. You wanted to shrink away from it, to hide yourself.[8]

Cornelius's bullying did an incalculable amount of harm to his vulnerable son, who could never understand the contrast between the harmonious togetherness of his grandparents and the venomous quarrels of his parents. Nor did Edwina ever get used to her husband's rough way of claiming his marital rights, and the children were scared when they heard screams from their parents' bedroom.[9]

After nearly two years in Nashville and a few months in Canton, Reverend Dakin became rector of St. George's Church in Clarksdale, Mississippi, eighty miles south of Memphis. The family moved there late in 1915. Unsettling though they were, the moves did not destroy the children's happiness, but Edwina's name is conspicuously missing from the list of people Tom credits as responsible for the "joyously innocent" home life he enjoyed throughout the first eight years of his life. It was his "beloved Dakin grandparents," Walter and "Grand," as the children called Rose, who provided the "beneficent homelife," while he enjoyed "the wild and sweet half-imaginary world in which my sister and our beautiful black nurse Ozzie existed, separate, almost invisible to anyone but our little cabalistic circle of three."[10]

We sailed paper boats in wash-tubs of water, cut lovely paper-dolls out of huge mail-order catalogs, kept two white rabbits under the back porch, baked mud pies in the

Rose at the age of 18 months

Below: The young Tom with Ozzie,
"our beautiful black nurse"

sun upon the front walk, climbed up and slid down the big wood pile, collected from neighboring alleys and trash-piles bits of colored glass that were diamonds and rubies and sapphires and emeralds. And in the evenings when the white moonlight streamed over our bed, before we were asleep, our Negro nurse Ozzie, as warm and black as a moonless Mississippi night, would lean above our bed, telling in a low, rich voice her amazing tales about foxes and bears and rabbits and wolves that behaved like human beings.[11]

Like many frustrated actresses and singers, Edwina cheered herself up by performing to her children. She acted out the stories she read, as well as singing hymns and ballads. They were a responsive audience, while she was appreciative of Tom's qualities, noticing how observant he was. Whenever he picked a flower, he would stand peering into it "as though trying to discover the secret of its life." He used to run after his grandfather on visits to sick parishioners and listen carefully to what was said. "I always thought of Tom as a small pitcher with big ears; he would sit perfectly quiet never saying a word, listening with every sinew."[12]

In retrospect, time spent in his grandparents' homes seemed happy, but between the ages of five and eight the boy's life was disrupted—by sickness, the departure of Ozzie, and separation from his beloved grandparents. At five he almost died from what was thought to be diphtheria. For nine successive nights Edwina slept in his room so that she could keep changing the ice packs on his throat.[13] When his temperature went down, she let him get up, but instead of walking he sat on a stool and pushed himself around the room to reach his toys. The doctor, who was called again, diagnosed Bright's disease. The diphtheria, he said, had affected Tom's kidneys and paralyzed his legs. Edwina assumed that poison from the infected tonsils had damaged his system. Unable to use his legs for nearly two years, he could not play outdoors with other children. Edwina bought him an Irish Mail—a toy that enabled him to move around the room without putting any weight on his legs.

Spending so much time in bed, Tom had to devise his own entertainment: he invented a game of solitaire based on the *Iliad.* The red and black cards represented the opposing armies in the Trojan War, and he slapped red and black cards together, tossing them in the air. The soldiers that fell on the bedspread face down were dead; the others could fight on. Besides playing games he invented, he could enjoy the pictures that vividly presented themselves when he closed his eyes. "I get only dim images now," he said in 1945, "but when I was little, I'd see whole scenes, like the *Arabian Nights*."[14]

If two years of solitude helped to prime his imagination for his future career as a writer, they also (according to him) helped to undermine his masculinity. "My mother's overly solicitous attention planted in me the makings of a sissy, much to my father's discontent."[15]

Tom's legs gradually regained their strength, but he had to learn how to walk all over again. He practiced painfully on the sidewalk outside the house.[16] It was during the torrid summer of 1918, while he was recovering, that Cornelius was appointed sales manager of the International Shoe Company in St. Louis, where shoemaking was one of the biggest of the expanding local industries. Cornelius, who was finally settling down to a desk job after some nine years on the road, decided to move his wife and children there. Edwina by that time was pregnant with her third baby and also had the mumps, but she stayed with her husband at a boardinghouse while she hunted for the first home in which she and Cornelius were to live independently of her parents. She eventually found a six-room apartment in one of the city's most fashionable districts. Situated on the ground floor of a building in Westminster Place, the apartment was long, narrow, and so dark that lights had to be left on throughout most of the day.

Tom, who was given a tiny bedroom off a side hall, later used his memories of this home in *The Glass Menagerie*. The family lives in "one of those vast hive-like conglomerations of cellular living units that flower as warty growths in overcrowded urban centers of lower middle-class population and are symptomatic of the impulse of this largest and fundamentally enslaved section of American society to avoid fluidity and differentiation and to exist and function as one interfused mass of automatism." The building is "flanked on both sides by dark, narrow alleys which run into murky canyons of tangled clotheslines, garbage cans, and the sinister latticework of neighboring fire-escapes." In spite of the play's unflattering description, the building was later renamed the Glass Menagerie Apartments.

As grandchildren of the minister, Tom and Rose had enjoyed privileged status in Columbus, Nashville, Canton, and Clarksdale, but now, marooned in the country's fourth largest city, they felt like aliens. Tom was sent to Eugene Field Public School, where he was ridiculed for his Southern accent, for his smallness, and for being a sissy. Still unable to run, he could not take part in games and did not want to talk about his illness. One day, when he was sitting on a bench watching the other boys play, each passing boy kicked him hard on the ankle, and he went home with bruises on both legs. Nor were the teachers any more friendly. "Anybody can tell you're from the South," one of them told him. "You're as slow as January molasses."[17]

Going to school was an ordeal. "I was scared to death of everyone on earth and particularly of public school boys and public school teachers and public school principals, most of all. That name, public school, kept stabbing at my guts till I wanted, old as I was, to sit down and cry."[18] He gave up trying to make friends with boys of his own age. He went on playing with Rose, played by himself, and spent a lot of time reading.

During Tom's nine years in St. Louis the family moved nine times. Unable to afford a house in a fashionable district, they kept looking for roomier apartments or houses they could rent. Each time they moved, they seemed—as Dakin, the Williamses' third child (born 21 February 1919), later put it—to be "following in the footsteps of the Jameson family."[19] Cornelius's boss, Paul Jameson, was an admirer of Edwina and the family's generous protector. He provided furniture for their first apartment and paid for Cornelius and Edwina to travel west so that she could recuperate from the Spanish flu. Dakin inherited a baby carriage and later a bicycle from Jameson's son, and though Cornelius took no part in the outings, the rest of the family picnicked with the Jamesons almost every Sunday in Forest Park.[20]

Benefiting from Jameson's patronage, Cornelius was promoted to a managerial position at the warehouse on Washington Avenue, but in 1921 Edwina suffered a miscarriage, and her ensuing depression was so exacerbated by his drunkenness, gambling, and womanizing that she never fully recovered her health. The happiest moments in the children's lives came when their grandparents arrived for a visit. When "Grand" was there they would have "nickels for ice cream, quarters for movies, picnics in Forest Park." There would be "soft and gay laughter like the laughter of girls between our mother and her mother." Better still, Grand's presence guaranteed an interval of peace to a household that was under attack whenever Cornelius came home. "'Grand' was all we knew of God in our lives."[21]

Later, retrospectively tolerant, Tom blamed his father's alcoholism on the frustrations of office life after the freedom of life as a traveling salesman. Cornelius held his liquor fairly well: he was never arrested for drunken

Edwina and Dakin in St. Louis

driving or for being drunk and disorderly. Throughout the week he kept to a regular routine, arriving home for dinner with his family punctually at six o'clock and rarely drinking either before or afterward—at least not as far as the children could tell. After dinner he usually collapsed on the sofa and listened to the radio. Having to get up at six, he went to bed before midnight. The charm he undoubtedly had was a commodity he was unwilling to waste on the family, but most of his attacks on Edwina were verbal, and she was rarely bested.[22]

During their first twelve years in St. Louis, Edwina had eight operations, including a hysterectomy, while Rose suffered almost as much as her mother. Terrified Edwina would die, leaving her at the mercy of a violent father, Rose developed symptoms identical with her mother's and suffered from delusions—the food was being poisoned, and they were all going to be slaughtered by strangers. Suddenly Tom could no longer rely on the one element in his life that had seemed stable—his symbiotic companionship with the ideal playmate.

Rose had been the inspiration for Tom's earliest literary work—a comic paper called "The Rainbow," that he produced for her when he was nine. It contained childish sketches of her with captions, the flattery tinged with gentle mockery. The "Wido" R. L. Williams is depicted with her tenth husband: "All the rest committed suicid [sic] because she was so strict." Her rival is "Mrs. Jane h Rothchild," who "is a sufraget and is afraid." She is afraid because "Miss Rose Williams will paint up so much That she will get all the million men."[23]

That her illness was pushing him toward a literary career and toward homosexuality is suggested by an autobiographical story, "The Resemblance between a Violin Case and a Coffin," which he wrote in 1949. The story indicates that Rose was beginning to go mad when she fell in love for the first time.

In the story the first symptom is an odd look. One day the narrator's fourteen-year-old sister gets up later than usual, "as though she'd received some painful or frightening surprise." Their mother and grandmother start to treat her differently, addressing her in hushed and solicitous voices, escorting her to the table for breakfast as if she were in danger of toppling over. When the girl looks at her brother, she does so resentfully, as if he had attacked her, and when he speaks to her, she ignores him. Instead of wanting

roung for.
Mrs Jane H. Rothchild
is a sufreget. and is afraid
Miss Rose Williams will
paint up so much
That she will get all The
million men

W 100 A L Williams

Mrs Jane hR.

has her Tenth
husband. all
The Rest
commided suicid because
she was so strict

*The nine-year-old Tom makes Rose the main
character in a comic paper he produces for her*

to go on a bike ride with him, she sits down to practice the piano and, when he protests, gets up in a flood of tears.

A gulf has opened between brother and sister; the mother and grandmother appear to be doing everything they can to widen it. Why had Tom failed to make friends with other children? It is improper for his sister to go around without stockings, they say, and for him to go into her room without knocking. But the adults are still unaware of a wildness in the children that cannot be repressed. "My mother and maternal grandmother came of a calmer blood than my sister and I. They were unable to suspect the hazards that we were faced with, having in us the turbulent blood of our father. Irreconcilables fought for supremacy in us; peace could never be made: at best a smoldering sort of armistice might be reached after many battles. Childhood had held those clashes in abeyance. They were somehow timed to explode at adolescence, silently, shaking the earth where we were standing."

Tom becomes aware of his sister's beauty on the day her long, coppery curls are cut off. She is taken downtown, and he notices when she comes back through the front door that she has "begun to imitate the walk of grown ladies, the graceful and quick and decorous steps of my mother, and that she kept her arms at her sides instead of flung out as if brushing curtains aside as she sprang forward in the abruptly lost days." The mother and grandmother comment on her resemblance to Isabel, her father's beautiful sister, who had died young. When the girl, after strolling into the parlor, stands by the mantelpiece mirror to be admired, her brother knows he has lost the companion who used to cut out paper dolls and go for bike races with him. It was then, he says, that he "began to find life unsatisfactory as an explanation of itself and was forced to adopt the method of the artist of not explaining but putting the blocks together in some other way that seems more significant to him. Which is a rather fancy way of saying I started writing."

It was at this time that Rose Williams, thanks to advice and financial help from her grandparents, began to take piano and violin lessons. The story describes how the girl becomes a star pupil of the spinsterish Miss Aehle. The girl accompanies the other star pupil, a seventeen-year-old violinist called Richard Miles. His name is constantly on the girl's lips, which makes the fiercely resentful Tom dream about him. Seeing his sister has fallen in love with Richard, Tom follows suit. "He was one of those people who move in light, provided by practically everything about them. . . . And for

Rose at the time of her debut

the first time, prematurely, I was aware of skin as an attraction. A thing it might be desirable to touch." But when Richard, meeting the girl and Tom in the street, holds out his hand, Tom ducks shyly away, mumbling, and takes refuge in a drug store.

When Richard comes to the rectory to practice with the sister for their duet at a concert Miss Aehle's pupils are going to give in the parish house, Tom hides shamefully in his bedroom, but his interest has been transferred from Rose to Richard.

When I recall what a little Puritan I was in those days, there must have been a shocking ambivalence in my thoughts and sensations. . . . How on earth did I explain to myself, at that time, the fascination of his physical being without, at the same time, confessing to myself that I was a little monster of sensuality? . . . The sheer white cloth in which I had originally seen his upper body was always worn by it, and now . . . the white material became diaphanous with light, the torso shone through it, faintly pink and silver, the nipples on the chest and the armpits a little darker, and the diaphragm visibly pulsing as he breathed.

On the evening of the concert the girl's cheeks are red and her temples are sweaty. She orders Tom out of the room when he appears at the doorway as she is changing into a grownup-looking dress. She has to play without sheet music, and her memory lets her down. In the story she keeps repeating passages she has already played, finally sitting motionless and stunned at the keyboard. In reality Rose Williams played Papini's "Romance" at a "costume violin recital" organized in a YMCA hall by the Elise Aehle School of Music in December 1922. She was paralyzed with terror in the middle of her performance. Shaking and weeping, she was taken away by her family.[24]

For her brother, perception of Rose's mental imbalance blurred into realization that he was losing her. It was inevitable that he would feel upset and betrayed when the process of growing into a woman separated Rose from him. But adolescence is not usually accompanied by insanity, and Tom also had to contend with Rose's illness. He reacted by withdrawing from family life to write, using a secondhand portable typewriter that Edwina had bought him for his schoolwork. Writing "immediately became my place of retreat, my cave, my refuge."[25]

His shyness increased, and he started to blush a great deal. As he remembered it, the affliction started in a geometry class when he noticed a dark, attractive girl was looking at him. His face started to burn, and afterward, whenever he saw another pair of eyes looking into his, he would feel his face burning with a blush.[26] The need to write was nurtured by his discomfort and his inability to discuss it. He was thirteen when he started making serious attempts to write, and he remembered this as "an escape from a world of reality in which I felt acutely uncomfortable."[27]

He wrote poems and stories for the school newspaper. In October 1924 his ghost story "A Great Tale Told at Katrina's Party" appeared in the Halloween issue of the Ben Blewett Junior High newspaper, *Junior Life*. Two of his poems were accepted soon after, and his essay on downtown factory fumes, "Demon Smoke," was published during June 1925 in the school yearbook. After he was moved to Soldan High School, he wrote film reviews for the school newspaper. One of his first subjects was a 1925 silent movie, *Stella Dallas*, directed by Henry King.

But writing created new anxieties. Looking back twenty-four years later on these early efforts, Williams remembered that within a week of starting to write he began to suffer from writer's block. Having so little self-confidence, he was leery of wanting anything badly. Would it be wiser not to place himself in such a vulnerable position? Almost certainly he would fail to get what he wanted, even if his only ambition was to finish a story or a poem. As he says, "Having, always, to contend with this adversary of fear, which was sometimes terror, gave me a certain tendency toward an atmosphere of hysteria and violence in my writing, an atmosphere that has existed in it since the beginning."[28]

As the family moved from apartment to apartment, he moved from school to school, which reduced his chances of doing well either academically or socially. His grades were no better than average, and he gave teachers the impression of being ill-adjusted. But he persevered with his writing and in May 1927 earned five dollars by winning third prize in a competition run by the magazine *Smart Set*. The question he had to answer was "Can a Good Wife Be a Good Sport?" and he wrote as if he were a man whose wife was dating other men.[29] He had a natural instinct for inventing situations that generated dramatic tension.

He was still a seventeen-year-old pupil at University City High School in 1928 when he earned thirty-five dollars for a horror story he submitted to the magazine *Weird Tales*. Derived partly from reading Herodotus and partly from his preoccupation with brother-sister relationships, "The

17

Vengeance of Nitocris" centers on an Egyptian queen who avenges her brother's death by inviting the men who condemned him to a feast and then, as she floods the banquet hall, gloatingly watches the death agonies of her victims. The story was published in June.[30]

The only close friendship Tom formed during these years was with a plump redheaded girl, Hazel Kramer, whom he met when he rescued her from boys who were throwing stones at her in an alley. They were both nine. She lived around the corner, and they continued to meet, playing in her attic, inventing games, making up stories and illustrating them. By the time Tom was sixteen, Hazel was taller than he, and he noticed that she hunched down to make herself look smaller when they were together in the street, but his parents disapproved of her. In his memoirs he accuses only his mother of opposing the friendship (on the grounds that Hazel's mother was too "common");[31] but Cornelius seems to have intervened more strenuously. A 1962 letter shows that he forbade Tom to enroll at the University of Missouri if Hazel did. This letter claims that love for Hazel was "the deepest thing" in Tom's life, and although there was no question of arguing his father's "Jovian" edict, Tom felt more rebellious inwardly than ever before, and uncomfortable under the same roof as the tyrant.

It is difficult to reconstruct the relationship with Hazel because Williams gave contradictory accounts of it. In 1973 he told *Playboy* he was constantly thinking about sex but she was frigid. "Tom," she said, "we're much too young to think about these things," and she made him count to ten before he kissed her. But she was the object of his desire when he had his first spontaneous ejaculation.[32] He describes the episode in his memoirs. They were on a river boat in St. Louis. He was wearing white flannel trousers and she was in a pale green chiffon party dress with no sleeves. "We went up on the dark upper deck and I put my arm around those delicious shoulders and I 'came' in my white flannels. . . . No mention was made between us of the tattletale wet spot on my pants front but Hazel said, 'Let's stay up here and walk around the deck, I don't think we ought to dance now. . . . ' "[33]

Tom was equally frustrated in his home life. His brother, Dakin, confirms that

life at home was terrible, just terrible. By the late 1920s mother and father were in open warfare, and both were good combatants. He came home drunk and picked up a bill—perhaps for Tom's clothing or schoolbooks—and he'd fly into a rage. "How dare you spend money on Tom—books! a coat!" and he'd scream something terrific

The warring parents on a porch in the Ozarks

and there'd be a vicious row and finally mother would do her famous fainting act—always managing to fall on the couch of course, so that she wouldn't hurt herself. Once, however, it was so terrible that she ran into the bedroom and locked herself in. He broke down the door and in doing so the door hit her and broke her nose. That time she really fainted.[34]

In the summer of 1928 Tom went abroad for the first time. Reverend Dakin, who was organizing a European tour for his parishioners, arranged for his grandson to travel with them. The rest of the party consisted entirely of women, mostly middle-aged or elderly. Before sailing they spent four days in New York, where Tom was given his first taste of Broadway when they went to see *Showboat*. They crossed the ocean on the *Homeric*, which had been one of Kaiser Wilhelm's flagships. It sailed at midnight, with a brass band playing and streamers being tossed between the ship and the dock. On their first day at sea, Tom tasted alcohol for the first time, drinking a crème de menthe at the bar on deck. Within half an hour he was violently sick, and went on feeling ill for the five days of the trip, spending most of the time in his airless cabin. But he recovered sufficiently to enjoy dancing with a woman of about twenty-seven, a dancing teacher whose lover became jealous and took his revenge by making ominous remarks about the boy's sexual "future". The young woman tried to defend him: how could anyone be sure when he was still only seventeen?[35]

In Paris Tom drank champagne, looked at the paintings in the Louvre, took in the Folies Bergère and the Moulin Rouge, heard Gounod's *Romeo et Juliette* at the Opera, and visited Versailles. But he had two bad experiences. At the Eiffel Tower a pickpocket made off with the hundred dollars Cornelius had given him as spending money. The other he describes as a "nearly psychotic crisis." He was walking toward the Hotel Rochambeau, where they were staying, when he suddenly started thinking about the thinking process—which struck him as both complex and mysterious. He found himself walking faster, as if to outpace the idea, but his heartbeat accelerated. He was sweating and, by the time he reached the hotel, trembling. "At least a month of the tour was enveloped for me by this phobia about the process of thought, and the phobia grew and grew till I think I was within a hairsbreadth of going quite mad from it."[36]

They went on to Marseilles, Monte Carlo, Venice, Milan, and Interlaken, then traveled by steamer along the Rhine to Cologne, where the phobia reached its climax. Seized by panic in the cathedral, Tom knelt down

The seventeen-year-old Tom (left) on the deck of the S.S. Homeric *(1928)*

Below: The parishioners that Reverend Dakin took to Venice (1928)

to pray and went on praying after the others had left. Suddenly he felt as if a hand were lifting the phobia away. He was certain Jesus had touched his head with mercy. For about a week he felt better. The phobia returned in Amsterdam, where the Olympic Games were being held. The party attended the equestrian competition, and it was afterward, going out at night into the streets, that Tom succeeded in exorcising his malaise by composing a short piece of verse about the multiplicity and interconnectedness of humanity. In his final couplet his "hot woe / cools like a cinder dropped on snow," which reminds him that his existence could dissolve as lightly as anyone else's.

Back at school he was told to write an essay on his European travels. Drawing on the diary he had kept, he mentioned the sensation in the cathedral and the poem. Suddenly his prestige increased because he was the only boy in his class who had been abroad. A series of excerpts from his travel essay appeared in the school newspaper. But he was still too shy to speak in the classroom and, resigning themselves to this, the teachers stopped asking him questions.[37] Tom concentrated more on his newspaper articles than his math, and his schoolwork deteriorated. By the end of his senior year he was ranked fifty-third in the class of eighty-three.[38]

2

Columbia and Washington

In 1929 Tom was accepted at the University of Missouri at Columbia, 150 miles west of St. Louis. His grandparents paid the tuition—forty dollars a term—while his father gave him a monthly allowance for living expenses. Accompanying him to Columbia, Edwina selected a residence hall where male and female students met only at meals. On the first night, Tom's roommate, a tall blond boy, climbed almost somnambulistically into his bed but got out again when greeted with a cry of dismay and never returned—though Tom was rather hoping he would.[1]

From the beginning of his university career, Tom's inclinations were uncomfortably at odds with his father's plans for him. Not interested in literature and unconcerned about any preparations Tom might want to make for writing poetry, Cornelius wanted him to equip himself for a career as a journalist. When the stock market crashed in October 1929, about a month after the term began, Cornelius would have taken his son out of college if the Dakins had not sent a thousand dollars.

After this Tom wrote regular letters to his grandparents. In November he told his grandfather that his aunt Belle had "sent Rose and I a very warm invitation." Grammar would never be his forte, and neither would spelling. He had been reading a biography of "Shelly," who "seems to have been the wild, passionate and dissolute type of genius, which makes him very entertaining to read about." Although Tom obviously felt attracted to the kind of life Shelley had led, he was not expecting to become a man of letters: he was thinking of taking a short business course after he graduated.[2]

Wanting his son to be as similar to himself as possible, Cornelius tried to exert influence on him without taking account of either his personality or his potential. All students were obliged to enroll for two years in the military training program, and Tom was told he should take an active part in the Reserve Officers' Training Corps (ROTC). Cornelius also put pressure on him to join Alpha Tau Omega, an exclusive fraternity with strict rules. Tom capitulated on both fronts, and his reluctance to join the fraternity was eroded rapidly when he saw the mock-Tudor fraternity house then under construction. He was expecting to be at the university for four years, and life would be more comfortable in the new building.

But after pledging and moving in, Tom was repeatedly hauled in front of the fraternity's kangaroo court. Some of his misdemeanors originated out of the penury consequent on the meagerness of his monthly allowance. Required by the rules to appear at dinner in a clean shirt, and never ready when the bell rang at six in the evening, Tom would rush into a brother's room and borrow a white shirt, hoping to return it stealthily later on. Too impoverished to pay his bills at bars, he wrote checks on banks where he had no account, and when the chapter gave a formal dance, he would bring girls whose names were not listed as acceptable. The punishment was known as paddling, the paddle being an oar. The victim had to bend over, presenting his bared bottom to a brother who would sprint across the long front room to deliver up to ten hefty thwacks. After receiving the maximum, as he often did, Tom found it hard either to walk or to find a comfortable position in bed.[3]

In his first year he took courses in English composition, intermediate French, citizenship, and geology. He struck up friendships with two members of the fraternity and a girl called Esmeralda Mayes. At lunchtime he picnicked with her, avidly discussing art and literature, and they went to the town's two movie theaters. But at the end of the year his marks were unimpressive. He had no As, received Bs in composition, citizenship, and French, Cs in geology and literature, while ROTC had given him an F. It was no consolation to Cornelius that Tom had published a short story, "The Lady's Beaded Bag," in the campus literary magazine or that his one-act play *Beauty Is the Word* had been the first freshman play to win an honorable mention from the contest judges of the Dramatic Arts Club. The plot

Rose: the ideal playmate grows into a young woman

revolves around a prudish missionary and his family. According to the *Missourian*, it was based on "an original and constructive idea, but the handling is too didactic and the dialogue often too moralistic."[4]

During the summer vacation of 1930 Tom earned money in St. Louis by joining a team of boys paid twenty-one dollars a week for trying to sell subscriptions to a women's magazine, *Pictorial Review*, door-to-door. They had to work from nine in the morning till eight-thirty in the evening. They were lodged in a hotel on Grand Avenue, and, supervised by the regional sales manager, they worked in pairs, knocking on doors and ringing bells. Tom was sent to some of the worst areas in the city, and the people summoned to their front doors were often abusive. This was the first year of the Depression, and the campaign was so unsuccessful that everyone was fired after about two weeks. Tom's partner, a blond boy from Tulsa, stayed on in St. Louis, and, taking him on a double date with Hazel and a friend of hers, Tom understood neither the boy's lack of interest in girls nor the meaning of the question: "Wouldn't we have more fun if we went to the bars?"[5]

Tom was spending a lot of time with Hazel, and a lot with Rose. Physically he and Rose were shy of each other, never touching except when they played records and danced together, but they took evening strolls through Delmar, "that long, long street which probably began near the Mississippi River in downtown St. Louis and continued through University City and on out into the country."[6] They stopped to buy root beer and stared at the clothes in the shop windows. Rose loved clothes but had little money to spend. When they went home, Tom followed her into her bedroom to carry on the desultory conversation.

After going back to college in the autumn of 1930 for his second year, he fell innocently in love with his new roommate. The young man was tall, well-built, and dark-haired, with "large and luminous eyes which gleamed at night like a fire-cat's."[7] During "Old Home Week," when the frat house was packed with alumni, they shared a bunk in the dormitory on the third floor. One night they were both wearing underwear, and after lights out Tom felt fingers caressing his upper arms and shoulders. He then felt the pressure of another male body against his buttocks. To *Playboy*, forty-three years later, he explained that he was "deeply in love" with this boy, "but neither of us knew what to do about it. If he came to my bed, I'd say, 'What do you want?' I was so puritanical I wouldn't permit him to kiss me. But he could just touch my arm and I'd come. Nothing planned, just spontaneous orgasms."[8]

As the year went on, they fell more deeply in love with each other. On a spring night when Tom was lying on the lawn, the boy put his big fingers under Tom's shirt to caress his chest, which made him start trembling. The relationship was never consummated. They got no further than amorous wrestling and a few unsuccessful attempts the roommate made to kiss Tom on the mouth. Once, when they seemed to be on the point of making love, Tom was so nervous that he was sick on the floor. His friend cleaned up the mess, undressed him, put him to bed, climbed in next to the shaking body, and held it in a tight grip. But they did not make love. One night in St. Louis when they shared the double bed in Rose's room (she had gone to the hospital for a check-up) they embraced innocently. None of the other fraternity brothers suspected them of homosexuality.[9]

Though capable of working extremely hard when he was his own taskmaster, Tom reacted negatively to academic pressure. During his second year his grades were even lower: only one B, in literature; Cs in journalism,

Cornelius before he lost all his hair

composition, logic, history, and zoology; Ds in Greek history and French; and another F in military science. Angry that his son was doing so badly in ROTC, the veteran of the Spanish-American War decreed that Tom was to have extra training. The weekly routine involved two classes in military science and a Wednesday afternoon parade on the quadrangle wearing uniform—white trousers and blue coat. But the absentminded Tom often forgot his white trousers, and spectators were amused to see a pair of blue trousers among the eight hundred white pairs.[10]

Cornelius punished him for his low grades by making him work through the summer vacation of 1931 as a temporary clerk in the company's Continental Shoe division. They would drive to work together in the morning, but the rapport between father and son was steadily deteriorating. Tom remembers: "I used to try to think of something to say to him. I would compose about three sentences in my mind, . . . something like 'the smog is heavy today,' or 'the traffic is bad,' you know, and to each one he would grunt in some disparaging way: 'What's this son-of-a-bitch trying to talk to me for.'. . . We were just so tongue tied with each other."[11]

Tom blamed Edwina. "If Mother hadn't held me so fiercely close to her, the situation might not have got so bad between us that I *froze* when he entered the house. I might even have got to know him as a man—and I sometimes feel he *wanted* to know me, but the trouble lay in the fact that, knowing I *was* afraid of him, he resented that knowledge so much that he turned against me."[12]

In September, back at the university, Tom entered the School of Journalism. He was still living at the frat house, and, eager to win points for Alpha Tau Omega, he agreed to take part in a wrestling match. Although he lost his two fights—he was pitted against muscular farm boys—he fought with enough courage and aggressiveness to earn the nickname "Tiger Williams."[13] Academically, though, he did badly. He got Cs in English and one of his two journalism courses, Ds in the other and in political science, while ROTC again graded him F. These poor grades gave Cornelius a pretext for pulling him out of college. According to Edwina, "Tom wanted with all his heart to get a degree, to keep learning, to be able to write more effectively. I think he would have given anything to remain in college. But he did not defy his father. I can only guess what it must have cost him psychically."[14]

First he studied shorthand and typing in night classes, hoping to get a clerical job with the International Shoe Company. According to his memoirs he spent three years earning sixty-five dollars a month at the warehouse for onerous menial and secretarial work that included dusting shoes in the sample rooms, typing factory orders, and carrying packing cases of samples. One afternoon, riding on a bus, Edwina saw a young man carrying a box nearly as long as a sofa and trying to cross a busy street. She felt sorry for him without at first recognizing him as her son. He was on the staff at the warehouse for only ten months (June 1934 to April 1935), but he may have worked before this on a daily basis and been paid out of petty cash or the department's budget.[15]

He had his first experiences of theatergoing at the only theater in St. Louis, the American. He sat in the balcony. The third play he saw was Ibsen's *Ghosts*, with Alla Nazimova. "And it was so fabulous, so terrifyingly exciting that I couldn't stay in my seat! I suddenly jumped up and rushed out and began pacing the corridor of the peanut gallery, trying to hear what was

*The unhappy shoe salesman
who would have preferred
to be at college*

*Alla Nazimova as
Mrs. Alving in Ibsen's*
Ghosts *(1934)*

being said on the stage, but at the same time I couldn't stand to watch it anymore."[16]

But he had to put up with a great deal that was hard to bear. Generally, his situation could hardly have been worse. Hazel Kramer was on the point of getting married. Rose's stability was becoming more precarious, while Cornelius made no secret of his preference for his younger son, Dakin, who was taller and more masculine and enjoyed being taken to ball games. If Tom wanted to borrow the car, Cornelius lent it grudgingly, afterward complaining about dents that had already been there, but he willingly let Dakin use it.[17]

Cornelius was still drinking and behaving outrageously. Rose got used to seeing him order her mother out of the house, and once, when Edwina told him to go, he packed a bag and left, only to return the next day. One evening, when Rose had invited a young man to the house, Cornelius refused to move from his supine position on the sofa in the living room, where he was listening to the radio. She telephoned the young man to cancel the date and protested to her father, who slapped her. She ran out into the street, saying she was going to find a policeman and have her crazy father locked up. For days she would not speak to him, and she went on complaining of pains in her stomach, saying that someone was trying to poison her. When she was taken to the hospital for an examination, the doctors suggested she should see a psychiatrist, and when she started going to one regularly, he persuaded Cornelius to give her an allowance. But she went on complaining about him to the psychiatrist, saying a common truck driver was more of a gentleman than he was.

She stayed indoors day after day, staring into space. The psychiatrist recommended a period in a sanatorium, and she was sent to St. Vincent's, a Catholic institution staffed by nuns. Dakin, who was in his senior year at the University City High School, often drove his mother, and sometimes his father, to the sanatorium. Dakin testifies: "Rose was like a wild animal. Often I would hear her screaming long before the Catholic sisters would usher us into her presence. . . . Between screams and the most vile cursing, she would be chain-smoking or pacing up and down the corridor or visiting room." Finally the Mother Superior asked for her to be taken somewhere else.[18]

She came home, but her condition deteriorated again after a widower who had befriended her was killed by a truck. Once in the middle of the

*Rose outside the Catholic sanatorium in
St. Louis*

night she heard Cornelius pounding on the front door, unable to get in, and she went downstairs. Edwina never found out what he said or did to Rose, who fled upstairs and used furniture to barricade herself in her room. The next day she said she was moving out. Tom carried her suitcase to the car, but after driving her around, he and Edwina tried to persuade her to come back. She refused adamantly, and in the end they took her to the psychiatric ward of a general hospital.

Tom reacted by putting more pressure on himself and releasing it through writing. Throughout 1933 and 1934 he went on writing short poems modeled on the work of Sara Teasdale, a lyric poet who wrote in a simple style, expressing moods and using quatrains almost devoid of imagery. She committed suicide in January 1933 at the age of forty-eight. Tom submitted his lyrics—sometimes successfully—to such periodicals as *Neophyte, Inspiration, Counterpoint, L'Alouette,* and *Voices.* He also worked hard at short stories, offering them perseveringly to the magazine *Story,* which invariably rejected them. "Stella for Star," the twenty-third story he submitted, eventually won him ten dollars when he was awarded first prize in the Winifred Irwin competition. He was also pleased when the alumni magazine of the University of Missouri gave him an honorable mention in a story contest, and the chairman of the English department at the university sent him an encouraging letter. He worked late every night at his stories, keeping himself awake with coffee, and surviving on little sleep. Once, after seeing him at the table when she went to bed, Edwina found him sitting in the same position when she got up, and he often went on working till he was too exhausted to take his clothes off. In the morning she found him sprawled across his bed fully dressed, with a cloud of tobacco smoke around him and an empty coffee pot next to him.[19]

His 1937 story "The Field of Blue Children" helps to explain the pressures behind his writing. The central character is a girl. Since the beginning of her adolescence Myra has written a little verse, and begins to write regularly in her final spring at the state university.

Whenever the rising well of unexplainable emotion became so full that its hurt was intolerable, she found that it helped her a little to scribble things down on paper. Single lines or couplets, sometimes whole stanzas, leapt into her mind with the instant completeness of slides flashed on the screen of a magic lantern. Their beauty startled her: sometimes it was like a moment of religious exaltation. She stood in a frozen attitude; her breath was released in a sigh. Each time she felt as though she were about to penetrate some new area of human thought. She had the sensation of standing upon a verge of a shadowy vastness which might momentarily flower into a marvelous crystal of light.

As if to compensate for giving this experience to a woman, Williams introduces a portrait of himself, in the character of Homer, a poet: "He was rather short, stocky and dark. Myra thought him good-looking, but certainly not in any usual way. He had intense black eyes, a straight nose with flaring nostrils, full, mobile lips that sometimes jerked nervously at the corners. All of his movements were overcharged. When he rose from a chair he would nearly upset it. When he lighted a cigarette his face would twist into a terrible scowl and he would fling the burnt match away like a lighted firecracker."

Of all the pressures on Tom the most insidious was created by the problem of whether to stay at home and do his best to protect Rose or to escape, abandoning her. In the apartment the only room where he felt at home was hers. He had helped her paint the walls and furniture white and put up the shelves that housed her collection of glass animals. "As I thought about it the glass animals came to represent the fragile, delicate ties that must be broken, that you inevitably break, when you try to fulfill yourself."[20] Guilt feelings were tightly bound up in the image of the glass menagerie.

While fighting to repress his anger against the father who had aborted his studies and forced him into work that seemed pointless, Tom at first did what he could to help Rose, who was losing her self-confidence and becoming depressed. She applied for a job as a dress model at a shop called Scruggs but was told that she was too short. Edwina enrolled her in a secretarial course, which proved too taxing, and she failed to last for long in her one job, as a dentist's receptionist.[21] Like Edwina's efforts to help her, Tom's were often counterproductive. He took her to a Halloween dance in 1933, but the costumes and masks frightened her. She also had strange delusions, such as thinking that the woman next door, Mrs. Wright, was her half-sister. She responded with great enthusiasm to the doctor, who seemed to be helping her.

Believing that all her daughter needed was a boyfriend, Edwina made arrangements for her to receive a series of "gentleman callers." The phrase, which was current at the time, has become familiar to us through the 1944 play *The Glass Menagerie*, but this is less directly autobiographical than the story "Portrait of a Girl in Glass," which was started in February 1941. The narrator is named Tom, but his sister is called Laura. She is described as someone who "made no positive motion toward the world but stood at the edge of the water. . . . She'd never have budged an inch, I'm pretty sure, if my mother who was a relatively aggressive sort of woman had not shoved her roughly forward, when Laura was nearly twenty years old, by enrolling her as a student in a nearby business college." Every evening after dinner, Laura sits at home for hours in front of a chart, trying to memorize the typewriter keyboard while she polishes her collection of glass ornaments. But she fails so abjectly in her secretarial work that without admitting she is staying away from school, she walks around the park every day for six hours until their mother discovers her defection. After this Laura seldom leaves her bedroom. "She kept the shades drawn down, and as Mother would not permit the use of electric current except when needed, her days were spent almost in perpetual twilight." Apart from the bed, there is no furniture in the room except a bureau and a chair, but the walls are covered with shelves of little glass ornaments. "These she washed and polished with endless care. When you entered the room there was always this soft, transparent radiance in it which came from the glass absorbing whatever faint light had come in through the shades." On her 1920 victrola she plays records from the same period, and sings the songs quietly to herself.

I think that was why I always wrote such strange and sorrowful poems in those days. Because I had in my ears the wispy sound of my sister serenading her pieces of colored glass, washing them while she sang or merely looking down at them with her vague blue eyes until the points of gem-like radiance in them gently drew the arching particles of reality from her mind and finally produced a state of hypnotic calm. . . . I don't believe that my sister was actually foolish. I think the petals of her mind had simply closed through fear.

Encouraged by his mother to invite a friend to dinner, because "it might be nice for your sister," Tom brings Jim Delaney, "a big red-haired Irishman who had the scrubbed and polished look of well-kept chinaware." Sitting next to Jim at the table, Laura keeps her eyes averted. Her face is feverishly bright and one eyelid develops a nervous tic. She and Tom are embarrassed when their mother cross-examines Jim about his home and family, but after the meal Jim expresses interest in Laura's records, and they dance together happily. When her mother comes into the room, Jim is trying to pay Laura a compliment: "She's as light as a feather! With a little more practice she'd dance as good as Betty!" Asked by the crestfallen mother who Betty is, Jim admits she is his fiancée. But Laura gives no sign of being upset.

The story, in which Tom has introduced himself as a poet with a job in a warehouse, ends when he is fired for writing a poem on the lid of a shoe box. He leaves St. Louis and travels from place to place. "The cities swept about me like dead leaves. . . . My nature changed. I grew to be firm and sufficient. . . . But once in a while, usually in a strange town before I have found companions, the shell of deliberate hardness is broken through. . . . I see the faint and sorrowful radiance of the glass, hundreds of little transparent pieces of it in very delicate colors. I hold my breath, for if my sister's face appears among them—the night is hers!"

At the beginning of 1935 Rose would eat only Campbell's tomato soup, and she tore the labels off the cans as if they were discount coupons. According to Dakin, she became "increasingly unhappy and threatened and depressed"; Tom, he says, became "terribly fragile at the same time."[22]

Already a handicap in college, Tom's absentmindedness increased. He got into trouble at the warehouse when a fifty-thousand-dollar order was ignored: he had put the papers in his pocket and forgotten them. Some of his depressive feelings are filtered into his namesake in *The Glass Menagerie*. Tom knows he seems dreamy, but inside, he says, he is boiling. "Whenever I pick up a shoe, I shudder a little thinking how short life is and what I am doing! Whatever that means, I know it doesn't mean shoes—except as something to wear on a traveler's feet!" He has been going to the movies most evenings, but has come to disapprove of them. "You know what happens? People go to the *movies* instead of *moving!* Hollywood characters are supposed to have all the adventures for everybody in America, while everybody in America sits in a dark room and watches them have them!"

Neither the play nor the story says anything about homosexuality, but Tom's uncertainty about his sexual nature was adding to his worries. He was losing weight, which together with lack of sleep, overwork, anxiety, and too much caffeine, probably fomented what he made out to be a heart attack in the spring of 1935. He may have exaggerated symptoms in order to make more of an impression on Cornelius. To recuperate, Tom was sent to stay with his grandparents in Memphis, where he spent the afternoons reading either in the municipal public library or in the University of Tennessee library. He was invited to collaborate with a neighbor's daughter, Bernice Dorothy Shapiro, on a one-act play for local amateurs. She wrote only the prologue and epilogue; he wrote the play—*Cairo! Shanghai! Bombay!*—which is about two sailors who on shore leave pick up a couple of prostitutes and go on an imaginary trip round the world.

He enjoyed rehearsals, in spite of a leading lady "who bawls her lines so loudly that she sounds like she is selling fish."[23] When he saw the play performed he found it so funny that he joined in the audience's laughter.[24] He came to regard this summer in Memphis as a turning point in his life. Staying with his beloved grandparents, he felt as if he were being reborn: he recovered his health and had his first play produced.

3

Student Playwright

By September 1935, when Tom returned to St. Louis, Cornelius's annual salary had increased to $7,500, which meant that they could rent a bigger house in a better district, and that Tom could resume his university career. They moved first to Pershing Avenue and then to a large red-brick colonial house on 42 Aberdeen Place, not far from Washington University, where Tom enrolled for courses in general literature and philosophy. After he made friends with two other students who wanted to write, Clark Mills and William Jay Smith, the three of them formed what they called a "literary factory." But, meeting in Aberdeen Place, they were inhibited by Edwina's garrulity. According to Smith, "She never stopped talking, although there was little inflection or warmth in the steady flow of her speech. One topic, no matter how trivial, received the same emphasis as the next, which might be utterly tragic. I had the impression listening to her that the words she produced were like the red balls in a game of Chinese checkers, all suddenly released and clicking quickly and aimlessly about the board."[1]

Rose's presence was an obstacle to Tom's new friendships. One weekend when his parents were away, he was entertaining Mills and several other friends in the house when one of them, drunker than the rest, went up to the telephone on the landing and began to make obscene telephone calls. Rose told Edwina, who forbade Tom to invite any of these friends to the house. Furious at being betrayed, he turned on Rose "like a wildcat and I hissed at

*TW in the back garden of the house on
Aberdeen Place*

her: 'I hate the sight of your ugly old face!' Wordless, stricken and crouching, she stood there motionless in a corner of the landing as I rushed on out of the house. This is the cruelest thing I have done in my life, I suspect, and one for which I can never properly atone."[2]

It was infuriating that Mills had been banished from the house. Though less handsome than Smith, he was good-looking and, in Tom's view, "brilliantly talented." Smith had a high regard for Tom, who he said "had fanatical and inexhaustible energy in his writing. His persistence was almost grotesque. It was Dionysian, demoniac. He wasn't aiming basically at material success. He wrote because it was a fatal need."[3] This derived partly from compulsion to justify himself in the face of spoken and unspoken criticism from his parents and Rose, who all disapproved of the way he was living.

In "The Accent of a Coming Foot" Bud's sister Cecilia pokes fun at him. Shy, withdrawn, and absent-minded, he has dropped out of college, and now, at twenty-three, spends most of his time in the attic, pounding at an old typewriter he bought in a junk shop. He does not even bother to put on all his clothes, as Cecilia complains to his girlfriend, Catharine, "just a sweatshirt and a pair of old pants like he was training for a championship prizefight or something. . . . He shaves about once every week, he never combs his hair and it seems like Mother just has to *make* him take a bath!" Though his poetry is published in the little magazines, he receives no payment. Still more than half in love with him, Catharine understands how easily scared he is. He moves "like a tall, vague shadow, one hand stretched slightly before him like the feeling hand of the blind, suspicious even of air." But she feels deeply hurt when he comes in and, seeing her, goes out again.

One function of stories like this one was to question what Tom could achieve by pounding away at his typewriter, but at the same time he was at least partly validating his activity by winning prizes. In a poetry contest arranged by the Wednesday Club he was awarded the first prize of twenty-five dollars for his three "Sonnets for Spring," while his poems appeared in

Triumph of a short sonneteer. The twenty-four-year-old Thomas L. Williams with the chairman of the judges for a poetry contest and a sixteen-year-old prizewinner.

TW (front row, far left) at Washington University, St. Louis, with other students who worked on The Eliot, *the literary magazine*

the college poetry society's journal, *College Verse*, and in the university literary magazine, *The Eliot*, which was named after T. S. Eliot's grandfather, founder and chancellor of the university.

All this time Tom remained phenomenally diffident. Smith describes him as "the shyest, quietest person I had ever met. His stonyfaced silence often put people off: he appeared disdainful of what was going on around him, never joining in the quick give-and-take of a conversation, but rather listening carefully and taking it all in. He would sit quietly in a gathering for long periods of time until suddenly like a volcano erupting he would burst out with a high cackle and then with resounding and uncontrollable laughter."[4]

It was Edwina who told him about a one-act-play competition that was being organized by a suburban amateur group, the Webster Groves Theatre Guild. She had read about it in a newspaper. The deadline was tight, but he worked rapidly to turn out *The Magic Tower*, which centers on the relationship between a young artist and his wife, an ex-actress, who live in a garret, calling it their magic tower. They are happy there until he loses confidence in his talent.

Tom's self-confidence was bolstered in the summer of 1936 when his story "27 Wagons Full of Cotton" was published in the magazine *Manuscript*. On a hot day, while a man on a Southern plantation is busy ginning twenty-seven wagon-loads of cotton, his big wife sits on the veranda flirting with the plantation manager, a small man. Eventually she invites him to her bedroom, pleading with him not to hurt her.

Edwina and Rose both disapproved of the story, and, as Tom told his grandparents, "Mother forbids me to send the magazine to anybody. She thinks it is too shocking. It is supposed to be humorous but she and Rose don't take it that way."[5]

Returning to college in the autumn of 1936, he took courses in drama, literature, philosophy, French, Greek, and government. But he cared more about his writing, and he scored another success in October when *The Magic Tower* was finally staged by the Webster Groves Theatre Guild. The critic of the *St. Louis News-Times* called the play "a poignant little tragedy with a touch of warm fantasy."[6]

The performances coincided with preparations by another amateur group, the Mummers of St. Louis, for a production of Irwin Shaw's antiwar play *Bury the Dead*. Finding it ran for less than two hours, the producer, Willard Holland, asked Tom for a twelve-minute curtain raiser based on headlines and pacifist statements. Working rapidly, he produced four episodes: an Armistice Day address by a local senator, a send-up of a local politician, and two sketches about life in St. Louis—one about society and the other about school. *Headlines* was given three performances, starting on 11 November 1936 at the Wednesday Club auditorium, which the Mummers rented for their shows. Standing at the back, Tom enjoyed the audience's laughter.

He got no credit in the program, but thought highly of the group. "Dynamism was what the Mummers had. . . . There was about them that kind of excessive romanticism which is youth and which is the best and purest part of life." He described Holland as "a great director. . . . Everything that he touched he charged with electricity."[7] Holland remembered Tom as "easy to work with . . . He had no temperament about his plays. . . . There was an immersion in his work that was staggering . . . [and] he had the most inane laugh I ever heard, a high squeaky cackle, a shriek."[8]

It was Holland who produced Tom's first full-length play, *Candles to the Sun*, which was bad in Williams's own retrospective opinion, though it "was a smash hit. It even got rave notices out of all three papers, and there was a real demonstration on the opening night with shouts and cheers and stamping, and the pink-faced author took his first bow among the gray-faced coal miners that he had created out of an imagination never stimulated by the sight of an actual coal mine."[9] Writing about people whose lives are adversely affected by the coal-mining company, even when they do not work for it, Williams was contrasting the candlelight of individual consciousness with the sunlight of collective thinking. A Communist is praised because "He ain't in it for what he can get out of it like everybody else seems to be. He talks about society."

Tom went on to write another play for the senior class play-writing competition at the university. *Me, Vasbya!* is about a First World War munitions worker and his oddball wife. After hearing that William Carson, the judging professor, had rejected the play, Tom surprised himself by storming into Carson's office and shouting at him.

Giving priority to his plays, Tom had neglected his academic work, and he failed Greek, which stopped him from graduating. His other main problem was that Rose's condition was deteriorating. Afterward he felt sure she had known she was going mad. She became exceedingly quiet, and seemed to be suffering from insomnia. At night, when she went to bed, she left a pitcher of ice water outside her bedroom door. As Tom spent more time with his new friends, she became more attached to the little Boston bull terrier, Jiggs, holding and hugging him till Edwina ordered her to put him down.

In 1937, after two periods of treatment as an out-patient at the state asylum in Farmington, Missouri, Rose was sent back to St. Vincent's mental hospital. When she came home she was prone to hallucinations and wild outbursts. Sometimes she threatened Cornelius with physical violence, and he reacted brutally, especially when drunk. Once, when he beat her, he induced a fit of hysterical raving, and it may have been in an effort to calm her that he said or did something she interpreted as a sexual advance.

Her hysteria lasted for several days, and the doctors failed to calm her. At least twice more during the summer of 1937 she was admitted to the state asylum, and when Tom visited her there, she led him through a ward full of narrow beds and wooden benches, with a catatonic young girl crouching under one of them. The only occasion on which Edwina saw her mother weep was during a visit to Farmington, when Rose stared blankly at them through the bars.[10]

Rose with Jiggs at the sanatorium

The theater at the University of Iowa

In the autumn of 1937 Tom needed to escape from the trap. He was half-way through his twenty-seventh year, and had always lived with the family, except for the three years of being at the University of Missouri during term-time. Shorter than his nineteen-year-old brother, who was treated so much better by Cornelius, Tom could neither assert himself during family quarrels nor retreat, as he used to, into his sister's bedroom. Had he stayed at home, he might have been able to save her from brain surgery. But though he knew she would be in danger, he decided not to stay in St. Louis.

He had tried, unsuccessfully, to help her, though it was depressing to watch her progressive deterioration. When he left home, he was both escaping from this unpleasant spectacle and seizing an opportunity to make himself into a better playwright by attending the play-writing course at the University of Iowa. This was directed by the head of the drama department, E. C. Mabie, who was later to teach in New York at the New School for Social Research, while other teachers at the university included Elsworth P. Conkle, a successful dramatist.

At first Tom stayed in the Alpha Tau Omega house, but he soon moved into a two-room apartment. He took English literature, Shakespeare, modern drama, experimental play writing, and speech. The first play he wrote for the dramatic production course was a sentimental love story, *Spring Storm*, and when he read it out in class, Mabie's eyes "had a glassy look as though he had drifted into a state of trance." At the end he broke the embarrassed silence with the comment: "Well, we all have to paint our nudes!"[11]

When Willard Holland wanted another play for the Mummers, Tom sent "Not about Nightingales," which ignored private emotion in favor of a social issue, though he could base his story on neither strong feelings nor personal experience. The plot concerns a prison riot after some convicts have been burned alive while being "disciplined" in a room as hot as an oven.[12] The play remained unperformed, but Holland liked another play of Tom's, "Fugitive Kind," enough to stage it in the Wednesday Club auditorium at the end of November. In it a criminal on the run falls in love with

E. C. Mabie, head of the drama department at the University of Iowa. He had a brain tumor and was prone to fits of rage.

the adopted daughter of a man who runs a flophouse. The theme prefigures much of Williams's later work, and the setting reflects his view of the individual as a refugee from the destructive forces generated by urbanization: "A large glass window admits a skyline of the city whose towers are outlined at night by a faint electric glow, so that we are always conscious of the city as a great implacable force, pressing in upon the shabby room and crowding its fugitive inhabitants back against their last wall."

The main character is a petty gangster who sees himself as "a sort of one man revolution. I haven't got any flags or ideal or stuff like that to fight for. All I got is myself an' what I need an' what I want." The *St. Louis Star-Times* called the play "vital and absorbing. . . . Thomas Lanier Williams is a playwright to watch." He wanted "to say something forceful and true about the chaos of modern life" and his theatrical craftsmanship was "first-rate."[13]

Though he was only twenty-six, his hypochondria predisposed him to be scared of impotence. He was cured of this phobia, at least temporarily, by a heterosexual affair. The initiative was taken by Bette Reitz, a hedonistic fellow student. She "had a sort of Etruscan profile, I mean the forehead and nose were on a straight line, the mouth full and sensual and her breath always pleasantly scented by tobacco and beer. She had a terrific build, especially her breasts, which were about the most prominent on campus."[14] He was still handicapped by the puritanism that had kept his virginity intact throughout so many homosexual flirtations, and their first evening together was a fiasco. She had borrowed an apartment from a friend, but when they were naked together on the sofa, he suddenly felt "nauseated from the liquor consumed and from the nervous strain and embarrassment. I rushed into the bathroom and puked, came out with a towel around me, hangdog with shame over my failed test of virility."[15] He made amends the next evening, and having sex regularly, he improved his technique, learning to give more satisfaction as they went on. He had assumed that what attracted her to him was his achievement of writing a play that was about to be produced in St. Louis by the Mummers, but her attitude toward him did not change when "Fugitive Kind" flopped.

He lost all sexual interest in boys, but after the Christmas holidays she refused to meet him. Something had happened, she said. She would tell him later. Several days went by before they met, and when she said she was pregnant, he did not believe her. The truth was that she had a new lover. Tom tried half-heartedly to date other girls, but his interest in boys gradually revived, encouraged by glimpses of seminaked young actors and by a comment made when two students—a man named Lomax and his black girlfriend—made him up for the role of a page boy in Clemence Dane's *Richard of Bordeaux*. Together they rouged his cheeks, colored his lips, tousled his hair into curls. After helping him into the costume, Lomax led him to the woman: "See what I mean?" What he meant, as Tom saw when he stared into the mirror, was that he looked feminine.[16]

Two other factors were poverty and lingering puritanism. He was better off with men, he decided, because he could not afford to go out with women. Nor could he relax sufficiently to give his virility a chance. Before losing his virginity to Bette, he had never achieved orgasm by penetrating someone else's body, and he claimed never to have even masturbated until about a year earlier. "I didn't know what such a thing *was*. Well, I'd heard of it, but it never occurred to me to practice it."[17]

After losing Bette he felt lonely in Iowa City. When summer came, he took to wandering the streets at night, partly to escape from the overpowering heat of his room, partly in quest of adventure. He enjoyed the great trees and the town's old-fashioned charm. But he was full of anxiety. "I didn't know the next step. I was finally fully persuaded that I was 'queer,' but had no idea what to do about it. I didn't even know how to accept a boy on the rare occasions when one would offer himself to me."[18]

Throughout Tom's time at the university Rose had been sinking farther into madness. Her fits had become more violent, and, reacting against the genteel puritanism Edwina had tried to impose, she often shocked her mother by talking explicitly about sex. She said, for instance, that the girls at her college had abused themselves with altar candles they stole from the chapel.[19] She was also threatening to avenge herself for the incestuous assault Cornelius had made on her by launching a physical attack on him. Easily frightened, he believed himself to be in danger. Unfortunately for Rose, one of the doctors gave his support to this fear, while a local psychiatrist recommended lobotomy as a new way of helping the mentally ill. Rose's skull would be opened and the brain surgeon would sever the nerve fibers between the thalamus and the frontal lobes. Few lobotomies had yet been performed in the United States, and even in New York it would have been difficult to get informed advice about the risks involved in his kind of surgery.

We know neither how many doctors were consulted nor whether it is true that Cornelius left his wife to take a unilateral decision. In her 1963 memoir Edwina writes: "We relied on the advice of a local psychiatrist."[20] The local psychiatrist was Dr. Emmett Hoctor at the Farmington Asylum; one of the pioneer brain surgeons, he had been experimenting in prefrontal lobotomy. Six years later, when she was eighty-five and in poor mental health, Edwina claimed that two of the three doctors who advised her had been in favor of the operation, that she had been given six weeks to make a decision, and that Cornelius took no part in it. Certainly, as she says in the memoir, he "was in poor health because of his drinking, and once a month would have to go to the hospital for treatment."[21] In a 1981 interview Williams said that his father had not wanted the operation and had wept on hearing about it. But this may not be true, and even if Cornelius took no part in the decision, Edwina made it at a time when she was still strongly influenced by him—and by knowing what his priorities were. Fearful of what his daughter might do, he was also short of money, and the lobotomy was being offered as an unrepeatable bargain. It would have cost thousands of dollars had it been performed at a private clinic, but this surgeon was going to operate for no fee on thirty selected patients.[22]

We may never know when Tom found out about the lobotomy. According to his published statements, he knew nothing about it until afterward, and this is implicitly confirmed by what Edwina wrote: "I think Tom always felt as though he had failed Rose, that had he been on hand when the big decision was made, he might have been able to stop the lobotomy."[23] He was not on hand when the operation was performed in the autumn of 1937, but according to some of his friends he admitted privately that he had not been kept in complete ignorance of the plan to lobotomize his sister, and that if he had come home, he might have been able to protect her. He took a different view from his mother of what was wrong with Rose. According to him, her fits were no more than hysterical expressions of frustrated sexual desire. "I think [Edwina] was frightened by Rose's sexual fantasies. But that's all they were—fantasies. . . . My mother panicked because she said my sister had begun using four-letter words. 'Do anything! Don't let her talk like that!'"[24] In 1963, twenty-six years after the damage was done, Edwina still described lobotomy as "a very delicate operation on the brain which destroys the chain of memory, in large part, so that one lives without being tortured by fantasies."[25]

Suddenly Last Summer, which was written in 1957, is a perfunctorily camouflaged condemnation of Edwina for authorizing the operation, and it leaves Cornelius out of the picture. A genteel harridan—a monster without any of the extenuating qualities that the mother has in *The Glass Menagerie*—Mrs. Venable is a rich woman with no husband to boss her about. She wants her niece to have brain surgery, the aim being to silence her—to "cut that horrible story out of her brain." To the aunt, whose son has been killed, it does not matter whether the story is true: it is a story that must never be told.

At the University of Iowa Tom found the theater was well equipped, and his classes provided practical experience of acting, stage management, and even building sets. In a "living newspaper" sketch Tom played the black chairman of a church convention condemning the Ku Klux Klan, while he earned extra money by working as a waiter in the cafeteria of the university hospital.[26]

TW (second from left) as one of Falstaff's soldiers in Henry IV, Part I *at the University of Iowa (1938)*

TW (far right) in Marcus Bach's Calvario
at the University of Iowa (1938)

Mabie was liable to throw tantrums. He had a brain tumor and was periodically confined in the mental ward of the university hospital. Once, dissatisfied with a dress rehearsal, he threw his spectacles at the actors and kept them rehearsing from eight in the evening till noon the following day.[27] Generally Tom found the lectures more useful than at the University of Missouri or Washington University, and in his first semester Mabie had given him an A in the experimental play writing course. His other grades were two Bs and two Cs. Students were required to write radio scripts for an Iowa station, and, because Elsworth Conkle recommended Tom's scripts, a series of them was broadcast. At the end of the year, Conkle wanted to have him awarded a scholarship and keep him on, but Mabie was less enthusiastic about his work. He was given a B in creative writing, experimental drama, and literature and he got Ds in modern and classical drama and zoology, which meant he could not graduate unless he took a summer-school course. To pay for it he washed dishes in a doctors' cafeteria, where he was given free meals. On 5 August 1938 he finally acquired a degree in English literature. He was twenty-seven.

According to Donald Windham, who got to know him well shortly afterward, Tom was under a great deal of pressure from his father, who had

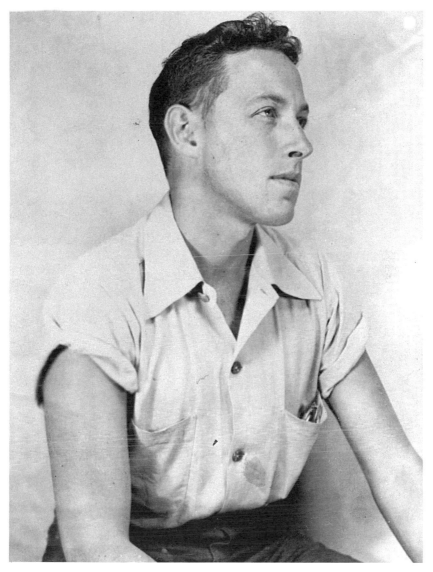

*The twenty-seven-year-old TW at the time
of his graduation from the University of Iowa
(1938)*

delivered an ultimatum, insisting that he should get a job.[28] Knowing he could not stay on at home without doing so, Tom left for Chicago.

The choice of Chicago was determined partly by Lomax and his black girlfriend, who invited him to travel with them, and partly by Conkle, who told him about the Federal Writers' Project of the Works Progress Administration (WPA). Under a scheme that had been started during the Depression, jobs were being provided for needy writers.

But Tom came back to St. Louis empty-handed. Clark Mills was there, and with other friends they went on picnics along the Meramec River. There were times when Cornelius seemed less unfriendly, less reluctant to lend Tom the car, but without Rose, who was kept in the hospital after her operation, home life was intolerable: nothing distracted him from the facade of genteel refinement Edwina had erected like a barricade against Cornelius's crudity and miserliness. In Chicago Tom had been recommended to apply for work in New Orleans, where the Writers' Project needed a larger staff, and at the end of the year, when he left home, Edwina was not expecting him to come back.[29]

4

Exit Tom,
Enter Tennessee

In December 1938 Tom traveled by bus from St. Louis to New Orleans. He felt—or so it seemed retrospectively—as if he were "a migratory bird going to a more congenial climate."[1] It was almost like arriving in a different country. A. J. Liebling has said New Orleans is less like the southernmost point of the United States than the northernmost point of Costa Rica. Tom was suddenly in a more lackadaisical society where little attention was paid to either propriety or punctuality. In contrast to the Garden District and other respectable uptown areas, the French Quarter, where he settled, was slummy and sexually permissive. Prostitutes and strip bars were easier to find than anywhere else in the country. Today the bawdiest street is Bourbon Street, but in 1938 the red-light district had its center on Dauphine Street. Tom was walking down it one night when he heard "metallic tappings on the shutters" and "ladies whispering through the shutters, you know, 'Come in, baby,' offering various enticements."[2]

People in the French Quarter were friendly, food was cheap, and he felt at home. The new sense of freedom was intensely enjoyable. As he said later, "I've never known anybody who lived in, or even visited the Quarter, who wasn't slightly intoxicated—without booze."[3] The French Quarter was not what it has since become. Since the turn of the century, it had, like Greenwich Village, offered a refuge from pressure. In one story he calls New Orleans "the cheapest and most comfortable place in America for fugitives

"The cheapest and most comfortable place in America for fugitives from the economic struggle." New Orleans, the French Quarter, corner of Toulouse and Burgundy Streets.

from economic struggle," while another of his stories describes the city as having a "lunar atmosphere," which "draws me back whenever the waves of energy which removed me to more vital towns have spent themselves and a time of recession is called for. Each time I have felt some rather profound psychic wound, a loss or a failure, I have returned to this city. At such periods I would seem to belong there and no place else in the country."[4]

After a brief stay with people he knew on St. Peter Street, he moved toward the end of December into a small hotel at 431 Royal Street, where he was given a clean little room for three dollars a week. At a New Year's Eve party he met Lyle Saxon, who ran the local WPA office and did his best to help Tom, but the Writers' Project was gradually being dismantled, and Saxon could do no more than provide a list of trade journals that could commission articles. Tom started calling at their offices, and tried to sell plays to the radio stations.[5]

722 Toulouse Street

Early in January 1939 he moved into a boardinghouse at 722 Toulouse Street, paying ten dollars a month. The staircase is still what he describes in the stage directions of his 1977 play, *Vieux Carré*, ascending from "a dark narrow passageway" between the front door and a kitchen area. The house was owned by Mrs. Anderson, "a lovely Mississippi lady," who provided well-cooked meals for twenty-five cents. This gave Tom an idea he passed on. Why not make part of the first floor into a café? Desperately short of money, he had pawned almost everything he owned while working at a variety of odd jobs, but it would be better to get involved in the café, which they called the Quarter Eat Shop. Having thought up the slogan, "Meals for a Quarter in the Quarter," he earned wages by giving out hand-printed cards in the street and then going indoors to work as waiter and cashier.

But the café did not survive for long. After a week the sixty-seven-year-old cook, Mrs. Nesbit, called to say that her son would not let her come to work because she had been so exhausted the previous night after doing all the kitchen work as well as all the cooking. Unable to find another cook, Mrs. Anderson was thinking of selling out for $350—a price that would include both the lease and the furniture. But before she could find a buyer, she got herself into trouble with the police. She had been, as Tom put it, having "a hard time adjusting herself to the Bohemian spirit of the Vieux Carré," and when the tenant of the first-floor studio, which was just underneath her bedroom, held a noisy party, she retaliated by pouring a bucket of water through his ceiling. She was taken to the nearest police station and charged with malicious mischief and disturbing the peace. Tom had to appear in court as a witness, and, eager to help her, but unwilling to lie under oath, he equivocated by saying he thought it highly unlikely that any lady would do such a thing as pour water through a ceiling. She was fined fifteen dollars.[6]

The house at 722 Toulouse Street, which now contains the offices of the Historic New Orleans Collection, dates from the early nineteenth century. Today it has only two stories, but it had three then, and he was given an attic room with a dormer window. The other attic room was occupied by a tubercular painter who earned money by making quick sketches of customers at a restaurant around the corner, the Court of Two Sisters, and it seems to have been this man who initiated the young writer into homosexuality.

In his 1973 interview with *Playboy* Williams claimed that his first "real encounter" had been in New Orleans after a New Year's Eve party when he was twenty-eight. He was twenty-seven in December 1938 when he arrived in the city, but he left before his twenty-eighth birthday and long before the war started. He did not return until September 1941, when he was thirty. The incident he described to the interviewer could have occurred in the house where he was living on New Year's Day 1942. What happened, he says, is that "a very handsome paratrooper climbed up to my grilled veranda and said, 'Come down to my place,' and I did, and he said, 'Would you like a sunlamp treatment?' and I said, 'Fine,' and I got under one and he proceeded to do me. That was my coming out and I enjoyed it."[7] By the end of

1941 the United States had entered the war, and the port of New Orleans was in use as a naval base. Tom is more likely to have slept with a paratrooper then, but if he did, the one-night stand was certainly not his "coming out." He had been having homosexual affairs in New York at the beginning of 1940, and he told another interviewer that he kept falling in love during the summer of 1940, which he remembered as the happiest in his life.

He probably "came out" during his first visit to New Orleans. It was here, he says, that he found "a kind of freedom I had always needed. And the shock of it against the Puritanism of my nature has given me a subject, a theme, which I have never ceased exploiting."[8] In *Vieux Carré*, the Writer speculates on what first attracted him to the French Quarter: "I couldn't have consciously, deliberately, selected a better place than here to discover—to encounter— my true nature." Later he tells his landlady how ignorant he had been when he arrived. "This place has been a—I ought to pay you—tuition."

In the short story "The Angel in the Alcove," which Williams wrote in October 1943 and which was to serve, thirty-four years later, as the basis for *Vieux Carré*, he describes a New Orleans boardinghouse that he locates on Bourbon Street. There the narrator is jolted out of his sleep by someone who has come into his room and is crouching over the bed. "I jumped up and nearly cried out, but the arms of the visitor passionately restrained me. He whispered his name which was that of a tubercular young artist who slept in the room adjoining. I want to, I want to, he whispered. So I lay back and let him do what he wanted until he was finished. Then without any speech he got up and left my room. For a while afterwards I heard him coughing and muttering to himself through the wall between us. Turbulent feelings were on both sides of the wall."

The fiction seems to contain more of the facts about Tom's first homosexual affair than the *Playboy* interview. He may have thought the truth too squalid to be compatible with the image he was trying to project in 1973, and possibly, having told the story once, he thought it better to serve up a new incident than to repeat an old one. The tubercular artist is resurrected in the 1977 play, but here his advances are gently rebuffed.

By 1973 Williams may himself have been muddling his first stay in New Orleans with his second. We cannot be sure of his motives for covering his tracks in such a way that the biographer is forced to rely on guesswork. His first homosexual experience was a turning point in his life, and if it did occur early in 1939, it coincided with an effort at self-transformation. He had already sent out a few scripts under the name Tennessee Williams, but he now began to use this alternative name consistently. He was changing more than his name. Instead of dressing conservatively in a dark suit with a shirt and tie, and wearing shoes that might have been bought from the International Shoe Company, he started to sport sandals and flamboyant shirts and jackets. Encouraging himself to be less diffident, he built up a collection of fashionably casual shoes, three-piece suits, bow ties, and silk handkerchiefs for his jacket pocket. But his hair was unruly, and there was always something discordant in his appearance. The shirt clashed with the tie, or he went out with no socks on.[9]

Nor did he feel obliged to admit that Tennessee Williams was as old as Tom Williams. The habit of subtracting three years from his age started in February 1939, after he heard about a competition for playwrights under the age of twenty-five. He was within a month of his twenty-eighth birthday, but since competitors were not required to submit proof of their age, he decided to enter "Fugitive Kind," "Not about Nightingales," and four one-act plays.

The competition was organized by the Group Theatre, which had been founded in 1931 by Harold Clurman and Lee Strasberg, who were now running it with Elia Kazan and Cheryl Crawford. Tennessee was still waiting for news about the result when a young jazz clarinetist, Jim Parrott, offered him a free ride to California. Jim was hoping to work with a band in Los Angeles, and Tennessee accepted, wanting to try his luck as a Hollywood scriptwriter.

After setting out on 18 February, they lived on fifty cents a day, cooking over open fires by the roadside and sleeping in an old army tent. In Los Angeles Jim got a job in an airplane factory, but Tennessee's attempts to find work were hampered by a cataract forming in his left eye. After three weeks on the road, he settled for a job on a chicken ranch in Hawthorne, twenty miles from Los Angeles. For each chicken they killed and plucked, the workers would put a feather into a milk bottle, and they were paid according to the number of feathers. After killing and plucking between sixty and a hundred chickens a day, Tennessee had to drive them on a truck to the market. A job he relished even less was looking after the chicken farmer, who got drunk every evening, moving on to another bar whenever a

Jim Parrott and TW in front of the "Pigeon Ranch" (1939)

bartender refused to go on serving him. He usually ended up singing "O Takki" at the top of his voice while Tennessee drove him home.[10]

After losing his job at the factory, Jim rejoined his friend, but by the end of March Tennessee had left the farm to work for a couple of weeks at Clark's Bootery in Culver City, where he earned $12.50 a week for about sixty hours of work—nine to six on weekdays; nine to nine on Saturdays. He got the job through Cornelius, who had been in touch with a colleague at the west coast branch of the International Shoe Company. Twice a day Tennessee had to cycle the twelve miles between Hawthorne and Culver City.

He had just started the job in the shoe store when a telegram arrived from New York. The Group Theatre had decided to award him a special prize of a hundred dollars for the one-act plays. Elia Kazan's wife, Molly Day Thacher, had been the one to spot his talent. Though the first prize of five hundred dollars was awarded to another playwright, Ramon Naya, Clurman had agreed to Thacher's idea of creating a special award for Tennessee. She also sent his plays to an influential agent, Audrey Wood.

After hearing the good news, Tennessee and Jim biked down to the Mexican border. They stayed in a Tijuana cantina, where they lost most of their money, and, making their way back up the California coast, had to sleep in the open air until, in a canyon outside Laguna Beach, they found jobs on another chicken ranch. The elderly owners needed someone to look after the birds while they went to Canada for a vacation. In lieu of pay, Tennessee and Jim were given permission to sleep in a small cabin at the end of the chicken run.[11]

Work at the chicken farm was complicated by the vagueness of the instructions that had been left. He and Jim had been told to give the small chicks "enough growing mash so that they'll never be without it." Since they ate continuously, it was hard to gauge how much was enough, and one morning the boys found the food trough empty and three birds dead. In one of the coops a small bantam rooster was alone with eight big hens. "His activities . . . make me doubt, almost, the superiority of the human race."[12]

It was during this summer—through correspondence—that Tennessee launched into a relationship crucial to his career as a playwright. Once Audrey Wood had begun to show interest in his work, he took advantage of the distance between Laguna Beach and New York to brew up an appetizing account of himself, spiced with fiction. With undisguised relish for the task of introducing himself in letters, he presented himself as a young man of twenty-five, a native of Mississippi, descended from "Indian-fighting Tennessee pioneers." He had first become interested in writing for the theater, he told her, during his last year at the University of Iowa, so he had not benefited much from the excellent dramatic training available there. The truth was that he had spent only a year in Iowa (1937 – 38) and had been busily writing plays since his first one-acter—*Cairo! Shanghai! Bombay!*—had been staged by amateurs in the summer of 1935. His ambition, he told her, was to settle for a year in a cabin he had discovered on a lonely Mexican arroyo, where he could live simply and concentrate on writing a long, careful play. He now had only thirty dollars left, he said, and once that money was spent, he would have to pawn his typewriter and his guitar, while writing to his parents, pleading for money.[13]

Tennessee wanted to write a play about the poet Vachel Lindsay, basing it on the biography by Edgar Lee Masters, but by the middle of July D. H. Lawrence had emerged as a more enticing subject. At the same time Tennessee was thinking about a nonbiographical play, and by the end of the month had worked out the plot in considerable detail. A woman is dying of cancer while her husband is out getting drunk. Fugitives from life, they have both been waiting unrealistically for a future in which the past fulfills the promises it had seemed to be making. The husband, Jonathan, had once been the golden-haired glamour boy of a small lakeside town in upstate New York. Always given star parts in school plays, he also played the saxophone, and had become president of every school society, while Ida had been a shy, sensitive girl who wrote verse. (The idea has some of its roots in such short stories as "The Accent of a Coming Foot" and "The Field of Blue Children.") When Ida and Jonathan married, she still believed his future would be in line with his past, but instead of becoming a movie star, he worked as a barman and developed into a drunkard. Still in love with him, she dies before he returns home. At the end of July, outlining the action in a letter to Audrey Wood, Tennessee claimed that "with its emphasis on atmosphere and character-touches," it was "the sort of thing for which I have a particular facility."[14] But she wrote back discouragingly: nearly all the action was in the past.

To earn money while living at the chicken farm, Tennessee took an additional job during July at a bowling alley in Laguna Beach, setting up pins. In August there was an epidemic among the chickens. One morning he and Jim emerged from their cabin to find at least a third of the birds dead and the survivors wandering dizzily around as if about to collapse. Scared, Jim escaped in an old car he had recently acquired, and Tennessee, who had already lost his job at the bowling alley, had to survive for about ten days with no money and no food except for avocados stolen from a nearby grove. Without explaining what had led him to this conclusion, he wrote to tell Audrey Wood that it was impossible to starve in rural California, where there were so many orchards and truck farms. In his view, anyway, it was more dignified to climb a fence and steal avocados than to line up outside a soup kitchen.[15]

But he did not steal enough to stave off hunger pangs. "I discovered that after the third day, you stop feeling hungry. You just drift into a strangely peaceful condition which is ideal for meditation."[16] After he had survived two weeks of near-starvation Jim reappeared. By playing his clarinet in a nightclub near Los Angeles he had managed to earn enough money to get them both into the San Bernardino Mountains for a period of recuperation.

Frieda Lawrence: "Still magnificent, a Valkyrie who runs and plunges about the ranch like a female bull"

Before they met, Audrey Wood had begun to play an active role in Tennessee's life. She sold "The Field of Blue Children" to the magazine *Story* for twenty-five dollars, and as soon as he said that he wanted to settle in New York, she advanced money for bus fares. He traveled via Taos, New Mexico, so that he could visit D. H. Lawrence's widow, Frieda, at her ranch in the Lobo Mountains. Six years older than Lawrence, who had died of tuberculosis in 1930 at the age of forty-five, she was fifty-nine and "still magnificent, a Valkyrie who runs and plunges about the ranch like a female bull." She was "not a member of the female sex," he decided. She had "thick yellow straw hair" and piercing blue eyes. She had recently taken a new lover, an Italian. Meeting her made Tennessee even more keen to write about Lawrence.

At the end of September Tennessee traveled from Taos to New York by bus, arriving in the early morning. Unshaven, he went straight to Wood's office in the RCA Building in Rockefeller Center. Audrey Wood was "a very small and dainty woman with red hair, a porcelain complexion and a look of cool perspicacity in her eyes." Her partner in the agency was her husband, William Liebling, who called her "the little giant of the American theatre." Shaking Tennessee's hand, she said: "Well, well, you've finally made it." His answer was "Not yet," but he was expecting to make it soon, and she was not alone in feeling confident that he would.[17] Writing to his grandfather on 13 October about theater people he had met in New York, Tennessee said they were looking at him as if he were a goose about to lay a golden egg, while some of them called him the gentile Clifford Odets.

He was paying $4.50 for a room in a West 108th Street block of studios rented to tyro artists and actors. To his grandfather he described it as sort of club for young men and women, mostly college graduates.[18] He was still there at the beginning of October, but, feeling lonely, he moved to Morningside Drive to live with Marion Galloway, a Kentucky woman he had met in Ohio.

Working on the play about Lawrence, Williams began at the end, writing the death scene. According to William Jay Smith, "Tom's great god was D. H. Lawrence."[19] In a preface to the play Williams wrote: "Lawrence felt the mystery and power of sex as the primal life urge, and was the lifelong adversary of those who wanted to keep the subject locked away in the cellars of prudery. . . . All in all his work is probably the greatest monument to the dark roots of creation." Made into a character in the play, Frieda says: "The meaning of Lawrence escapes you. In all of his work he celebrates the body." The play was going to focus on her devotion to him. Tennessee saw him both as a genius and as "a would-be satyr never quite released from the umbilicus." But Audrey Wood dissuaded him from investing time in the project, and the death scene became a one-act play. He called it *I Rise in Flame, Cried the Phoenix*.

She threw herself wholeheartedly into the task of finding ways Tennessee could earn money until his work was staged. She advised him to apply for a grant from the Rockefeller Foundation. Looking for backers to option his plays, she persuaded the actor Hume Cronyn to pay Tennessee fifty dollars a month for production rights to the nine one-act plays. She also gave Tennessee money and paid bills for him, and as the autumn became colder persuaded friends to give him unwanted clothes. But after staying briefly at the Men's Residence Club on West 56th Street, he left for St. Louis, though he did not have enough money for the whole trip. Two weeks later he was still stranded in Dodge City, Kansas.

When he finally made it back to his family in St. Louis, he spent most of his time in the attic, working on a full-length play, *Battle of Angels*, which incorporated some of his ideas from the play about the drunk who had once been a golden boy, but there was also a strong autobiographical element in it, and he called it an "emotional record" of his youth. Busy on it in early November, he kept Audrey Wood in touch with developments: in a postcard dated 7 November, he told her that the fire motif in the play had suddenly struck him as atrociously silly, and the climax of the third act was "sheer melodrama." He thought of cutting the act completely, but four days later he was intending to keep it and to call the play "Figures in Flame". He was being pulled between artistic and commercial considerations. He had started out with the intention of writing a play that would make a lot of money, but he was hoping "that the final result will have some artistic merit as well." He was also nervous of leaving his manuscript in the attic: it was possible that his mother would go up there when he was out, read what he had been writing, and "launch one of her literary purges."[20]

Though reluctant to stay on in St. Louis, he was kept there "by necessity, the *smother* of invention." There was "a kind of spiritual fungus or gangrene" that set in after the second or third month, and if he stayed for a fourth, he would be "pronounced incurable." But he was still there in December, and still writing prolifically. He told Audrey Wood he was planning a trilogy of plays about the South—"Spring Storm," *Battle of Angels*, and "The Aristocrats." As she must have observed, he said, there was only one major theme in his work—"the destructive impact of society on the sensitive, non-conformist individual." The nonconformist in "The Aristocrats" was going to be an extraordinarily gifted young female artist who would be forced into prostitution. He was also thinking of using her as the central figure in a novel called "Americans."[21]

The necessity that had been smothering invention was financial, and he was released from it when he heard that the Dramatists Guild, using a grant from the Rockefeller Foundation, had awarded him a writing fellowship of a thousand dollars. He could return to New York at the beginning of January 1940, and he accepted Audrey Wood's suggestion that she should keep the money and pay him monthly installments of a hundred dollars.

He stayed at the YMCA on West 63rd Street, where the weekly rent of $7.50 gave him the right to use the swimming pool. The critic John Gassner, who was an administrator of the Theatre Guild, invited him to attend a play-writing seminar at the New School for Social Research, where E. C. Mabie was now teaching. In Gassner's seminar Tennessee revised *Battle of Angels*, which Gassner liked so much that he showed it to the playwright Elmer Rice and recommended it to Theresa Helburn and Lawrence Langner of the Theatre Guild, which had been the most influential management in New York since the end of the First World War. Tennessee was allowed to sit in on rehearsals of the Guild's production of a play by Clifford Odets, *Night Music*. He also went out with Odets's sister, Florence. "Unfortunately she's Jewish," he wrote to his grandfather. "But very nice."[22]

Donald Windham

Tennessee was unimpressed by most of the productions he saw. "There is a pitiful lot of plays going on right now," he wrote to Edwina, confident that his own work would soon be taken up by the commercial theater. He was happy to be meeting so many exciting people, but it seemed unlikely that he would ever be able to concentrate on writing in New York. "So many interesting things to do that the days slip by unnoticed."[23]

In January a poetry editor he knew, Harold Vinal, invited a few friends to his small apartment on 52nd Street, where Tennessee started dancing with a good-looking boy of nineteen, Donald Windham, who had been working in an Atlanta barrel factory and had come to Manhattan because his lover, Fred Melton, was working as a show card letterer in a department store. Not knowing about Fred, Tennessee started kissing Donald, but desisted when an Indian boy told him to cool it. "His lover doesn't like it."[24]

Donald's first impression was that Tennessee was a loner, shy but also bold, and this view remained unchanged as their friendship developed. "His quotidian goal was to end up in bed with a partner at least once before the twenty-four hours was over. . . . His practice in a room of half a dozen more or less presentable males was to make a pass at the one he found most attractive and then, if it was not successful, to go on down the line." Among his possessions, still stored untidily in a suitcase and footlocker in the YMCA, "he kept, besides a jar of Vaseline, a bottle of Cuprex, against crabs, and a tube of prophylactic salve, against gonorrhea. A small drawstring bag, like the bags cigarette tobacco was sold in then, accompanied the tube of salve, to tie around his genitals . . . after the salve was applied."[25] After so many puritanical years of unconsummated love, Tennessee, as if trying to make up for wasted time, put diffidence resolutely behind him in his compulsive search for sexual pleasure.

His astigmatic left eye was now covered by a milky white cataract, which, in combination with his rakish smile, gave "the impression of a continual conspiratorial wink." Smoking a cigarette in a long black holder, he "looked provocatively into your eyes" and, while still talking, "let his focus fade to unseeing and, with a tap of his finger, knocked the cigarette ashes in your direction, as though no longer aware of your presence."[26]

His plays were not taken up by the commercial theater as quickly as he had expected, and within two months he was tiring of New York and making plans for another stay in Mexico. Early in March, writing to Anne Bretzfelder, a young sculptor who lived in St. Louis, he told her his desk, cluttered with fragments of plays and stray bits of stories, was surmounted by an immense travel poster of Mexico. It would cost fifty-five dollars to sail to Vera Cruz, traveling second-class, and he was planning to leave on the twenty-second, four days before his birthday. He wanted to go on to Mexico City and Acapulco. In the meantime he was going to stay up all night to watch the *Queen Elizabeth* dock at 5:00 A.M. in New York harbor.[27]

What kept him in New York was news that in April students at the New School for Social Research were going to stage *The Long Goodbye*, his play about a young man who seems to be losing his past as the furniture is moved out of his apartment. As in so many of Tennessee's early plays and stories, the writing is impelled by a mixture of guilt and resentment at his family situation. In most of these fictions he takes revenge against Cornelius by leaving him out of the picture. The typical Williams family consists of a mother abandoned by her husband and living with two grown children, a daughter and a son who writes verse. But the feckless father appears in *The Long Goodbye*. The nagging mother reproaches the poet for not taking better care of his sister, Myra, who picks up men at a swimming pool. Trying to cultivate a stoic detachment, the poet recognizes that life consists of saying goodbye to one thing after another. The performances given on 9 and 10 April were so well attended that a third was mounted on the fourteenth.

In reality it was Tennessee who was picking up men at a swimming pool. At the YMCA he found both the pool and the steam room were good places for making new friends, as were the bars of Times Square, if you drank there late at night. Claiming to be twenty-five, Tennessee, with his boyish looks and high spirits, seemed scarcely older than the nineteen-year-old Donald. They went swimming together at the YMCA, walked through a snowstorm to see a performance of *The Long Goodbye* at the New School, and on Easter Sunday attended the morning service at the Cathedral of St. John the Divine. Tennessee was wearing a new straw hat. Donald noticed how productive he was: "He put writing before knowing where he was going to sleep or where his next meal was coming from."[28]

Often he was "humbly eager for companionship," and he had great charm, but usually ignored other people's needs and expectations. He paid no attention to mealtimes, eating whenever he felt hungry. On his way to meet his agent or an interested producer, he would notice a café and announce that he wanted to eat rice pudding. Inside, he ordered chicken croquettes or a bowl of soup. While eating he sucked his teeth, smacked his lips, and licked food from around his mouth. If Donald reminded him about the agent or producer, he answered: "Oh, I don't imagine they'll be expecting me now." He then suggested they should go back to the Y for a swim, but when they got there, he sat down at his typewriter and worked.[29]

At the end of April he was still in New York, but he was packing the things he wanted to leave in St. Louis before sailing south. On the Sunday morning before he was due to leave New York, he rang Donald and Fred, asking them to come over and help him pack. They found him kneeling on the floor, surrounded chaotically by his possessions. Desk, bed, and windowsill were cluttered with manuscripts, and he could not decide which to throw away, which to leave in St. Louis, and which to pack in his suitcase. He had no hesitation about taking the collected poems of Hart Crane, the book that accompanied him everywhere. Finally Donald and Fred helped him to carry his things to the railroad station. Apart from the suitcase, there were a cardboard box tied with cord, a trunk, a portable typewriter, a rented radio, several coats, and an envelope of manuscripts that Donald would deliver to the Liebling-Wood office.

In the Clover Bar at the old Pennsylvania Station Tennessee bought them drinks and introduced them to another friend who had come to see him off, but he got no farther than Memphis, where he was staying with his grandparents when a telegram arrived: the Theatre Guild had optioned *Battle of Angels*. He returned to New York, but casting was still incomplete, and, almost as reluctant to stay in New York as in St. Louis, he left again for Lake George, in upstate New York, expecting the swimming to be good, but the water was too cold, and he returned to the city, where Donald and Fred had a chance of subletting a duplex beginning the first of June. Tennessee agreed to move in with them.

He took the top floor, a large studio with three windows that had striped awnings over them and a large table where he set up his typewriter and the victrola, which he played while he worked. He rewrote each story and play again and again, not revising the previous draft but tossing it away, to work from memory. "For each of these revisions," according to Donald, "Tennessee held in, often for phenomenal lengths of time, everything in his backlog of emotions that was seeking release, everything he felt, until he could rush through it blindly, furiously, to a climax of achievement."[30]

Gratified though he was that at last one of his full-length plays was to be given a full-scale Broadway production, he became so depressed that Paul Bigelow, a Theatre Guild executive who had befriended him, often putting him up at his apartment on East 73rd Street when he had nowhere else to stay, persuaded him to leave for Provincetown, on Cape Cod. His spirits had never been lower than when he made the trip. "I actually hoped that my bad cough was tuberculosis or that some convenient accident would occur on the road and I would be relieved of the tedious problem of remaining alive."[31]

In Provincetown he took a room for twenty dollars a week in a cottage on a pier overlooking the harbor. "The sun has come out," he wrote to Donald at the end of June, "and the lonely sand-dunes, sea-gulls and blue ocean is an excellent katharsis for a 'sin-sick soul.'"[32] While there he met a handsome young Jewish Canadian dance student, nephew of the

Russian bass Alexander Kipnis. An illegal immigrant, the young man was studying at the Hanya Holm school and earning money by modeling in an art school under the name Kip Kiernan. When the affair began, Tennessee was so unnerved at having his passion reciprocated that he went on laughing and crying for what seemed like an hour or two, unable to get out of bed. Once, when Kip stayed out all night, Tennessee was acutely anxious, thinking he had found another lover. In fact he had settled down alone on the beach "because he needed some sleep. Doesn't get much with me. But that's his own fault for being so incredibly beautiful." Tennessee was much happier, feeling loved. He was certain that "nobody ever loved me before so completely." He went swimming every day and worked on a long narrative poem.[33]

But the affair lasted only six weeks, and it is hard to be sure why. According to Tennessee, Kip became interested in a girl; according to Donald, Kip was not promiscuous, and it was Tennessee who ran away, "fleeing from a fear of emotional commitment." Afterward Tennessee claimed that the breakup "was only an incident in a long cumulation of tensions and difficulties, actual and psychic, and the result was a sort of temporary obliteration of everything solid in me and all I thought of was my own immediate preservation through change, escape, travel, new scenes, new people."[34]

Tennessee was probably thinking of himself when, in the story "Rubio y Morena," which he may have started about this time, he describes the writer Kamrowski as unable to endure the realization that someone loves him. The discovery "broke finally all the way through the encrusted shell of his ego, which had never before been broken all the way through, and he was released. He was let out of the small but apparently rather light and comfortable room of his known self into a space that lacked the comfort of limits. He entered a space of bewildering dark and immensity, and yet not dark, of which light is really the darker side of the sphere. He was not at home in it. It gave him unbearable fright, and so he crawled back." In September Tennessee started out on the trip he had intended to make in March: he sailed for Mexico.

5

You   Old   Bitch!

Every morning when I get up I look at myself in the mirror and say with surprise and scorn and a kind of amused tolerance, "Well, there you still are, you old bitch!" Now, that is definitely a ruder remark than anyone has addressed to me, except myself. — Tennessee Williams in Acapulco, 25 or 26 September 1940

In Mexico City, on his last night before leaving for Taxeo and Acapulco, Tennessee was accosted on the street by some of the male whores and taken to the house of Juanita, their queen, where he was entertained, though he spoke no Spanish and they spoke no English. Their price was only two pesos—about forty cents—and one of them was so attractive that a kiss and an embrace from him was enough to give Tennessee an orgasm. He stayed out of bed, though, suspecting that they were all riddled with disease, but he soon had a new lover, Carlos, who also spoke no English. By now the affair with Kip had dwindled in Tennessee's memory. "Probably because you [meaning 'I'] never really got to know, you simply surrounded him with fiction, so when that fiction was shed by separation or loss, there was nothing left."[1]

In Acapulco Tennessee stayed at the Hotel Costa Verde. "The tranquil spirit of the tropics, hours of swimming and sun-bathing and a few sympathetic friends and a new lover have restored my faith in the possibility of going on with this strange business called life."[2] The town was full of Germans exuberant about the blitz on London. When Tennessee said "Hello"

The twenty-nine-year-old TW in Acapulco (1940)

to an attractive German girl at the hotel, her response was: "Sorry, I don't speak Yiddish."[3]

Paul and Jane Bowles were living in the town, and he made friends with them, though he describes the first conversation as being mainly about dyspepsia and the food that Paul Bowles could digest. Short of cash, Tennessee was in danger of being thrown out of the hotel when a check arrived—his advance on *Battle of Angels*—and soon afterward he heard that movie star Miriam Hopkins might be willing to play the leading part if she could fit it in with her Hollywood commitments.[4] He had wanted to do more work on the script, but things started to happen too quickly. The director chosen by the Guild was Margaret Webster, an Englishwoman with more experience of directing Shakespearean drama than of working with writers on new plays.

Before returning to New York for rehearsals Tennessee stayed in St. Louis, where he worked on a play he had started in the summer, "Stairs to the Roof." But before the end of October he was installed again at the YMCA, eager for his first experience of preparing for a Broadway opening. To earn money he took a job at a bookstore, the Gotham Book Mart on West 47th Street, but he was fired on his first day. He met Margaret Webster in her hotel suite with Miriam Hopkins. Margaret Webster described him as

a short, sturdy young man with crew-cut hair, pebble-thick glasses and an even thicker Southern accent, dressed in a shabby corduroy jacket and muddy riding boots. He greeted us amiably; Miriam said she hoped he had enjoyed his ride; he replied that he never went riding but that he liked the boots. He then sat down on the spotless yellow chaise-longue and put them up on it. We started to talk about the play; he didn't seem much interested; once, when Miriam became a little vehement, he prefaced his reply with "As far as I can gather from all this hysteria."[5]

He was in a state of near-panic because the Guild was planning to open the play in Boston on 30 December and after two weeks there bring it to New York. Tennessee was afraid he would be expected to rewrite dialogue during rehearsals.

Without being directly autobiographical, the play contains ingredients and themes that were so important to him that he went on writing variations on them throughout his life. While treating *Battle of Angels* like the first draft of a script he revised it compulsively till it was staged in 1957 under the title *Orpheus Descending*.

Among the titles Audrey Wood dissuaded him from using was "The Fugitive Kind." As in *The Glass Menagerie*, Tennessee wanted to show sensitivity being crushed by brutality. Val Xavier is a poet, young, homeless, impoverished, imaginative, virile but fragile. After being given both a job and a home by Myra Torrance, who lives above the confectionery store she runs, he turns out to be irresistibly attractive not only to Myra, whose aging husband is dying of cancer, but to Vee Talbot, an eccentric painter, wife of the sheriff, and to Cassandra Whiteside, a local woman with a tendency to nymphomania. "You and me," Cassandra tells Val, "belong to the fugitive kind. We live on motion . . . Nothing but motion, motion, mile after mile, keeping up with the wind."

Dedicated to the memory of D. H. Lawrence, *Battle of Angels* is reminiscent of his work in both its symbolism and its glorification of rudimentary sexual drives. When Myra becomes pregnant by Val, her husband, Jabe, reveals that it was he who killed her father, and the violence, which has been suspensefully and melodramatically wound up like a spring, is released at the end, when Jabe shoots Myra and puts the blame on Val, who is hanged by the sheriff's posse.

Tennessee wrote to Edwina that he was getting his own way with the production, but only after a lot of fighting. "The lady has a strong will. I have had to develop a strong one also to manage her." Edwina never found out whether he meant Miriam Hopkins or Theresa Helburn, one of the Theatre Guild managers, who suggested a great many script changes. Forced into several compromises, Tennessee never satisfactorily solved the problem of how to end the play. Miriam Hopkins was determined to be on stage throughout most of the last act, and the Theatre Guild insisted on a script that satisfied her in this respect.[6]

Tennessee had rented a fairly elegant room in a shabby apartment that belonged to a titled lady. It was on Fifty-eighth Street, and before the company left for Boston he gave a Saturday-afternoon cocktail party in his new room. Donald was among the guests who turned up to find a pint of whisky on the mantelpiece and a message from Tennessee inviting them to help themselves. He would be late, it said, and he was so late that none of them waited for him.[7]

Battle of Angels made inordinate technical demands, especially at the end, when the set had to be destroyed by fire. The smoke pots were ineffectual in rehearsal and overwhelming on the first night in Boston, when the cast and what remained of the audience were enveloped in thick smoke. Some of the audience had already left, outraged when Vee Talbot unveiled her painting of a Jesus with an unmistakable resemblance to Val. Coming forward to take her curtain call, Miriam Hopkins waved her hands at the smoke, coughing and smiling apologetically.[8]

The *Boston Herald* reviewer, Alexander Williams, paid tribute to "an astonishing play, one of the strangest mixtures of poetry, realism, melodrama, comedy, whimsy and eroticism that it has ever been our privilege to see upon the boards. . . . There is something for every taste and equally something that will irritate every customer who more or less knows his mind about theatrical matters." In the *Boston Post* Elliot Norton called Williams's talent "most interesting," praising his compassion and his "gift for vividness."[9] Though the play survived in Boston for two weeks, complaints were made to the City Council, and at a meeting held on the morning after the first night, the Guild decided not to open the play in New York. William Jay Smith, who was in Boston and saw the performance, was asked to stay with Tennessee, who was deeply depressed. "He said nothing about *Battle of Angels* but went to his suitcase and took out an anthology of poetry and asked me to read aloud to him the poems of John Donne, which I did for the next few hours."[10]

Tennessee was given a check for two hundred dollars and told to rewrite the play, but hopes of making a breakthrough had receded. According to Donald Windham, "He was penniless, borrowing when he could, no longer living in the comparative affluence of option money and grants."[11] Homeless, he accepted hospitality from whoever offered it, and after an operation on his cataract, convalesced in the Greenwich Village apartment of a New Orleans painter he had met in Provincetown, Fritz Bultman, who reports: "He had this great sweetness and charm and humor, and then he could be cold and abusive as ice. Very soon it was a nuisance to have him in the apartment. He would drag home a stranger during the night and then expect me to get rid of the fellow later. This went on when he visited again the following winter, but then I had to ask Tennessee to leave."[12]

In January 1941 Tennessee worked on the play during the day and at night wandered the streets near the West Side piers, but he was restless in New York and at the end of the month, receiving a Rockefeller Foundation grant of five hundred dollars, he took off for Miami, where, missing the check that Audrey Wood had mailed to Key West, he had to stay at the YMCA and work for two days washing dishes at a luncheonette. Sending her a postcard of the Bahai Honda Bridge, he said one day in Miami would have been enough.[13]

He met up with Jim Parrott, who gave him a lift to Key West. The southernmost point in the United States, it was certain to offer warmer swimming

THE TRADE WINDS   KEY WEST, FLORIDA

A postcard showing the Trade Winds in Key West

in February than Lake George had offered in May. Seeing a handsome mahogany frame house with verandas on all four sides, upstairs and downstairs, they pulled up and found it belonged to Cora Black, widow of an Episcopal minister. When Tennessee told her about his grandfather Dakin, she gladly gave him and Jim a downstairs bedroom. Jim, who was working in Miami, had to leave in the morning, but she offered Tennessee the small cabin that had been built for servants. She installed a shower, and charged him only about $7.50 a week.

Still unspoiled, Key West seemed to belong more to the Caribbean world than to the American. The houses were mostly white clapboard shanties which had weathered gray, and they had wide verandas. Hemingway had lived there, and fishermen like the ones he described in *To Have and Have Not* were still to be seen in the streets, as were other attractive faces. In 1973, when Key West was no longer the same, Tennessee nostalgically remembered that it "once had the most beautiful people I've ever met in my life, mostly blacks—before Howard Johnson and Ramada Inns arrived."[14]

His impressions are summarized in a letter to Jo Healy, a friendly young woman who had been switchboard operator at the Theatre Guild when *Battle of Angels* was in production. Key West was the most fantastic place he had ever seen in America, he said, even more colorful than New Orleans,

San Francisco, or Santa Fe. There were comparatively few tourists, and the town was "the real stuff." It still belonged to the natives, who were known as "conks." The main activities were sponge collecting and deep-sea fishing. The nets could be seen drying on the front porches, and there were bushes of flaming poinsettia in the yards.[15]

Tennessee rented a bike, and in the mornings he rode down to a restaurant where he could wake himself up with coffee. "This Cuban coffee really was dynamite. It wasn't doing my heart any good but I have a funny heart. Sometimes it seems to thrive on punishment."[16] Back at the cabin he worked on poems and stories, as well as rewriting *Battle of Angels*.

In the evenings he went to a bar on Duval Street, Sloppy Joe's, where Hemingway had left his signature on one of the stools.[17] There was a long front-to-rear bar, and a good black dance band. Tennessee often went there with Cora Black's good-looking daughter, Marion, who married into the Vaccaro family, which owned a fruit-trading company, but her husband was an alcoholic, who was being treated with ether. Marion became a close friend: Tennessee confided in her as he had in no one since Rose, and they danced together at Sloppy Joe's. In his story "Two on a Party" Marion appears as the nymphomaniac Cora, who befriends the homosexual, Billy. "She was the kindest person that Billy had ever met. She said and meant everything kindly . . . ; she hadn't a single malicious bone in her body, not a particle of jealousy or suspicion or evil in her nature, and that was what made it so sad that Cora was a lush." They start going around together because "they were mutually advantageous as a team for cruising the Broadway bars." They are also in agreement about the conformist majority:

Getting around the squares, evading, defying the phony rules of convention, that was maybe responsible for half their pleasure in their outlaw existence. They were a pair of kids playing cops and robbers; except for that element, the thrill of something lawless, they probably would have gotten bored with cruising. But . . . the various people involved in the niggardly control of funds, almost everybody that you passed when you were drunk and hilariously gay on the street, especially all those bull-like middle-aged couples that stood off sharply and glared at you as you swept through a hotel lobby with your blushing trade—all, all, all of these were natural enemies to them.

But Marion could not save Tennessee from becoming almost suicidally depressed. At the end of February he was writing to tell Audrey Wood that he felt like a piece of broken string. This was a one-way street he had chosen, and he would have to "follow it through with all the confidence or courage that necessity gives you." He was thinking, he said, of hitchhiking around the state, and eleven days later he was considering whether to join a branch of the military.[18]

But he was not too depressed to work on *Battle of Angels*. A new idea he announced in mid-March was that Val should meet a woman in an oil field near Waco, Texas, and become involved with her, only to be accused of rape when he tries to abandon her. "She's a symbol of the animal sexuality that dogs Val's footsteps wherever he goes." But Tennessee was still worried about ending the play with a "big holocaust." It was all overwritten, he said, and he would have to tone it down.[19]

On 20 March he sent Audrey Wood a telegram saying he had been evicted from the Key West boardinghouse: would she wire him twenty dollars immediately? Within three weeks he had gotten himself into a different kind of trouble. Cora Black's drunken son-in-law had run up gambling debts, and because his life was in danger, Tennessee promised to smuggle him to Brunswick, Georgia, and keep him sober until Marion arrived. They got no farther than Miami, where the man was put into a sanatorium, and Tennessee was soon on his way to Georgia, where he had been invited to stay on the Vaccaros' farm. But he never reached Georgia. After three days he had got no farther than St. Augustine, but at least he was filling his notebook with "Southern Americana." He arrived at St. Simon's Island with raging flu and a racking cough. He had a check, but there was no one to cash it, and he was forced to sleep on the beach, where he would "probably have perished but for the timely intervention of some friends from California met by chance."[20] His depressed letters made Audrey Wood so anxious that she persuaded him he should come back to New York. En route he spent a few days in St. Louis. He arrived in New York to find that the Guild had lost interest in his play.

Despondent and restless, he left in the summer of 1941 for the Massachusetts coast. During July he was in Provincetown again, staying in an apartment with two men and a woman. Watching the quadrilateral of relationships with amused detachment, he described it in a letter to Paul Bigelow. The woman had slept with both the other men, Joe and "the skeezo," but neither had given her an orgasm, and, wanting sex with her again, they had both been trying to rape her, but she was attracted to homosexuals, and the whole of "her great, throbbing heart" belonged to Tennessee. She insisted on sleeping in his room and abased herself, washing his feet, buttering his bread, lighting his cigarettes, and even buttoning his trousers. But he was staying on in Provincetown because of a blond boy who was indifferent to him. When Tennessee embraced him wildly, declaring his love, the young man laughed, saying: "Tennessee, you amaze me!" Frustrated, he had accumulated enough sexual potency "to blast the Atlantic fleet out of Brooklyn."[21]

At the end of the month he returned to New York, where he stayed briefly in Bigelow's East 73rd Street apartment before leaving again for New Orleans in September. There was no question of living anywhere but the French Quarter, and at first he settled for what he called a "slum room." His depression had been exacerbated by the failure of his play, but he fought back by working furiously, revising *Battle of Angels* and dividing the rest of his time between "Stairs to the Roof," *I Rise in Flame, Cried the Phoenix*, and short stories. By the end of October he was also working on a libretto for a short opera about blacks and on the twenty-seventh he sent Audrey Wood two one-act plays written in two days. Short of money, he worked as a waiter at a restaurant on Royal Street, Gluck's, and, needing to smoke while he settled down to write in the morning, he was sometimes reduced to bumming cigarettes from strangers.[22]

Though he was glad to be back in New Orleans, the city was no longer the same. The war had ruined it, "virtually broken up all the gaiety."[23] Alternating between exuberance and depression, he often thought about death, and during the last week of September he wrote to give Audrey Wood detailed instructions on what to do if he was killed, as he might be at any minute, he said, thanks to defective vision and absentmindedness. A truck might run him over, for instance, on the new bike he had bought. If this happened, she should tell his parents he had asked her to have copies made at their expense of everything he had written. She would have no difficulty in making them pay, but she must not surrender any of his work to them. Edwina had complained that the one-act plays he had submitted to the Guild were "ugly details about indecent people" and a disgrace to the kinfolk mentioned in the program. Tennessee was apprehensive she would burn his work to save his reputation.[24] Within a month he did have an accident on his bike, colliding with a cow, who damaged one of the wheels so badly that he had to hitchhike until it was repaired.

431 Royal Street, New Orleans

Everything felt so insecure that there was no point in avoiding risks. He took a great many chances with casual pickups, sometimes moving in with them. In the space of a month, he stayed at four boardinghouses. One of these was on Royal Street, opposite a gay bar, the St. James. Tennessee could sit on his balcony, wishing he had a mantilla to throw across it, and he felt he was hovering "like a bright angel over the troubled waters of homo-society."[25]

The most serious of his sexual entanglements was with Eloi Bordelon, who belonged to one of the oldest families in the city and owned a boarding-house on Toulouse Street. Taking his usual pleasure in discussing men as if they were women, Tennessee described him as a "Creole belle." "Homo-society" was full of belles: "such delicious belles you have never seen." Tennessee was regarded as "butch" and as an "outdoor type." Eloi was the queen bee of butch society, and at first Tennessee was delighted with the liaison, but Eloi became so possessive that it was almost like the affair with Kip, and when Tennessee tried to extricate himself, Eloi became "horribly vicious. . . . Hell hath no fury. . . ." After "a violent and rather bloody matrimonial break-up" in November, Tennessee retreated.

By 3 November he was on his way to St. Louis, knowing his father was away, and intending to leave before Cornelius returned. Tennessee went to Baton Rouge, where he had "a lovely lover," going on to Jackson, Mississippi, congratulating himself on having distanced himself from Eloi Bordelon and evading "the displeasure which I must admit was somewhat justly provoked—marriage is not for me."[26] But he was back in New Orleans by the middle of December, and the meeting with the handsome paratrooper may have occurred on New Year's Eve.

Needing another cataract operation, Tennessee went back to New York early in 1942 and stayed—until he was ejected—in the Greenwich Village apartment of Fritz Bultman. Tennessee wrote during the day and worked in the Village during the evenings at the Beggar's Bar, which was run by Valesca Gert, a refugee cabaret performer from Berlin. She surrounded herself with eccentrics, and Tennessee never found out whether the singer she employed was a male or a female transvestite. Over the eye on which the cataract operation had been performed, Tennessee wore a black eye patch with an eye painted on it. His work consisted not only of waiting but also of reciting poems, but he earned no wage—only tips. One day, when Valesca Gert ordered the three waiters to pool their tips and share them with her, a friend of Tennessee's started throwing quart soda bottles at her, which left her needing several stitches in her scalp and Tennessee needing a new job.[27]

There are conflicting explanations of why Bultman finally ejected his guest. According to Donald, Tennessee was in the habit of putting a coffeepot on the stove to heat, forgetting about it, and wondering whether the smell of burning meant there was a fire in the neighborhood. According to Jean Bultman, Tennessee was an inconsiderate guest who brought sailors back to the apartment and regularly left the place in a mess. This tallies with Fritz Bultman's explanation, but according to Tennessee, Bultman used to send him and another friend they called "the pilot fish" out on the streets every evening "to fetch home carefully specified kinds of visitors." Most of were satisfactory, but one evening Tennessee and the pilot fish brought home "some guests of a roguish nature" who stole several valuable objects from the apartment, and it was after this that Tennessee was ejected.[28]

Needing alternative accommodation and not wanting to earn money for rent by taking a job that would stop him from writing, Tennessee latched onto a rich homosexual songwriter who kept him for four months in his Madison Avenue penthouse. Tennessee and Donald had decided to collaborate on making a play out of D. H. Lawrence's story "You Touched Me," and they worked every day in Donald's room at the YMCA. According to Donald, Tennessee, though proud of being attractive to the men he called "old aunties," grimaced with disgust whenever he mentioned them. One day he made a dramatic entrance. "Dropping his mangy topcoat to the floor, he recounts the fagging night he has passed with the songwriter and his alcoholic friends and vows that he could not have survived it without my companionship to look forward to."[29]

A story Tennessee started in March, "Desire and the Black Masseur," is self-revealing without being directly autobiographical. The central character was modeled on an acquaintance, but in empathizing, Tennessee also projected many of his own personality traits. The character is a timid clerk who since childhood "had betrayed an instinct for being included in things that swallowed him up." Sitting in a movie theater, Anthony feels "like a particle of food dissolving in a big hot mouth." He still moves like a child in the presence of critical adults. Overcoming the fear that is the constant concomitant of his desires, he accepts the invitation proffered by a red neon sign: "Turkish Baths and Massage." After leaving him alone in the steam room, the gigantic black masseur treats him roughly, but the pain brings him to orgasm. Addictively he keeps going back to the masseur, who senses that he is "in search of atonement." The massage becomes progressively more violent until, in the surrealistically macabre ending, the little man is killed and eaten by the big masseur.

Like Tennessee's hypochondria, his irrational belief that he was dying was grounded in an equally irrational conviction that he did not deserve to stay alive. His masochism, which surfaces in this story, adds tension in his plays to the logic by which characters are punished for their life-denying resistance to healthy sexuality or to homosexuality. The punishment meted out by the black masseur is gratuitous, but in the plays characters are penalized for rejecting the Lawrentian gospel and refusing to celebrate the body. In punishing them Tennessee is vicariously punishing himself.

The script of the dramatization of the Lawrence story now looks like a blueprint for much of his subsequent work. A retired factory owner threatens to disinherit his daughter, Matilda, unless she marries his adopted son, Hadrian, but the marriage works out well, redeeming her from the emptiness of her life. The play vulgarizes the story, changing Matilda's younger sister, Emmie, into a maiden aunt who stands for what Tennessee called "aggressive sterility," while the thin, big-nosed thirty-two-year-old Matilda is transformed into a shy young woman of twenty. Hadrian—a scheming little soldier in the story—becomes a clean-cut, muscular lieutenant in the Canadian air force, while the factory owner becomes an alcoholic old sea captain.

The action deteriorates into a simplistic battle between those in favor of sexuality and those against it, the benighted bad guys being Emmie and an impotent clergyman who wants to marry her. This points forward to the way Tennessee went on to abuse the theme of sexuality, writing as if all problems could be solved by casting abstinence aside.

It was impossible to raise any option money on the first draft of *You Touched Me*, and when he found it unbearable to go on living with the songwriter, he moved in with Paul Bigelow. After Bigelow accepted an invitation to spend the summer with friends in Georgia, Tennessee could have stayed on in the apartment, but, not wanting to be alone, he wrote to ask whether he could join them. Arriving in mid-June, he found Bigelow was occupying an attic room, which they had to share. Later a third house guest was billeted in the attic, a retarded young man who sweated a great deal but never changed his socks or bathed. Not that the odor stopped Tennessee from working on poems, short stories, and "Stairs to the Roof." He was earning some money busing tables in a local restaurant, the Pig 'n Whistle, but even a routine like this seemed preferable to the life he would have lived in New York. At the beginning of August he was saying he never wanted to go back there unless he had a job or a play in production. "Otherwise I'll stay in the South which I hate and love so intensely."[30]

Before the end of the month he set out for Key West, but got no farther than Jacksonville, Florida, where he earned money by working until mid-November for the War Department in the U.S. Engineers' office, operating a teletype machine between eleven at night and seven in the morning for $120 a month. The nocturnal wakefulness led him to reflect on the way he was conducting his life, questioning his priorities. Writing to Audrey Wood, he quoted what he had said to Bigelow: "There *aren't* any good *plans* but there are a few acceptable expedients." The great trauma of his life had been the experience of his sister, who had "the same precarious balance of nerves that I have to live with, and who found it too much and escaped."

Was he using his plays as an escape? He knew there were dangers in writing about himself so much. On the other hand it would have been cowardly not to deal with the things he knew best.[31]

Back in New York at the end of the year, he continued his random succession of jobs, working as an elevator operator in a hotel and as an usher in a movie house. The uniform he had to wear in the afternoon looked like the school uniform at Eton; in the evening he wore a midnight-blue uniform with satin lapels, "and we are drilled like a regiment."[32] But when he was off duty, he was taking little trouble over his appearance. "His heart is faint," wrote Donald on 7 November, "and his eyesight weak and his constitution worn from much abuse." He stayed nowhere for long, moving between cheap hotels and friends' apartments. In his diary for 18 November Donald wrote: "After I got off work I came and moved Tenn downtown to Butch's. His room was desolate confusion, clothes and folded typewriter mss piled intermixed between each other, suitcases full and overflowing onto the floor, cigarette ashes and butts, empty wadded cigarette packages, old magazines, shoes, underwear, dirty unwritten-on paper."[33]

He went on trying to find a job that would suit him better than the one as usher. After submitting some of his work, he went to meet the refugee German director Erwin Piscator, who had established his Drama Workshop at the New School for Social Research. Piscator lived in a palatial house, where Tennessee was kept waiting for thirty minutes before the German butler led him up to the bedroom where Piscator, wearing peach-colored pajamas, was lying in bed with a dinner tray. A fur robe was draped over the bed. Looking at Tennessee mournfully, he said: "Mr. Williams, you have written a Fascist play. All your characters are selfishly pursuing their little personal ends and aims in life with a ruthless disregard for the mistakes and sufferings of the world about them." But at the end of the meeting Tennessee was still hoping to be offered a job.[34]

He went home again in the spring of 1943, when his grandparents were staying with his parents at 53 Arundel Place, and his grandmother was dying. The domestic quarrels were worse than ever. "It has come to such a pass now that the family cannot even sit at the same table with each other. Father eats first, separately. He evidently opposed my coming here and has ordered me to do all sorts of absurd things such as transferring the woodpile from one corner of the garden to the other and washing windows in the garage." Rose wrote home from the state hospital in Farmington.

Tennessee was lucky, she said, to be in the penitentiary because "hordes of hungry people are clamoring at the gates of the city."[35]

He was writing "The Gentleman Caller." He had been thinking of Rose's fragility when he was working on *You Touched Me:* Matilda is described as having "the delicate, almost transparent quality of glass." Both Laura and Matilda are shy, intensely vulnerable, cut off from the life around them, but Laura's gentleman caller brings her only momentarily to life, and Tennessee was again drawing freely on his family situation for the new play. "I might also call it 'The Not so Beautiful People' or 'The Human Tragedy,' as it is taking on the atmosphere of 53 Arundel Place." He made rapid progress but felt uncertain whether he should go back to New York. Perhaps it would be better to leave for New Mexico or to "head West and just forget New York and the theatre." He had never entirely shaken off the superstitious feeling that by wanting something he was reducing his chances of getting it. Perhaps he would achieve success only if he stopped thinking about it and planning for it. It would be better just to write a play, put it aside, and write another. "That is why it is so bad to be in New York and listening for telephones and watching for letters and notices. Success is like a shy mouse—he won't come out while you're watching."[36]

But at the end of April Audrey Wood decided his fate by helping him to fulfill the ambition that had been born four years earlier when he traveled from New Orleans to California, wanting to try his luck as a scriptwriter. She secured for him a six-month contract as a screenwriter at M-G-M, for $250 a week. To protect his copyright control over the writing he had already completed, she sent the studio a list of his works, which included 10 full-length plays, 12 "long short" plays, 17 one-act plays, 19 stories, and over 250 poems. For a man of thirty-two, this is an impressive quantity of work.

6

Hollywood Worm

In Hollywood I was a worm. Prostrate and crawling. Pathetic and evil. . . . Worms need worms.

The man who was effectively Tennessee's boss at M-G-M was the thirty-eight-year-old producer Pandro Berman. Son of the general manager at Universal, he had worked as assistant director and as film editor before becoming David O. Selznick's assistant. A producer since 1931, Berman had been responsible for many prestigious movies, including several starring Fred Astaire and Ginger Rogers. Tennessee described him as a nice guy who knew more about showbiz than about writers.[1]

Berman was having an affair with the twenty-three-year-old Lana Turner. Daughter of a mine foreman and a beautician, she had become one of America's favorite pinup girls and had already appeared in about twenty films. The first of her seven husbands was the bandleader Artie Shaw, who married her when she was twenty and divorced her a year later. She was known as "the sweater girl" because of the bosom that had made light-weight sweaters look so interesting in so many pictures, but, according to Tennessee she "couldn't act her way out of her form-fitting cashmeres."[2] In May 1943, saying he wanted to break Tennessee in on something simple, Berman gave him *Marriage Is a Private Affair*, a script intended for her. She was pregnant, but this was to be her first film after having the baby. Written by Lenore Coffee, it contained "every cliché situation you've ever seen in a Grade B picture." Tennessee was expected to give it "freshness and vitality," but to keep it as "a Lana Turner sort of thing. . . . I feel like an obstetrician required to successfully deliver a mastodon from a beaver." But at first Berman liked what he was doing.[3]

Tennessee was pleased with the office he was given at the studio. It had an easy chair, a table lamp, a big typewriter, and venetian blinds. But the apartment he chose reminded him of "the frightful little flat" his father had selected for his mother in St. Louis. "She looked at it and laughed and cried."[4] With a friend, David Gregory, Tennessee had settled into two rented rooms in a boardinghouse on Ocean Avenue, Santa Monica — "nothing at all grand, in fact a very honky-tonk air about it with stained wallpaper . . . and very gaudy curtains."[5] There was a plaster model of Mae West on the mantelpiece and a picture of Saint Theresa above the sink. The rooms overlooked the Palisades, a big park on a promontory above the beach. Two paths wound between the palm trees, and there were summer houses in the arbors.

The landlady, who drank a quart of beer for breakfast, was "a lecherous communist woman of about forty-five with a great blown-up body. She sleeps with any man in the house who will have her, and has a frail, sour little husband named Ernie who does all the house-work, bed-making, Etc., while she soaks up the sun on the porch steps or a big raggedy mattress she has flung out in the back-yard near the tomato patch, with a cocker spaniel resting its head on her belly."[6] The landlady's first name was Zola, and she was accustomed to keeping a copy of Zola's *The Human Beast* on her table. When she entertained soldiers, she told them it was her biography, and they believed her.[7]

While working on the screenplay — Tennessee felt as if he had been hired to tailor a "celluloid brassiere" for Lana Turner — he developed his story about Rose, "Portrait of a Girl in Glass." He had already used the ten-page story as a basis for two one-act plays. Ever since Rose's lobotomy, he had been plagued by guilt feelings, and he tried to articulate some of these in the two plays. In "The Spinning Song" a doctor argues with a mother who is ruining her life through "useless devotion to a sick person whose disease is a type that would keep you both withdrawn from the world as much as if this house were barred as a prison." In "The Front Porch Girl," which was later developed into another play, "If You Breathe, It Breaks! or Portrait of a Girl in Glass," Miriam Wingfield collects glass animals that are "so—*delicate*—they're so—easily *broken!* When you look at them sometimes it—makes you cry! . . . Oh, not just for them—you understand. . . . Not just for the little glass objects but everything else in the world that—people break to pieces because they're—easily broken."

A photograph of Rose stood on the desk in his office, confronting him while he reworked the material, his energy still pepped up by guilt feelings. His first version of "The Gentleman Caller" was a one-act play. It then struck him that the material could be made into a film, and at the end of May he sent Audrey Wood an outline. By mid-June he had completed a new, twenty-eight-page story, also called "The Gentleman Caller," which he described as a minor excursion into the material he was using for the stage version of the story.[8] By the end of July he had written a detailed screen treatment, which he offered to M-G-M, but it was rejected. Retreating to the idea of theater, he wrote a sixty-page script for a play in five scenes. About twenty pages of this were incorporated into the next version, which extended to over a hundred pages, divided into seven scenes. The version that was finally staged in 1944 had eight scenes, but he reverted to the seven-scene version when the script was published.

In the story a red-haired young Irishman, Jim Delaney, meets Laura for the first time when he comes to dinner; in the play he has the same name as a good-looking student Tennessee had met at the University of Missouri, Jim O'Connor, and the character is not meeting Rose for the first time. They knew each other at school, where she admired him.

Though the mother in the story was modeled directly on Edwina, she was sketched in only perfunctorily. Her attempts at matchmaking were strenuous and insensitive, but she was simply called Mother and she did not have any nostalgic speeches about her popularity when she was young. The story was started only two years after Tennessee began calling himself Tennessee. In the play, working in Hollywood and fortified with greater self-confidence, greater financial security, and greater distance in both time and space, he could look back with a mixture of bitterness, compassion, and objectivity on the domestic life he had escaped. He draws more deeply and more extensively on his memories of what Edwina had been like as a mother.

The success of the play rests mainly on the characterization of the mother, Amanda, who is garrulous and tiresome, but also funny and pathetic. She is described as "a little woman of great but confused vitality clinging frantically to another time and place. . . . She is not paranoiac, but her life is paranoia. . . . She has endurance and a kind of heroism, and though her foolishness makes her unwittingly cruel at times, there is tenderness in her slight person." Formerly a Southern belle, she once received seventeen gentlemen callers on one afternoon. Abandoned by her alcoholic husband, she is living in reduced circumstances, but she gives herself airs, and talks at length about the glorious past and the men who wanted to marry her. Vicariously ambitious for both her children, she nags them endlessly about the refinement they must cultivate. If her son brings a book by D. H. Lawrence into the house, she takes it back to the lending library. He complains of having nothing he can call his own, and he can seldom settle down to work without being interrupted.

The colorfulness of the characterization depends largely on Tennessee's skill in reproducing the Southern idiom, and on counterpointing its drawling relaxation with the neurotic tension in Amanda, who seems happy when she recalls her past, but becomes both anxious and autocratic when she plans for her children's future.

Neither Rose nor the Laura of the story was lame, but her lameness in the play exacerbates the family tendency to lose touch with reality, living through illusions. Laura is like Rose, though, in having what she calls "nervous indigestion," and in collecting glass animals, "too exquisitely fragile to move from the shelf." Intensely diffident, she has come to resemble these ornaments. Like Rose, she has dropped out from a business college and allowed her mother to go on thinking she was attending classes when actually she was going out for walks in the park.

In Hollywood, Tennessee made friends with Christopher Isherwood, who was about seven years his senior. They went out together for fish dinners on the pier at Santa Monica, and Isherwood visited him on Ocean Avenue, where he used to find Tennessee "sitting typing a film story in a yachting cap, amidst a litter of dirty coffee cups, crumpled bed linen, and old newspapers. . . . He works till he's tired, eats when he feels like it, sleeps when he can't stay awake."[9] Tennessee confirms in his memoirs that in those days he often worked for six or eight hours at a stretch. To Isherwood, who was shy, he seemed "very bold, very spontaneous. . . . He made contact with people very easily."[10] Combined with the need for sexual gratification, the need for contacts was voracious, but the casual encounters did nothing toward curing his loneliness. "As for loneliness," he told a friend, "very few people ever understand it. . . . It requires moodiness and inability to get on with most people — and lack of social charm always helps. (To acquire it.)"[11]

Because of the war and the danger of Japanese air raids, the Pacific coast was blacked out at night, which made it easier to pick up men. Young servicemen could be found wandering around on the Palisades, or enjoying the view over the curving stone balustrade. In the evening Tennessee would bike around until he found one who appealed to him. After pretending "to join him in his spurious enchantment with the view," Tennessee would light a cigarette. "If the match-light confirmed my first impression of his charms, I would mention that I had a pad only a few blocks away, and he would often accept the invitation." One of his most memorable pickups was a sailor: "I wouldn't believe it if it were not recorded in my journal of that summer, but I screwed him seven times that night."[12]

Several times a week Tennessee went to the movies in Hollywood, returning on the bus, which was blacked out, and sitting down next to anyone he found attractive. "After a few moments my right knee would permit itself to be jolted against his left knee. If the contact were permitted to continue, I would know that it would not be necessary, when I got off at Santa Monica, to resort to the Palisades."[13]

Toward the end of June, seeing that he was never going to come up with a suitable script for Lana Turner, Berman gave the job to another writer and the film *Marriage Is a Private Affair* was made in 1944. Tennessee was now given opportunities to write a story about Billy the Kid and a screenplay for the child actress Margaret O'Brien, whom he described as "a smaller and more loathsome edition of Shirley Temple before *that* one retired from the screen. I do indeed have a story idea for her, but it is unprintable."[14] But in August, because he was failing to do the work he was given, he was suspended for six weeks without pay.

He was still uncertain what he wanted to do with his talent and his opportunities. He was "frightened by the emotional deadness" of the hack writers and opportunistic directors who could thrive in Hollywood. Many of them had considerable talent, as well as technical savoir faire, but they nearly all seemed to be "withered inside." Most of them had been in Hollywood for a long time and had abandoned any ideals they might once have had. Tennessee knew it would be damaging to him if he stayed there for longer than about six months. What he had to do was "follow my heart with absolute willfulness where work is concerned." But it was easier to be willful in a story than in a play. So far as he could assess his own motives, he was writing the stories without any expectation of selling them to magazines, though with the faith that if he was patient enough, he would eventually find an outlet for everything he wrote, provided that it was written honestly and with "a sufficient degree of craftsmanship."[15]

What changed his fortunes as a playwright was the arrival of the producer-director Margo Jones, who had spent a year in India, written a book on Hindu philosophy, traveled around the world, and directed plays for seven years in Houston. Audrey Wood had shown her Tennessee's plays, and she wanted to stage *You Touched Me* in Cleveland, hoping to transfer it to the Pasadena Playbox, a smaller offshoot of the famous Pasadena Playhouse.

According to Tennessee, Margo Jones had "the energy of Niagara Falls and an enthusiasm which is either irresistible or overwhelming." Without consulting Donald Windham, he worked with her on revising the script, and later Windham found that his name was being featured less than Tennessee's in the prepublicity. "I hope you will bear in mind," Tennessee wrote, "that my *heart* (as well as so much labor, time, desperation) is threaded into this play. There are things in it, speeches, feelings, ideas, that are as deeply and intensely personal to me as all my past life — or any organ of my body, or life itself!"[16]

Margo Jones cast the production in New York, where she had a better choice of actors, but by September, when she was rehearsing it in Cleveland, Tennessee was on the M-G-M payroll again after his six weeks of suspension. He survived in Hollywood till October, but was fired in time to work on the play after it opened in Cleveland to moderately favorable reviews. The intention was to use big-name movie actors, including Agnes Moorehead, for the Pasadena production, but the Hollywood actors balked at the prospect of an hour's bus ride to and from rehearsals, and the play was recast with Pasadena residents.[17] The play opened in Pasadena on 29 November and closed on 5 December. Audience reactions were favorable, but it was a rule of the theater that no reviewers would be admitted.

While the play was in rehearsal, Tennessee had found that the formidable willpower of Margo Jones seemed to be focused on marrying him. Cornelius, who was in Los Angeles on business, came to a performance, bringing some of his salesmen. Margo, reported Tennessee, "was so bored that she got drunk on their liquor and performed a wild dance around the room." Cornelius was shocked, and, realizing she had set her heart on marrying Tennessee, warned him of the danger. This was the first serious conversation for years between father and son. Admitting he had always been a slave to drink, Cornelius warned Tennessee against marrying a drunken woman. The Williamses, who had all been drinkers, said Cornelius, needed to be restrained by their women. He was drinking throughout the conversation, and becoming maudlin. As Tennessee wrote Donald: "He feels probably correctly that his days are numbered, told me dolefully that 'the Parson' was 85 but would probably out-live him."[18]

Cornelius never came to Tennessee's apartment, but the publisher James Laughlin, founder of New Directions books, called when he was out and saw the chaos. The kitchen was "a garden of fungi and a paradise of microscopic organisms, dishes having remained unwashed for weeks, my worst manuscripts thrown about like a cyclone had struck them, joy-rags scattered all about the unmade bed together with all the little accoutrements and conveniences of pleasure. . . . The very odor of the place was appalling." The mess reflected a depression that included revulsion against his own work. "I wish I could crawl out of it like a snake from an old skin and begin all over again, more with life than with words."[19]

By the autumn of 1943, his grandmother was dying. Her weight had dropped to eighty-six pounds, and Tennessee knew he was expected to go home. A few months previously, after years of living on the minister's retirement pension of eighty-five dollars a month, his grandparents had given up their small house in Memphis to move in with their daughter, though they hated exposing themselves to the rudeness and aggression of their drunken son-in-law.

Arriving at the house late, Tennessee found that though everyone else had gone to bed, Grand had not only waited up but had kept a meal hot for him. She made light of her illness, saying she had come to help Edwina, who was exhausted and disturbed by Cornelius's behavior. Cornelius was still working as sales manager at a branch of the International Shoe Company, but his job was in danger, following the scandal caused by a poker fight in which half his left ear was bitten off. Cartilage from a rib had to be grafted onto it in the hospital. Sleeping in his brother's old room, which was next to their father's doorless room, Tennessee was awakened several times when Cornelius, talking to himself, stumbled out of bed to fetch whiskey from its hiding place.

Sometimes Edwina still ordered Tennessee to bed, saying late hours would wreck his health,[20] but he suffered more from his father's behavior, and from observing his grandparents' anguished reaction to it. Reverend Dakin was now deaf and almost blind. In the evenings, when Cornelius was due home from the office, Grand would wait near the front door, listening for the sound of the Studebaker in the drive. The words "Walter, Cornelius is coming" would send the old man scurrying up the stairs, but if the two men confronted each other, Walter's greeting would usually be answered only by a glare and a grunt. One evening, after coming home late and drunk, Cornelius exploded with rage at the dinner table. Why was Edwina looking so sorry for herself when he was keeping her parents in the house free of charge? Walter and Edwina got up from the table, but the old lady stayed. "My father crouches over his plate, eating like a wild beast eats his kill in the jungle. Then my grandmother's voice, quiet and gentle: 'Cornelius, do you want us to pay board here?' Silence again. My father stops eating, though. He doesn't look up as he says in a hoarse, shaky voice: 'No, I don't, Mrs. Dakin.' His inflamed blue eyes are suddenly filled with tears."[21]

On 3 January 1944 Tennessee wrote that Grand was "well—and radiantly beautiful, all silvery and warm," but a few days later she died of a lung hemorrhage. "She never spoke nor opened her eyes when the fatal bleeding started, though I am fairly sure she was conscious."[22] Not wanting to attend the funeral, he arranged to have an operation on his cataract that day.

The extremity of his mood changes is reflected in the story "Ori-flamme," which he wrote in January 1944, setting it in St. Louis. The unnamed tubercular girl has never liked the place. "Her hope had died in a basement of this city. Her faith had died in one of its smug churches. Her love had not survived a journey across it." For weeks she has been lying in bed ill, but the weight that had kept her down has been lifted away during the night. She wants to tell someone the good news but no one would understand. She hates the passionless conformism of the citizens, the "conspiracy of dullness in the world," the "universal plan to shut out the resurgences of spirit which might interfere with clockwork." Finding that none of the dresses in her wardrobe expresses the excitement she feels, she goes out to buy a red silk evening dress, and, braving the disapproval of the saleswoman, puts it on to wear in the street. She does not know where she is going. "Direction was unimportant. The world was lost. She felt it slipping behind her, a long way back." When she dies at the top of a hill, we understand the story's opening account of her feeling liberated from the weight that had kept her in bed.

If Grand's death and a recurrent fear of dying had helped Tennessee to empathize with the girl, his premature fears of the aging process helped him in his next story, "The Vine," to empathize with a man scared of losing his youthful attractiveness. Tennessee, who was still subtracting three years from his age, celebrated his thirty-third birthday as his thirtieth that year. In the story, Donald is an actor who has grown so dependent on the physical presence of his wife, Rachel, that in bed at night they seem to have a continuity between their bodies: there is always a vinelike contact between them. The narrative encompasses a number of blows to his sexual vanity. His hair seems to be thinning. When they finally decide to have a baby, the doctor says he is sterile. After dressing carefully in his white linen suit—Tennessee often wore a white linen suit—Donald notices his waist has thickened, and a girl laughs as she passes him in the street. He is severely told off when he tries to make a pass at the girl sitting next to him in the soda fountain, and humiliated even more bitterly when he tries to kiss a friend of Rachel's.

For Donald, Rachel's absence is intolerable. "When you came home alone after being alone on the street, how was it bearable not having someone to tell all the little things you had on your mind? When you really thought about it, when you got down to it, what was there to live for outside the all-encompassing and protecting intimacy of marriage? . . . Going to bed alone, the wall on one side of you, empty space on the other, no warmth but your own, no flesh in contact with yours! Such loneliness was indecent!"

Meaning Tennessee's own life was indecent. On 2 February 1944 he was intending to leave home the following week, though he was undecided about whether he should go to Texas, New York, New Orleans, or Mexico.[23] Instead he started on a new play, possibly *Summer and Smoke*, remaining in St. Louis till mid-March, when he went to New York, where he stayed in boardinghouses and hostels.

At the end of the month he was spending time in a Manhattan hospital, where Kip Kiernan was dying. Tennessee's former lover had married, and according to Tennessee, he was summoned to the hospital by a telephone call from a woman. According to Donald Windham, it was only after arriving in the hospital that he and Tennessee learned from Kip's wife that the operation for a brain tumor had been unsuccessful. On the way to the hospital Tennessee bought a shantung robe which he gave Kip. Still feeling an almost intolerable sexual desire for the young man, Tennessee sat by his bedside holding his hand. After Kip died, Tennessee took the robe away with him. He had no intention of leaving it for Kip's wife, he said, and for the next few years he wore it himself.[24]

At the end of April the American Academy of Arts and Letters awarded him a grant of one thousand dollars in recognition of his dramatic achievement. Encouraged, he left for Cape Cod, where he settled in Provincetown to work on "The Gentleman Caller," which was retitled *The Glass Menagerie*. The edgy rhetoric and the throbbing pathos derive some of their energy from the irrational guilt he still felt about Rose. In the final narrative monologue—which retains many phrases and rhythms from the original short story—the character Tom describes a restlessness strikingly similar to that of the real Tom. "I traveled around a great deal. The cities swept about me like dead leaves. . . . I would have stopped, but I was pursued by something. . . . Perhaps I am walking along a street at night, in some strange city, before I have found companions. . . . Then all at once my sister touches my shoulder. I turn around and look into her eyes. Oh, Laura, Laura, I tried to leave you behind me, but I am more faithful than I intended to be!" Tennessee wanted the play to serve as his farewell to traditional play writing: "It is the *last* play I will try to write for the *now* existing theatre."[25] But he was more faithful than he intended to be.

Audrey Wood showed the script to the actor-producer Eddie Dowling, who reacted favorably and wanted to play Tom, though, at forty-nine, he was too old, while Julie Haydon, the actress he wanted to cast as Laura, was thirty-four—also too old. Her mentor, the critic George Jean Nathan, suggested that the part of Amanda should be offered to Laurette Taylor, whose alcoholism had forced her into retirement. Though Tennessee managed to arrange for Margo Jones to be engaged as assistant producer, her indomitable energy was pitted against forces that seemed to be dragging the play toward certain failure. The backers wanted the play to have a happy ending in which the gentleman caller fell in love with the lame Laura, but Tennessee refused to give in.[26]

Rehearsals began in New York for a Chicago tryout at the end of December, but Tennessee retreated to St. Louis. A week before the opening, when he was summoned to Chicago, "Laurette Taylor did not seem to know her lines as Amanda Wingfield, hardly a fraction of them, and those she did seem to know she was delivering in a Southern accent which she had acquired from some long-ago black domestic."[27] At one rehearsal, after he had asked her to tone her accent down, she told him she was imitating his, and later on she found a black baby doll in her dressing room. Furiously, she threw it out, and it was some days before Julie Haydon confessed she had put it there. Tennessee was also worried by Laurette Taylor's "bright-eyed attentiveness to the other performances," which "seemed a symbol of lunacy, and so did the rapturous manner of dear Julie."[28] He told Donald Windham that Margo Jones was "like the scoutmaster of some very jolly but wayward troop."[29] On Christmas Eve Dowling was still asking for rewrites.

Laurette Taylor did know her lines: she had been deviating from them to interpolate improvisation. She was steered back to the script, but in effect she directed several of the scenes, particularly hers with Julie Haydon, and, according to Tennessee, "she did a top-notch job. She was continually working on her part, adding little things and taking them out. Almost every night in Chicago there was something new, but she never disturbed the central characterization."[30]

The play opened on 26 December to a small audience, which included Edwina, who sat with Tennessee and Donald. Donald had never found out the truth about his friend's age, but, looking in the program, Edwina said: "Why, son, this write-up has your age wrong."[31] Afterwards, when Edwina was taken backstage to meet the cast, Laurette Taylor asked: "Well, how did you like you'seff, Miz' Williams?" Later on in the evening Tennessee wanted to take his mother to a midnight service at the Episcopal church, but they failed to find a taxi.[32]

Box-office receipts were poor, and the next day the producers had already prepared the closing notice when two reviews made them change their minds. In the *Herald American* Ashton Stevens said the play had "the courage of true poetry couched in colloquial prose." In fifty years of going to first nights, he said, he had received "very few jolts so miraculously electrical" as the one Laurette Taylor had given him. In the *Chicago Daily Tribune* Claudia Cassidy said the play "holds in its shadowed fragility the stamina of success. . . . If it is your play, as it is mine, it reaches out . . . and you are caught in its spell." Both critics kept coming back to see the production and writing about it enthusiastically. By mid-January, it was sold out for

*Laurette Taylor (at table), Eddie Dowling
(center), and Julie Haydon (right) in* The
Glass Menagerie, *which opened on
Broadway in 1945*

the run. When Cornelius went to see it, an extra chair had to be placed in the
aisle for him. Having a date later on in the evening, Tennessee left him with
Laurette Taylor, who was furious. "How dare you leave me alone with that
dull old man?"[33]

Between the opening of a pre-Broadway tryout tour and the first night on
Broadway, few playwrights would be able to concentrate on another play,
but Tennessee was exceptional. Between 26 December 1944, when *The
Glass Menagerie* opened in Chicago, and the Broadway opening on 31 March
1945 he was working hard at a new play, designing it for forty-seven-year-
old Katharine Cornell, whom he had recently seen on Broadway as Masha
in Chekhov's *Three Sisters*. Tennessee's play was about two sisters in the
South. He did not yet have a title for it. Among those he scrapped were
"The Moth," "The Primary Colors," "Blanche's Chair in the Moon," and
"The Poker Night." At first, he said, he simply had a vision of a woman in

her late youth. "She was sitting in a chair all alone by a window with the moonlight streaming in on her desolate face, and she'd been stood up by the man she planned to marry."[34] The image derived, of course, from Rose, who had spent so much time waiting unhappily for the telephone to ring.

The epigraph for the manuscript entitled "The Primary Colors" is a quotation from St. John Perse: "And life! Life beautiful as a ram's skin painted red and nailed to the wall above a bolted doorway!" In this version the action is set in a two-room apartment in the downtown business district of Atlanta, Georgia. The only view from the rear window is of a vacant lot with billboards to the skyline.

A manuscript entitled "The Passion of a Moth" is prefaced with four lines from Tennessee's poem "Lament for the Moths":

Give them, O Mother of Moths and Mother of Men,
Strength to enter the heavy world again.
For delicate were the moths and badly wanted
Here in a world by mammoth figures haunted!

By 23 March, Tennessee could report that he had completed fifty-five to sixty pages of a first draft. Blanche, who is about thirty-four, has been running the ancestral home single-handed for five years, struggling to maintain the old order. Though essentially "decent and very delicate by nature," she has gone for protection to so many men that she has tarnished her reputation. Her sister, Stella, who is about thirty, has married a coarse man who unconsciously falls in love with Blanche just as she is on the point of making "the same adjustment" as Stella — buying protection and sexual satisfaction by settling for a man much coarser than herself. Tennessee had not yet made up his mind about the ending. There were three possibilities. After staying in her sister's apartment Blanche could leave without having anywhere to go. She could go mad, or she could throw herself in front of a train in the freight yards. The roar of the freight trains was to provide an ominous undertone for the whole action. "I know this is very heavy stuff," Tennessee admitted, but he was introducing as much lyrical and comic relief as was compatible with "the essentially tragic atmosphere."[35]

He was distracted from the new play by the success of *The Glass Menagerie*, which, a month before it opened on Broadway, was already earning him $250 a week. But he did not enjoy his first taste of success. "Being feted and lionized on a small scale has convinced me or rather confirmed my suspicion that success is a bore. People are never so unattractive as when they think you are worth impressing."[36]

As if to atone for the cruel portrait of his mother, he assigned her half his royalty income from future performances. The effect would be to emancipate her from Cornelius. Stagehands noticed the play was autobiographical. One of them commented: "Tennessee and only Tennessee laughed aloud at lines every time he came to a performance, lines that didn't seem to amuse anyone else."[37]

The production opened in New York, five days after Tennessee's thirty-fourth birthday. Neither of his parents was there: since they had both seen the play, Cornelius said, it would have been a waste of money to buy train tickets. The play was given a tremendous ovation, and the actors took over twenty curtain calls. Finally, in response to the shouts of "Author!" Tennessee let Eddie Dowling help him onto the stage. He was wearing a gray flannel suit with a button missing on the jacket, and he looked, according to one reporter, "more like a farmboy in his Sunday best than the author of a Broadway success."[38]

One reviewer, Burton Rascoe, wrote: "Here is make-believe so real it tears your heart out," and the *New York Times* reported that "Mr. Williams has a real ear for faintly sardonic dialogue, unexpected phrases and affection for his characters." The play won the New York Drama Critics' Circle Award as the best play of the season, and Arthur Miller later declared: *"The Glass Menagerie* in one stroke lifted lyricism to its highest level in our theatre's history, but it broke new ground in another way. What was new in Tennessee Williams was his rhapsodic insistence that form serve his utterance rather than dominating and cramping it. In him American theatre found, perhaps for the first time, an eloquence and an amplitude of feeling."[39]

Two years earlier, at the age of thirty-one, he had been working as an usher in a movie theater. Now he could afford to spend $125 on a suit and to sleep in a suite at a first-class Manhattan hotel. After "a life of clawing and scratching along a sheer surface and holding on tight with raw fingers to every inch of rock higher than the one caught hold of before," he suddenly found himself "on a level plateau with my arm still thrashing and my lungs still grabbing at air that no longer resisted." But he did not enjoy the hotel suite. Everything seemed to fall apart—an arm came off the sofa, cigarette burns "appeared" on the furniture. It should have been a great pleasure to order meals over the telephone and have them wheeled in on a trolley, but he could not take much interest in the food, and when he ordered a sirloin steak and a chocolate sundae, he mistook the chocolate sauce for gravy and poured it over the meat.[40]

7

Desire and Cemeteries

From now on Tennessee could live on a different level. The most dramatic turning point in his life was the transition from obscurity to fame and from poverty to wealth, but nothing was going to make him less restless. Since leaving college he had never stayed in one place for more than a few months. According to Paul Bowles, "he was more eager to get away from where he was than to get to another place." Again and again he felt "suddenly fed up with a place and the people in it."[1] In an essay called "On a Streetcar Named Success," he said that three months elapsed between the breakthrough and a cataract operation that allowed him "to withdraw from the world behind a gauze mask."[2] In fact, it was less than a month. Faced with a dizzying barrage of congratulation and flattery from acquaintances and strangers, he felt at ease only with people he knew well. He frequently turned up in the evening at Donald Windham's apartment, and they went to the theater or ate together with friends such as Margo Jones, Mary Hunter, and Jane Lawrence, a vivacious young actress who was distantly related to Tennessee and had played the juvenile lead in *Oklahoma!* Tennessee and Donald also saw a good deal of Edwina and Reverend Dakin when they came to New York.

When Tennessee decided to have his fourth cataract operation, he asked Donald to go to the hospital with him and stay till he came out of the operating room. For four days, both eyes were bandaged. Donald read to him every evening, and when he was discharged from the hospital, they went to stay for a weekend with friends in New Jersey.[3] Tennessee later wrote that the gauze mask "served a purpose":

While I was resting in the hospital, the friends whom I had neglected or affronted in one way or another began to call on me, and now that I was in pain and darkness, their voices seemed to have changed, or rather that unpleasant mutation which I had suspected earlier in the season had now disappeared and they sounded now as they had used to sound in the lamented days of my obscurity. Once more they were sincere and kindly voices with the ring of truth in them.[4]

But this did not stop him from running away.[5] In April 1945 he went to Mexico, where he settled into a guest-house on the edge of Lake Chapala, near Guadalajara, and resumed work on the play about the two sisters, Blanche and Stella.

Like Amanda Wingfield, Blanche is a faded beauty who affects a greater gentility than she has ever had, and like Laura she is crushed by the forces of brutality. At least half aware that he was telling and retelling the story of Cornelius's brutality, Edwina's delusions of refinement, and their brutal destruction of Rose, Tennessee would return to the same themes in play after play. The new play was conceived as a battle between coarse, working-class poker players and fragile Southern belles. In both plays a rhetorical style stands for a style of living that cannot be sustained. In the squalid setting of *Streetcar* Blanche's language seems no less fragile than Laura's glass animals.

Before leaving New York, Tennessee had learned about poker by inviting stagehands from the theater to his hotel room, where he provided cards, chips, food, and drink. He then took notes.[6] In Mexico he worked on the play every day till he left in mid-August for Dallas, where he saw Margo Jones. She bullied him into finishing a story he had started in New York during 1943. He had often handled the confrontation between the genuine emotion of the fugitive outsider and the rigid conformism of the legal and religious establishment, but he would previously have been incapable of twisting the theme into a wryly ironic ending. In "One Arm" Oliver Wine-miller, an ex-boxer, is a male prostitute who has murdered one of his customers. Before his sentence, he had been emotionally dead, believing that everyone he met was the same. Only when he is facing death in the electric chair and receiving hundreds of letters from the men who had picked him up does he recognize that these men had emotional as well as physical needs. Belatedly he recognizes their capacity for genuine emotion. Now that he has to die, he can see that there was, after all, something to live for.

The success of *The Glass Menagerie* at the Playhouse helped *You Touched Me* into existence in a production by Guthrie McClintic, with Edmund Gwenn as the old sea captain and the twenty-five-year-old Montgomery Clift as the young airman who arouses the love of the captain's daughter by touching her accidentally. Tennessee arrived in Boston at the end of August for the rehearsals and the start of the pre-Broadway tour. The play opened at the Booth Theatre, only three blocks from the Playhouse. Reviewers were lukewarm in their praise, but after so many years of seeming to be at the threshold of success, Tennessee was gratified to have two plays running simultaneously on Broadway.

Though he felt as if he were going into a physical decline, this did not stop him from enjoying himself. He was staying in a suite on the eighteenth floor of the Shelton Hotel, overlooking the East River. Of the hotel's amenities, none gave him more pleasure than the swimming pool and the steam room. As at the YMCA, both were good places for picking up attractive young men, and he admitted to Donald that he was practically using the hotel as a brothel.

Early in December, when his health was obviously deteriorating, he left for New Orleans, planning, on the doctor's advice, to live less strenuously. Though he had enjoyed himself in New York, he was always ambivalent in his feelings about the city, and he was glad to have left it. "Broadway seems like some revolting sickness that involves vomiting and shitting and eating all at once. One's ego becomes so sickly bloated with it, little vanities take the place of any real truth in living."[7]

His third visit to New Orleans, this was the first in which he did not have to economize. He stayed at the Hotel Pontchartrain, where he felt lonely, though his life was not "strictly celibate. My old friends have disappeared but while apartment hunting I ran into a group on the floor drinking wine, one of them in a Carmen Miranda head-dress devised from window-drapes." When he wrote this letter to Donald on 18 December, Tennessee was looking forward to an evening with these new friends, who were going to take him to a nightclub, the Goat House, where the program included "ether parties, which is something I haven't yet seen. Town is *wide* open."

Hotel Pontchartrain, New Orleans

On New Year's Day 1946 he moved into a furnished four-room apartment on the second floor of 710 Orleans Street, close to the St. Louis cathedral. "I never put on a shirt, just a leather jacket. I go unshaven for days. . . . I make my own coffee, have breakfast cream you have to dip out with a spoon."[8] The apartment had a balcony from which he could see the stone statue of Christ outside the cathedral, "his arms outstretched as if to invite the suffering world to come to him."[9]

Tennessee was soon sharing his new apartment with a good-looking young man who had been working in New Mexico as a receptionist at La Fonda de Taos Hotel, and had twice come to visit him in New Orleans. Pancho Rodriguez y Gonzalez "relieved me, during that period, of my greatest affliction, which is perhaps the major theme of my writings, the affliction of loneliness."[10] Ten years younger than Tennessee, Pancho became the first lover since Kip Kiernan to sustain a long-term, serious affair with him. But while Pancho wanted a quiet, stable relationship, Tennessee refused to give up the habit of going out almost every night to look for new men. His worst abuse of Pancho, though, according to Fritz Bultman, was to create real-life situations that were then translated into sequences in *A Streetcar Named Desire*.[11]

At the end of January 1946 Tennessee traveled to Washington for a command performance of *The Glass Menagerie*, but lost track of time and slept in his hotel, the Statler, all through the performance.

In New Orleans he had little contact with people outside the French Quarter until his friend Dick Orme gave a party for a debutante niece. Tennessee was sufficiently well known to find himself in demand as a guest at parties in the exclusive Garden District. He reciprocated by giving a party in his apartment but shocked some of his guests by showing them over the apartment, revealing that he and Pancho slept in the same bedroom. Later, Tennessee claims, one of the debutantes' escorts returned wearing nothing but a raincoat, which he promptly removed.[12]

After about four months in New Orleans Tennessee was on the move again. Sending Pancho to wait for him in Taos, he drove to St. Louis, where the family situation had deteriorated. Cornelius, who was sixty-five and had retired on the first of January from the International Shoe Company, had nothing to do but drink and quarrel. Life therefore became even more unpleasant for Tennessee's nonagenarian grandfather, who, almost blind, seldom dared to venture outside his room. Tennessee offered to find an apartment for him in New Orleans. Even more exposed to Cornelius's aggression, Edwina was scarcely benefiting from the financial independence *The Glass Menagerie* had given her. "As for Mother," Tennessee wrote, "she embodies all the errors and mistakes and misunderstandings that her time could produce," though he recognized she had once had "the makings of an awfully fine woman."[13]

Suffering from abdominal pain while he was in St. Louis, Tennessee was sent to be examined at a hospital in Wichita, Kansas, where the doctor diagnosed diverticulitis—the presence of small bulges or pockets at weak points in the large intestine—but Tennessee, refusing to be treated there, went on to Taos, where he arrived, suffering acute intestinal pain, in mid-May. He had in fact contracted a rare form of the disease, called Meckel's diverticulum—inflammation of a residual sac similar to the appendix. The operation he needed was only a minor one, but he alarmed his parents, Audrey Wood, and his friends by making out that his life was in danger. Pancho, he told them, was to be his sole heir. Tennessee went on cultivating his hypochondria: his life was more dramatic and his incentive to work all the greater if he could believe he would soon be felled by a disease no doctor had yet diagnosed.

The Algonquin Hotel, New York

In Taos Pancho nursed him through his convalescence, and they planned to spend the summer on the island of Nantucket after a brief visit to New York, where they stayed at the Royalton Hotel. Tennessee often met friends for drinks in the lobby of the Algonquin, across the street, and he was there one day with Donald and another man when Pancho rushed in, drunk and raging with sexual jealousy. After shouting abuse at the two men, he told Tennessee: "Go over to the Royalton and see what I've done." All Tennessee's clothes had been torn to shreds, and his typewriter had been smashed. But his manuscripts were still intact.[14]

On the island, he and Pancho rented one of the gray frame houses outside the town, and from now on, the main object of Pancho's jealousy was Carson McCullers. After reading her new novel, *The Member of the Wedding*, Tennessee had written to say how much he would like to meet her, and in response she came to Nantucket. "She got off the ferry looking very tall and wearing slacks and grinning her delightful crooked-toothed grin."[15] She moved into the house with them, sleeping in the downstairs guest room and doing most of the cooking. She was twenty-nine and married but bisexual.

She enjoyed swimming, bicycled round the island with Tennessee and Pancho, and set to work on a dramatization of her novel. She and Tennessee sat at opposite ends of the dining-room table, working, and at the end of the day they read out what they had written. Later in the summer he gave her a jade ring that had belonged to his sister; one of his biographers, Donald Spoto, is probably right to suggest that "he saw an opportunity to do for McCullers what he could not have done for Rose: to help keep her demands at bay, to sustain her unpredictable moods and her almost pathological selfishness."[16]

Williams was working on the play that was eventually to be called *Summer and Smoke* after he had, as usual, changed his mind about what to call it. "Chart of Anatomy" was one of the titles to be rejected. One of the characters is a doctor, whose preoccupation with the body is not merely professional. He and the other main character, Alma Winemiller, both suffer from what Williams calls incompleteness. The daughter of a Mississippi minister, Alma develops the spiritual side of her nature while remaining ignorant of physical passion; with qualities and deficiencies that are the opposite of hers, John is "brilliantly and restlessly alive in a stagnant society." As the grandson of a Mississippi minister, Williams understood the life-denying pressures that had made her into what she was, and he came to believe she "may very well be the best female portrait I have drawn in a play."[17] She remained his favorite character because he identified with her so deeply. Like him, she grew up "in the shadow of the rectory, and came only late to sexual experience."[18] Matilda in *You Touched Me* and Laura in *The Glass Menagerie* are similarly retarded in their sexual development, but they remain open to sexual experience, but Alma, like Tennessee for so many of his early years, rejects the sexuality that is offered to her, and in the canon of his plays that is a cardinal sin.

John and Alma fail to make contact, though each has what the other needs. Alma has the same surname—Winemiller—as Oliver, the ex-boxer in "One Arm," and, like him, she and John arrive too late at an understanding of what has been missing from their life. Just as John recognizes the insufficiency of mere physicality, she realizes it has been a mistake to reject sexuality, and turns to promiscuity. But the opposition between spiritual and carnal values is rather simplistic, and though Tennessee had rebelled against the life-denying pressures of puritanical religion, he found it hard to empathize with John, who "never seemed real to me, but always a cardboard figure."[19]

Katherine Balfour and Tod Andrews in the
Dallas production of Summer and Smoke
(1947)

Tennessee had formulated his ideas about incompleteness in the story "Desire and the Black Masseur," where desire is defined as "something that is made to occupy a larger space than that which is afforded by the individual being." Anthony's desire is so much too big for him that it swallows him up.

For the sins of the world are really only its partialities, its incompletions, and these are what sufferings must atone for. A wall that has been omitted from a house because the stones were exhausted, a room in a house left unfurnished because the householder's funds were not sufficient—these sorts of incompletion are usually covered up or glossed over by some kind of makeshift arrangement. The nature of man is full of such makeshift arrangements, devised by himself to cover his incompletion. He feels a part of himself to be like a missing wall or a room left unfurnished and he tries as well as he can to make up for it. The use of imagination, resorting to dreams or the loftier purpose of art, is a mask he devises to cover his incompletion.

Another mask is violence, whether in fighting between individuals, in warfare, or in the atonement that consists of surrendering the self to violent treatment. All three involve "a blind and senseless compensation for that which is not yet formed in human nature."

This imagery and these ideas have an underground connection with *Summer and Smoke*, in which the incompleteness of John and Alma has a physical counterpart in the missing walls of the set. In his production notes for the play, Tennessee even uses some of the words he had used in the story: "The walls are omitted or just barely suggested by certain necessary fragments such as might be needed to hang a picture or to contain a doorframe." Nor are his ideas for the set entirely separate from his handling of the characters: George Jean Nathan discerned "a scrim treatment of character . . . hiding real delineation behind pseudo-poetical gauze which blurs his audience's vision."

By mid-September illness had coincided once again with the need to move. Suffering from gastric pains, Tennessee returned to New York for a series of tests, which revealed a large tapeworm in his intestines. Morbidly, he insisted on interpreting its presence as a symptom of terminal cancer. It was only at the end of October that he was free to leave New York, but he again sent Pancho ahead—this time to organize winter quarters in New Orleans, where they settled into a beautifully furnished apartment on St. Peter Street, paying $150 a month. What Tennessee liked most of all was a long refectory table under a skylight that provided ideal conditions for working in the morning. He got up early, and after drinking black coffee, went straight to work. Through the skylight he could see the clouds. "New Orleans is slightly below sea level and maybe that's why . . . the clouds always seem just overhead. I suppose they are really vapor off the Mississippi more than genuine clouds and through that skylight they seemed so close that if the skylight were not glass, you could touch them. They were fleecy and in continual motion."[20] They left their mark on *Summer and Smoke:* in his production notes he asks for fleecy cloud forms to drift across the cyclorama.

632 St. Peter's Street, New Orleans

Alone in the apartment all day, he worked on the play, and when it was finished, he sent it to Audrey Wood with the suggestion that the English actress Celia Johnson would make a good Alma. But one night he read the script to a young man who kept yawning and finally asked: "How could the author of *The Glass Menagerie* write such a bad play as this?"[21]

Depressed, Tennessee went back to the play about the sisters, working on it from early morning till early afternoon. He was already preoccupied with the idea of death before he heard that Laurette Taylor had died at sixty-two, only four months after giving her last performance in *The Glass Menagerie*. Convinced that he was dying of pancreatic cancer, Tennessee worked furiously, trying to build memories of the past and feelings about the present into a play that could survive as his monument.

His irrational fear that he was dying was inseparable from his equally irrational conviction that he did not deserve to stay alive. Vestigial puritanism sharpened his discomfort at his homosexuality: should he be allowed to get away with it? In most of his insistent celebrations of the body, homosexual love is dressed in heterosexual disguise to make it look more appealing, and when he deals directly with homosexual subject matter, it is usually through narrative about past action, as in *A Streetcar Named Desire* and *Cat on a Hot Tin Roof*. Like Ibsen, who mines his plots with guilty secrets that explode when characters dig up the past, he often contrives tension that can be released only through narrative explanation of past action. Into Blanche's prehistory in *Streetcar*, Tennessee builds a variety of sins. She has sold the ancestral home without consulting her sister, she has been promiscuous, and she lies about her past, but what interests him most of all is the brutality of her reaction when she discovered that her young husband was bisexual. After catching him in bed with a young boy, she told him, while dancing with him, how much he disgusted her. Afterward he put a revolver into his mouth and fired, blowing off the back of his head.

In punishing her for this, Tennessee is also punishing himself for his ambivalence toward homosexuality. The moralist rubs shoulders with the masochist. The violence that encroaches on so many of his plays stems from the same ambivalence. The insistent glorification of the body gets caught up in an uncontrollable undercurrent: Tennessee is simultaneously trying to affirm and deny himself. He subjects his surrogates to a tension that often breaks into exorbitant violence. In spite of himself he ferociously punishes the characters he would most like to protect, while punishing himself for his irresolution.

In 1946, living on St. Peter Street, he could look out of the window and see "that rattletrap old streetcar" named Desire that ran up and down Royal Street day and night. Another streetcar was called Cemeteries, and "their indiscourageable progress up and down Royal Street struck me as having some symbolic bearing of a broad nature on the life in the Vieux Carré—and everywhere else, for that matter."[22] The play's title is explained in Blanche's first speech: "They told me to take a streetcar named Desire, and then transfer to one called Cemeteries and ride six blocks and get off at—Elysian Fields!" In fact the streetcar called Cemeteries ran up and down Canal Street, not Royal Street, and the street called Elysian Fields is outside the Quarter, but the stage directions describe a scene typical of the Quarter as it was then. The play benefits from the glimpses it affords of street life and relationships with neighbors, including a black woman. New Orleans, says a stage direction, "is a cosmopolitan city where there is a relatively warm and easy intermingling of races in the old part of the town." As in *Summer and Smoke*, the sky is visible, and it is described as "a peculiarly tender blue,

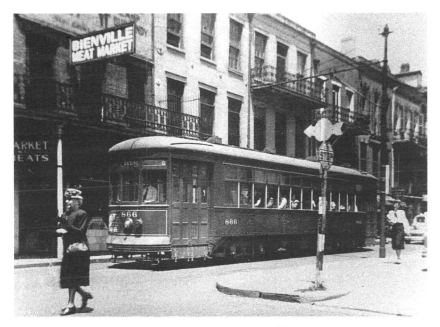

A streetcar named Desire: Royal Street, New Orleans (1945)

almost turquoise." It "invests the scene with a kind of lyricism and gracefully attenuates the atmosphere of decay." Music contributes substantially to the atmosphere of the play. In this part of New Orleans, we are told, "you are practically always just around the corner, or a few doors down the street, from a tinny piano being played with the infatuated fluency of brown fingers. This 'Blue Piano' expresses the spirit of the life which goes on here."

The "cemeteries" theme surfaces in frequent reminders of death. When a blind Mexican woman appears, wearing a dark shawl and selling the tin flowers that working-class Mexicans display at funerals, Blanche is scared, momentarily taking her for Death, and in the final scene Blanche fantasizes about dying at sea after eating an unwashed grape. Her hand will be touching the hand of a good-looking doctor with a blond moustache. She will be buried in the water, sewn up in a clean white sack and dropped overboard in the blaze of summer under a sky as blue as her first lover's eyes.

"I think my work is good," Tennessee once wrote, "in exact ratio to the degree of emotional tension which is released into it."[23] None of his plays had more tension released into it than *A Streetcar Named Desire*. He was always to some extent writing about himself, but never more ingeniously than here, and seldom less obviously. Alongside his fear of death, the most active ingredients were memories of his parents' feuding and more recent feuding with Pancho, sadness and incredulity at the loss of Rose's companionship, and guilt about his predatory homosexuality.

Cornelius's drunken brutality had made Tennessee an expert on domestic terrorism: the husband moves from aggression to maudlin remorse; accepting the reconciliation as compensation for the battering, the terrorized wife feels redeemed and renewed. Tennessee's relationship with Pancho had grown increasingly to resemble a marriage, and Stanley Kowalski's violent quarrels with Stella echo Tennessee's with Pancho as much as Cornelius's with Edwina. Elia Kazan noticed that "Tennessee liked Pancho for the same qualities he saw in Kowalski—that he'd break up the joint if he didn't like what was going on."[24] Like Stella, Tennessee would gladly put up with the brawling and the panic for the sake of the reconciliation and the sex that came afterward.

But the violence of the play also refers to Rose. The role of the victim is divided between the two sisters, Blanche and Stella. Stella, the survivor, will have to go on putting up with eruptions of domestic terrorism, but Blanche will lose everything she had once enjoyed, spending the rest of her life in an asylum.

She has been a schoolteacher, and her mannered speech is reminiscent of Amanda's in *Menagerie* and Alma's in *Summer and Smoke*. Like Edwina, all three characters use language that implies an outdated mode of manners and they hold their language up ineffectually, like an umbrella, against the assaults of a stormy reality. It can almost be said that Stella represents young America, torn between its loyalty to antiquated idealism and the brutal realism of the present, while Blanche incarnates the pretensions of the old South: its values and quaint manners echo through her quaintly mannered speech, while Belle Reve, the ancestral home that she was forced to sell, stands for the elegant life that was once lived on the plantations. Stanley's "Polack" bluntness contrasts with Blanche's quintessentially Southern refinement. As Tennessee had already shown in *Menagerie*, the rhythms and cadences of Edwina's endless tirades had impressed themselves on his memory, and for him her image would always blur with that of the archetypal Southern belle.

In sketching out the relationship between Blanche and Stella, he was drawing on memories of his boyhood with Rose and on fantasies about staying in the house of a married sibling who has become a stranger. Maybe he asked himself how he would have reacted to finding Rose in a shabby tenement, married to a hard-drinking working-class poker player.

Tennessee also rubs up against his own obsessions when he makes Stella refuse to believe Stanley has raped Blanche. Rejecting Rose's allegations against her father, Edwina had punished her with a lobotomy. In writing the poignant sequence in which Blanche is led away by the doctor and nurse to internment in a mental home, Tennessee was reenacting the family story. The wife of the rapist, Stella is left feeling guilty and distressed, just as Edwina, wife of a man who may have made incestuous demands on his daughter, should have felt guilty and distressed—as Tennessee did—about the fate of the innocuous Rose.

Another set of guilt feelings comes into play when Tennessee constructs Blanche's background. Suspecting she has kept all the proceeds from the sale of the family home, Stanley investigates her past. He discovers her nymphomaniac tendencies: she has acquired a reputation for seducing teenage boys, and we soon see her flirting with a young man who comes to the apartment collecting for the *Evening Star*. (Tennessee could draw on memories of ringing doorbells in St. Louis to solicit new subscribers for the *Pictorial Review*.) Making a feeble joke, asking the young man for a light, inquiring what the time is, prolonging the conversation by questioning him about what he drank in the soda bar, displaying her envy of his youth, complimenting him on his appearance, and planting a kiss on his lips without giving him a chance to refuse it, Blanche is going through gambits comparable to those Tennessee used when picking up young men, and she feels something of the same guilt.

New Orleans may seem like the only possible setting for the action, but earlier drafts were set in Chicago and Atlanta. At first the sisters and the younger one's husband were going to be Italian, and then, opting for Southern belles, Tennessee intended to make the husband Irish. In the first draft Stanley is a weakly good-looking young man with "a playful tenderness and vivacity which would amount to effeminacy if he were not Italian." Though he grows tougher when Tennessee makes him Irish, he still has enough feminine traits to remind Blanche of a vicious fourteen-year-old girl in one of her classes. As he evolved, Stanley became more like John Buchanan, who

*Perpetual feast of nectared sweat: Vivien
Leigh and Marlon Brando in the film of*
Streetcar

is described as "unmarked by the dissipations in which he relieves his demo-niac unrest." Stanley, a cruder man, more subtly characterized, is full of masculine pride in his robust sexuality.

The Italian Stanley of the early draft would have been closer to a self-portrait; the exuberantly macho American Pole resembles the virile work-ing-class alcoholics Tennessee had read about in D. H. Lawrence, but in reworking his new play, Tennessee was not so much discarding auto-biographical material as disguising it more subtly, while letting the script benefit from literary influences he had absorbed. The most potent of these — the one which contributes most to the play's resonance — was the in-fluence of Strindberg. Son of a maidservant, he had married a baroness, and, with shameless brilliance, he drew on his memories of awkwardness, ex-hilaration, and guilt-feelings when he wrote *Miss Julie*. But in echoing his own experience he was encapsulating European social history. Like Chek-hov in *The Cherry Orchard*, Strindberg showed the impractical aristocracy in the process of handing over power half-voluntarily to the rising proletariat.

Marlon Brando, Jessica Tandy, and Kim Hunter in Streetcar *on Broadway*

Miss Julie's valet, Jean, is "the type who founds a species," while she is torn between the values she has inherited and the allure of Jean, who combines virility with power to seize the initiative. Sexually, as Strindberg says, Jean is the aristocrat. In one sequence Julie talks about a dream in which she is sitting on top of a pillar, too scared and dizzy to climb down. But Jean dreams he is lying under a high tree in a dark wood, wishing he could climb up to steal the golden eggs in the bird's nest at the top. In *Streetcar*, Williams not only makes Stanley a sexual aristocrat of the Strindbergian kind but echoes this imagery. When Stella refers to Belle Reve, Stanley says: "I was common as dirt. You showed me the snapshot of the place with the columns. I pulled you down off them columns and how you loved it, having them colored lights going!"

But whereas only Julie obeys when Jean orders her to kill herself, Stanley has two Southern belles in his power. Irritated from the outset by Blanche's affectation and her mendacity, he exposes her sordid past and effectively destroys her by raping her. Afterward, like the lobotomized Rose, she is fit only for the asylum. The rape occurs while Stella is in the hospital giving birth to Stanley's child, but she has secured her tenure of the future by coming down to his level.

In spite of its international ingredients—Swedish, Norwegian, Irish, Italian, Polish—the play is deeply imbued with the South, and after finishing it Tennessee tried to make himself stop writing about the South. Undeniably, though, he was in love with it—not with the South as it really was, but with the South as he believed it used to be. "I don't write about the North, because I feel nothing for it but eagerness to get out of it. . . . I don't write about the North because—so far as I know—they never had anything to lose, culturally. But the South once had a way of life that I'm just old enough to remember—a culture that had grace, elegance . . . an inbred culture . . . not a society based on money, as in the North. I write out of regret for that."[25]

Toward the end of 1946 Tennessee's grandfather arrived for a visit. With cataracts on both eyes, Reverend Dakin could no longer read, but was not too deaf to enjoy radio programs, and his presence was comforting. "Whenever I'm disturbed or discouraged with my work, I just go and sit near him. Sometimes we don't speak at all, but even as we sit in silence I seem to get a great spiritual solace from him."[26] The old man's presence served as a reminder of the genteel Southern traditions Tennessee was commemorating in *Streetcar*; it also acted as a catalyst on the relationship with Pancho, who was drinking heavily, which intensified his jealousy. But, unable to fight or even quarrel in front of the nonagenarian, the two men collaborated on looking after him, and they took him with them in mid-January 1947 when they drove Tennessee's new Pontiac to Key West.

They crossed the Suwannee River and drove across Florida. "Grandfather was a wonderful traveling companion. Everything pleased him. He pretended to see clearly despite his cataracts and in those days you could shout to him and he'd hear you."[27] From their two-room suite on the top floor of La Concha Hotel in Key West they could see the Gulf of Mexico. In the morning Tennessee worked on *Streetcar*; in the afternoons they drove to the South Beach, where the old man sat letting the waves wash over him. They visited Hemingway's ex-wife Pauline in her Spanish colonial home, and Miriam Hopkins threw a party for them.

At the end of March Tennessee sent *A Streetcar Named Desire* to Audrey

Wood, who responded more positively and more quickly than she had to *Summer and Smoke*. The producer she wanted to involve was Irene Selznick, who arranged to meet Tennessee in Charleston. The director they agreed to approach was Elia Kazan, who had just scored a success with his production of Arthur Miller's *All My Sons*. Though not immediately enthusiastic about the script, Kazan accepted a deal giving him 20 percent of the profits. He was sensitive to the Strindbergian substructure, and the word *aristocrat* occurs in his notes on the play. Writing about Stanley he asks: "Why does he want to bring Blanche and, before her, Stella, *down to his level?* . . . It's the hoodlum aristocrat. He's deeply dissatisfied, deeply hopeless, deeply cynical. . . . Stanley is supremely indifferent to everything except his own pleasure and comfort."[28]

Like Strindberg, who could identify with both the female aristocrat and the male servant, Tennessee could identify with both Stanley and Blanche. Her self-hatred, her self-destructiveness, and the pleasure she takes in musing on her own death helped to provoke Kazan's comment: "Blanche DuBois, the woman, *is* Williams. Blanche comes into a house where someone is going to murder her. The interesting part of it is that Blanche DuBois-Williams is *attracted* to the person who's going to murder her. . . . I saw Blanche as Williams, an ambivalent figure who is attracted to the harshness and vulgarity around him at the same time as he fears it, because it threatens his life."[29]

Tennessee's life was often under threat as the relationship with Pancho deteriorated and his excesses of jealous hysteria became more envenomed and violent. But in June 1947 Tennessee left with Pancho for Provincetown, where they rented a shingled cottage by the sea. Tennessee worked on *Summer and Smoke*, which was due to open on 8 July in Dallas, directed by Margo Jones, who wanted him to sit in on rehearsals. When he said that what he euphemistically called his private life would be unappreciated in Dallas, she and her friend Joanna Albus came to stay in the Provincetown cottage. By then Tennessee's private life had begun to change. Of the infidelities that provoked Pancho, the one which turned out to be most important was with a twenty-five-year-old man who had been in the navy.

Frank Merlo was a second-generation American from a Sicilian family. He was short—an inch shorter than Tennessee—muscular, and attractive. "He had enormous brown eyes and a sort of equine face, which led a couple of years later to his nickname 'The Little Horse.'" He and Tennessee made

117

Atlantic House Bar, where Tennessee met Frank

love on the sand dunes. "It was a fantastic hour in the dunes for me that evening even though I have never regarded sand as an ideal or even a desirable surface on which to worship the little god. However the little god was given such devout service that he must still be smiling."[30]

Returning home later that evening, Tennessee was walking up a steep hill when he saw the headlights of a car approaching much too fast. He stepped off the road, and Pancho drove the car into a field of marsh grass "with what seemed to be the intention of running me down." Tennessee ran toward the beach, pursued by Pancho, who was yelling in Spanish and English. Seeing a wooden pier, Tennessee ran out and climbed down to the understructure, hiding just above the level of the waves until Pancho had left. Tennessee spent the rest of the night in a rented room, but the next day Pancho was in the best of moods, behaving as if nothing had gone wrong. The breakup came soon afterward.[31]

Before the Provincetown fiasco, Tennessee and Pancho had gone to California, where Hume Cronyn was restaging *Portrait of a Madonna*, one of three one-act Williams plays Cronyn had directed in January for the Actor's Lab in Los Angeles. His English wife, Jessica Tandy, had played the lead then, and Cronyn hoped that if Tennessee saw her in the part, he would want her to play Blanche. She could scarcely have had a better showcase, for her character, Lucretia Collins, was like a first draft for Blanche—a genteel Southerner who tries to sustain her pretensions in squalid surroundings. Eventually, when her mind gives way, she is committed to an asylum. Kazan and Irene Selznick, who came to see the performance, agreed with Tennessee that Jessica Tandy would make a good Blanche.

The casting of Stanley had been more problematic. Tennessee wanted John Garfield, who accepted the part, but only on condition that he should be released if he got a good movie offer. The twenty-three-year-old Marlon Brando, who had already played four parts on Broadway, was in Kazan's "beginners" class at the Actors Studio. Apparently Brando slept in a different bed every night, and it was hard to locate him, but Kazan tracked him down, gave him twenty dollars for his trip to Provincetown,. and called Tennessee to say a young actor was on his way to read for the part. Three days later he called Tennessee again, but no actor had materialized. Brando had used the twenty dollars to eat, and had then hitchhiked to Provincetown with a girlfriend.[32]

In the Provincetown cottage, electricity and plumbing had failed simultaneously: Brando and the girl were received in candlelight. "I never saw such raw talent in an individual," Tennessee wrote afterward. "Brando was a gentle, lovely guy, a man of extraordinary beauty when I first met him. He was very natural and helpful. He repaired the plumbing that had gone on the whack, and he repaired the lights that had gone off. And then he just sat calmly down and began to read."[33] Tennessee gave him his cues, and within ten minutes, Margo Jones was on her feet. "'Get Kazan on the phone right away! This is the greatest reading I've ever heard—in or outside of Texas!' Brando maybe smiled a little but didn't show any particular elation, such as the elation we all felt." He and the girl spent the night on the floor, curled up in a blanket, and in the morning Brando wanted Tennessee to go for a walk on the beach, but they walked in silence.[34]

According to Kazan, "Tennessee was quite shy during our early rehearsals, but he became less so as time went on. He never interfered but he was always there for us, always available."[35] He told them he was dying, that he had written his last play, and that he had too little energy left to make script changes, but he mustered the energy to get rid of Pancho—the resourceful Irene Selznick helped to negotiate a financial settlement which eroded Pancho's reluctance to leave.

As soon as *Streetcar* opened in Boston, favorable notices began to appear, and on the opening night in Philadelphia, Kazan grinned at Tennessee in the crowded lobby of the theater. "This smells like a hit." When the play opened on Broadway at the beginning of December 1947, the audience applauded as soon as the curtain went up on Jo Mielziner's re-creation of the New Orleans street, and at the end the ovation lasted for thirty minutes. Tennessee was called on stage, but felt worried afterward that he had bowed to the actors instead of the audience.[36]

In the *New York Times* Brooks Atkinson described the play as "a quietly woven study of intangibles. . . . It reveals Mr. Williams as a genuinely poetic playwright whose knowledge of people is honest and thorough and whose sympathy is profoundly human." In the *Herald-Tribune* Howard Barnes declared: "Williams is certainly the Eugene O'Neill of the present period," and in the *New Yorker*, Wolcott Gibbs hailed "a brilliant, implacable play about the disintegration of a woman, or if you like, a society." Afterward the play won the New York Drama Critics' Circle Award and the Pulitzer Prize.

8

Roman Spring

Lionized in New York at the end of 1947, Tennessee was as uncomfortable as he had expected to be. One consolation was that he met Greta Garbo, who said she would be willing to make another film, provided her role was neither male nor female. "In appearance she is really hermaphroditic, almost as flat as a boy, very thin, the eyes and the voice extraordinarily pure and beautiful, but she has the cold quality of a mermaid. . . . She scares me to death."[1]

She and Helen Hayes were star guests at a party he gave, but soon afterward, succumbing to his usual restlessness, he booked a passage on a steamer to Cherbourg. In Paris he stayed at the Hotel Georges V, which Garbo had recommended but, disliking it, moved to a hotel on the Left Bank. A heavy cold and an upset stomach helped to make his first impressions of Paris unfavorable: "I hate to say this, but Dallas, Texas, is better."[2] He asked Audrey Wood to send cans of condensed milk and instant coffee. Subsequent bulletins told her he was in the American Hospital at Neuilly with hepatitis, but as usual he was overinterpreting minor symptoms, and soon he was enjoying the night life, going regularly to Le Boeuf sur le Toit, the nightclub that was immortalized by Darius Milhaud and Jean Cocteau, and to Madame Arthur's, which staged a drag show.

Restless again in February 1948, he repeated the journey he had made twenty years earlier with his grandfather, taking a train along the Riviera to

Naples and Reggio de Calabria, then, after a brief stay in Sicily, going to Rome, where he stayed at the Hotel Ambasciatore. He was surprised that so much of the city had been destroyed during the war. Workmen were demolishing the damaged houses, and a lot of rebuilding was under way, but he felt there was nothing hopeful or vigorous about the reconstruction. The atmosphere seemed to smell of dust, "as if you were actually breathing that quality of ruin-beyond-repair which Vienna has."[3] But he soon changed his mind about the city, deciding he liked it even better than New Orleans.[4]

What mattered most was that boys seemed more attractive and more available than in any other city. As he said in a letter, the buttocks of Roman boys had been "celebrated by artists for many centuries." He had bedded any number of Michelangelo's "more delicate creations, in fact the abundance and accessibility is downright embarrassing." In the Roman streets "you can't walk a block without being accosted by someone you would spend a whole evening trying vainly to make in the New York bars. Of course it usually costs a thousand lire but that is only two bucks . . . and there is never any unpleasantness about it even though one does not know a word they are saying!" His pickups were impoverished and envious of his possessions, including the clothes in his wardrobe. "Soon as they enter the room they start trying on everything you have and pretend they can't understand English when you say 'No!'"[5] In general, though, Tennessee was pleased with their lack of inhibition. "You rarely see a young man on the street who does not have a slight erection. Often they walk along the Veneto with hand in pocket, caressing their genitals quite unconsciously, and this regardless of whether or not they are hustling or cruising."[6]

On his first night in the city Tennessee found a Neapolitan lightweight boxer with thick glossy black hair and "a small but imperial torso."[7] On his second night Tennessee saw a teenage boy in a shabby overcoat sitting in Doney's, the patisserie of the Hotel Excelsior, at a table from which he could smile at passersby. When Tennessee beckoned him outside, he came promptly, revealing shoes that were tied to his feet with string. Nervous about taking him into the sumptuous hotel, Tennessee tipped the elevator operator generously. The boy's name was Salvatore, he was seventeen, and he spoke little English. When they needed words, they looked them up in a pocket dictionary. Salvatore explained his father's occupation by finding the word *carabiniere,* and indicated that he was punished if he stayed out all night. But they arranged to meet again the next evening.

Tennessee soon rented a two-room apartment on the Via Aurora, just off the Via Veneto. The huge windows of the living room, which he kept full of mimosa, looked out on the old wall encircling the Villa Borghese, while the bedroom was occupied almost entirely by the big double bed. He had soon fitted Salvatore out with a new wardrobe and emancipated him from the tyranny of his father, arranging for him to spend alternate nights in the Via Aurora apartment and a small *pensione*. On those nights Tennessee would go cruising with friends.

Rome had not yet recovered its affluence, and there were few cars in the streets. Tennessee bought a jeep from a G.I. and used it on Salvatore's nights off to race up and down looking for boys. It was the oldest and noisiest thing on the Roman streets, "the grandfather of all jeeps," he claimed in a letter to Jo Healy, his old friend from the Theatre Guild. "It sounds like a pair of fire engines in a fit of passion." After he made friends with the American writer Gore Vidal, they went on trips together in the jeep to Sorrento and Amalfi. At first Tennessee got on well with Vidal "but only through the strenuous effort it took to overlook his conceit. He has studied ballet and is constantly doing pirouettes and flexing his legs, and the rest of the time he is comparing himself and Truman Capote . . . to such figures as Dostoevsky and Balzac."[8]

In March 1948 Tennessee met the English historian Harold Acton, who described him as "a pudgy, taciturn, mustachioed little man without any obvious distinction."[9] Vidal found Tennessee more sympathetic, in spite of his "indifference to place, art, history." According to Vidal, Tennessee "seldom reads a book and the only history he knows is his own; he depends, finally, on a romantic genius to get him through life."[10]

In Rome Tennessee wrote "Rubio y Morena," a story that reflects his reactions to being lionized. The writer, Kamrowski, "had lately become what is called a Name and received a good deal of attention." But he takes little pleasure in it. "He was essentially a lonely man, not self-sufficient but living as though he were. He had never been able to believe that anybody sincerely cared much about him. . . . Companionship was not a familiar or easy thing for Kamrowski." Only once, during an almost incomprehensible and largely wordless liaison with a half-Indian girl, does he make close contact with another human being, not during lovemaking but when she is weeping and hugging him to her so tightly that the pressure of her gaunt arms convinces him that she loves him, and this scares him. This story sheds light on

*"Meet my daughter," Tom Titt's 1948
cartoon accompanying review of the West
End production of* The Glass Menagerie

both Tennessee's constant need for intimate companionship and his difficulties in sustaining relationships with intimate companions.

Alongside the story he had been working on *Summer and Smoke*, which
was due to open on Broadway in October, under the direction of Margo
Jones. In June she arrived in Naples, wanting to work on the play. After
brief visits to Capri and Ischia, they went together to London. "England,"
he wrote, "is about the most unpleasant, uncomfortable and expensive place
where you could be right now."[11] Whatever his expectations of London
might have been, they were disappointed. "Christ, what a dull town and
what stuffy people! . . . I have only had one lay since I got here."[12] His first
hotel was the Cumberland, where he had "the barest and ugliest single
room that I've ever seen outside a YMCA."[13] He moved to the Savoy, and
met John Gielgud, who was to direct *The Glass Menagerie* in the West End,
starring Helen Hayes. Gielgud struck Tennessee as a prima donna, nervous
and high-handed. There seemed to be no prospect of a working relationship with give-and-take in it. Nor did Tennessee like Gielgud's entourage
of carefully dressed young men and "middle aged fags who still think they're
young and pretty." But Gielgud gave a party for him at the Savoy, inviting
Noël Coward, Laurence Olivier, and Vivien Leigh. At the party Tennessee
met a young actress of Russian origin, Maria Britneva, who found him sitting alone on a sofa. She brought him a drink and, eager to make friends

Tennessee bites his lip while Maria Britneva shows her teeth

with him, arranged to pick him up from his hotel the next day and take him to lunch at her mother's. Her friendliness, her original turn of phrase, and the sharpness of her tongue made her seem refreshingly different from everyone else at the party, and she became a friend.

Tennessee went to some of the rehearsals in Brighton, where the pre-London tour of *The Glass Menagerie* was to open, but Helen Hayes was predicting failure for the show, and he left for Paris, where he stayed with Gore Vidal at the Hôtel de l'Université. "The swimming pool *Bains Deligny* contains some rare beauties and one finds at *Boeuf* the handsomest kept boys of Europe like jewels in Tiffany's window to be admired but not touched."[14] His life in Paris was even more disorganized than his life in America. "Needless to say I am completely out of laundry and am wearing continuously a midnight blue shirt which does not show the dirt."[15]

He did not go back to London for the opening of his play on 28 July at the Haymarket, but a couple of days later he wrote:

My absence from the opening was not deliberate. At least I don't think it was. I had been quite ill for several days previous and with my usual hypochondria thought I was even worse than I was. I had been overworking. It was mostly nerves but I also had vomiting and diarrhea . . . so I had to put off making a plane reservation till the last evening. Then could only get one for 7 o'clock the following morning. I tried to stay awake all night, remained in my clothes and drank coffee. I don't think I really fell asleep—just blacked out or something—and the hotel has no call system. It was noon when I woke up, so I just said a little prayer for Helen and the players—and went back to work.[16]

Three-armed bandit: Truman Capote at the age of twenty-three

Not wanting to miss the Broadway premiere of *Summer and Smoke* he traveled to New York on the *Queen Mary*. Truman Capote was on board, and the two men had a good deal of fun together. At night they went sneaking along the first-class corridors, picking up shoes that had been left outside cabin doors to be cleaned, and putting them down outside the wrong cabins.[17]

In New York Tennessee always stayed in a different apartment. This time he chose a rather beautiful first-floor apartment in a three-story brownstone on East 58th Street, between Lexington and Third Avenues. When *Summer and Smoke* opened at the Music Box Theatre on 6 October, he saw that Margo Jones had done "a rather mediocre job" as a director. "Not inspired, not vital, as Kazan would have been and as the play so dreadfully needed."[18]

Brooks Atkinson, writing in the *New York Times*, called the piece a "tone poem" with "the same mystic frustration and the same languid doom" as *Menagerie* and *Streetcar*. But most of the reviews were unfavorable, and John Gassner diagnosed "the weaknesses I have suspected in the author for a long time—an insufficient exertion of intellect."[19] But the theater was full every night, and "a great many people, I would say about 60% of each audience—practically all women—are more or less—and sometimes to the point of tears—moved by it." Two weeks after the opening Tennessee gave what he called a "bad notice party." Marlon Brando came on his new motorcycle and took them all riding in turns. "I enjoyed the ride, clamping his buttocks between my knees as we flew along the East River and along the river drive."[20] But the momentary contact with Brando was not enough to lift Tennessee out of his depression. He felt "like a discredited old conjuror whose bag of tricks was exhausted."[21]

By the end of October he was reunited with the Little Horse, Frank Merlo, who moved into the apartment with him. Tennessee wanted the same arrangement he had made with Salvatore, committing himself only to alternate nights with Frank, but they soon settled into a more stable relationship. Christopher Isherwood confirms: "He was a support to Tennessee; he made everything work for him. He ran the house, he looked after him in a way that was uncanny. He was no goody-goody. He was just plain good. And he wasn't just some kind of faithful servitor. He was a lovable man with a strong will."[22]

Enthusing about the Italians, Tennessee wrote: "They are the last of the beautiful young comedians of the world." According to Maria Britneva, Frank's family was

an enormous brood of first-generation Sicilian immigrants who had settled in New Jersey or somewhere. His poor mother was tormented by the size and vociferousness of her family, and used often, after arguments, to climb the figtree in the backyard and sulk, sometimes for hours on end. I remember Frank telling me that after one particularly blinding row, she refused to come down. Having shouted at her and pleaded with her, her sons took an axe to the tree and brought the whole thing down, with her in it.

The family had no plumbing in the house, and Frank returned from one visit there with dysentery. "He said it was the goat's milk that did it. They brought the goat right into his bedroom and milked it beside the bed and handed him the milk and would not take no for an answer as the goat was a great prize."[23]

As soon as the two men had settled down together, wanderlust again took possession of Tennessee, who left for St. Louis. Cornelius had finally moved out—he was living in an apartment near his sister in Knoxville—leaving the Arundel Place apartment to Edwina and her father. Husband and wife arranged a legal separation. Tennessee's feelings were mixed. His father, he said, had "probably suffered as much as anyone, possibly even more, and I'm afraid it will be a lonely and bitter end to his blind and selfish life."[24]

"What lingo do they talk there?" Tennessee sails to Morocco (1948)

Tennessee went to visit Rose at Farmington, afterward arranging for her to have half the royalties from *Summer and Smoke*, and to be transferred to a private clinic in Connecticut. When he went back to New York, he felt no desire to stay there. "I can't live within phone-call of Broadway without feeling like a piece of a big machine, and a piece that doesn't fit properly."[25] He sailed with Frank for Tangier, where they met Paul and Jane Bowles. The four of them spent three weeks touring Tangier, Fez (where their hotel had once been a sultan's palace) and Casablanca.[26]

Tennessee and Frank began 1949 in Marseilles, driving along the Riviera toward Rome, where they stayed at the apartment on the Via Aurora. But life in Rome seemed to have "gone stale." After trying Florence and not liking it, Tennessee drove to Naples with Truman Capote, who infuriated him in a restaurant by giving an imitation of the actress Anne Jackson's imitation of a speech Margo Jones had made to the cast of *Summer and Smoke*, saying that the play was the work of a dying writer. Tennessee knocked over the table and stamped out of the restaurant. But he forgave Capote the next day, and they went to Ischia together.[27]

Intending to visit Sicily, Tennessee used Frank in the way he had often used Pancho, sending him ahead to make preparations, and taking advantage of his absence to resume not only the affair with Salvatore but also the habit of cruising. Though he was twelve years younger than his heroine, many of his experiences are reproduced in the novel he began at this time, *The Roman Spring of Mrs. Stone.* He had no ambitions as a novelist: his original motive for writing the book was to organize material for a film in which he hoped Greta Garbo would play the leading part. Karen Stone is an American actress who has settled in Rome and sometimes forgets she has recently lost her beauty. She goes to bed with a gigolo introduced to her by a mercenary contessa who hands on beautiful young men to rich women and then uses the men to prize money out of them. It was easy for Tennessee to empathize with an aging woman who has doubts about the quality of her talent and cannot resist "pretty young boys of the pimp or gigolo class." But, not really a novelist, he introduces a lot of self-criticism by setting up a conversation between Karen and a character who has no function in the story except to tell her a few home truths, an outspoken female journalist rather like Henrietta Stackpole in Henry James's *Portrait of a Lady:* "Even if you did have more energy than talent, what do you think you are going to do with that energy now? . . . Energy can't be put into anything but action, and by action I don't mean sexual promiscuity!"

Karen often has a disturbing sense of not being in control: her life has been "clouded over by a sense of irreality. . . . At such times there is a sense of drifting, if not of drowning, in a universe of turbulently rushing fluids or vapors." Later on she hesitates about whether she should pretend to believe the story the young man told her about a friend who has been cheated on the black market by a priest and urgently needs ten million lire. The central question is about the wrongness of buying sexual pleasure. But as in so many of Williams's fictions, the theme of buying sexual favors is dovetailed with the theme of aging, and Karen is presented as primarily a victim of the aging process. When she gets a tan from sunbathing, the gold on her body contains "tiny creases which would not disappear beneath the oily fingers of the masseuse who visited her daily." They are the "signatures of time."

Williams takes little trouble to establish Karen's earlier career as an actress. She has retired after playing Juliet when she was too old, but we get little notion of what she was like on the stage, and the narrative is unconvincing when Williams tries to explain how she stayed at the top of her profession. She used to be energetic about visiting theater people in the hospital, even members of the stage staff, and she was meticulous about sending

Kirk Douglas and Jane Wyman in the film
of The Glass Menagerie *(1950)*

greetings to acquaintances on their birthdays and letters of sympathy on the anniversaries of bereavements. But "everything that she did to court the favor of her professional associates, to create the legend of Mrs. Stone as a paragon of loyalty and goodness, was directed by the head as distinguished from the heart." Williams seems uninterested in what actors do; he seems to think that even Mrs. Stone would find playwrights more interesting and feel secretly jealous "because for them there must have been some freedom in the creative work but for her it was only the following out of a prescribed pattern of speeches and acts."

She is less unconvincing as a wife than she is as an actress, though the backward glances at her marriage are fairly superficial. She had needed an adult child, while Mr. Stone had needed "a living and young and adorable mother." What Tennessee needed, presumably, was a lover who could sometimes be an adult child and sometimes a young and adorable surrogate for both parents. But he knew that "substitute relationships" are only partially effective in curing loneliness. "The desiring fingers enclose a phantom object, the hungering lips are pressed to a ghostly mouth."

But if Tennessee was trying to warn himself against the life he was leading, he ignored the warning. Not only did he make little effort to resist temptation, he almost compulsively courted danger. Sometimes he picked up sailors, and soon he was experimenting with pills—phenobarbital and secobarbital—having supplies sent from New York.

In April 1949 he returned to London, where Laurence Olivier was preparing his production of *Streetcar* with Vivien Leigh as Blanche. Tennessee was unimpressed by her performance in Anouilh's *Antigone*, but her offstage personality suggested that she might be better as Blanche. He found the city "just as amazingly dull as ever. And to live here, Oh Jesus!"[28] Vivien Leigh was later to star opposite Brando in the film of the play, but in the West End her Stanley was Bonar Colleano. Mitch was played by Bernard Braden.

Frank Merlo, Elia Kazan, TW, and producer Charles Feldman during the filming of Streetcar

Olivier had no natural understanding of either the play's rhythms or its shifts between comedy and pathos. He wanted to cut Stella's line from scene 4: "But there are things that happen between a man and woman in the dark—that sort of make everything else seem—unimportant." Though the cut would not have affected her directly, Vivien Leigh challenged it: why did he want to get rid of the line? "Because it'll get a laugh," he said.[29] Over-cautious about the audience's sensitivity to sexual innuendo, he made extensive cuts in the play, writing Tennessee an eighteen-page letter to explain his reasons. "I thought if a man takes the trouble to write me an eighteen-page letter, then I should go along with him."

After sailing back to New York in September, Tennessee learned that the film rights to *Streetcar* had been sold for half a million dollars, and Kazan was secured as director. But even these two pieces of good news failed to make Tennessee happy. Because of the sentimentalized screenplay, he had been deeply dissatisfied with the screen treatment of *The Glass Menagerie*,

Elia Kazan directs Karl Malden during the filming of Streetcar

and though he had gone out to Hollywood, he had stayed away from the soundstage, leaving the director, Irving Rapper, to do whatever he liked.

Apprehensive about the new film, and in order to "rest my nerves which were quite shaken by all the traveling and excitement," he gave up both coffee and tea, but always went out with two boxes of pills in his pocket—phenobarbital and secobarbital.[30]

With winter coming on, Tennessee and Frank decided to go south, taking Reverend Dakin with them. Now that Tennessee had no contact with Cornelius, Reverend Dakin had become more than ever like a surrogate father. Collecting the old man from St. Louis, Tennessee and Frank set off to spend the winter of 1949–50 in Key West. This was Tennessee's first visit since 1941 to the island that was to become one of his two favorite places in America, the other being New Orleans. Key West, he said, was "the only place in this country where it's warm enough for me to swim every day of the year. The sky is always clear, and the water's so blue."[31]

He rented a three-room clapboard cottage—which he was later to buy—at 1431 Duncan Street, a "sort of Tom Thumb mansion, a snow white frame house of the Bahama type with a white picket fence and with lovely pink shutters and light green porch furniture."[32] The living room was only about twenty feet by ten, and most of the furniture was made of wicker, with cushions covered in faded chintz. Reverend Dakin was given the whole ground floor to himself. Tennessee worked at the end of the dining-room table. Reverend Dakin could hear almost nothing without his hearing aid, which mostly he refused to wear, and though he was now nearly blind, he soon learned to find his way about the cottage.

He appeared to have no misgivings about his grandson's homosexuality. He dictated a letter to Edwina saying he was enjoying the companionship of Tennessee and Frank, as well as the social life of Key West. He had never been happier, he said, but in fact he was often irritable. Donald Windham remembers how grumpy he became when, at a restaurant on a visit several years later, he was unable to distinguish between fried oysters, which he liked, and fried potatoes, which he hated. Tennessee, who by then was finding it easier to be patient with the old man than with Frank, separated the two for him.[33]

By Christmas Tennessee had finished a first draft of the play he was eventually to call *The Rose Tattoo*. It felt to him as if *The Glass Menagerie*, *Streetcar*, and *Summer and Smoke* had been produced by "a single burst of

*Enjoying his grandfather and sun in Key
West (1947)*

personal lyricism,"[34] but now, writing in a more comic vein, he depended
less on disguised autobiography. Once again he wanted to make the principal female character speak in an idiom that, like the etiolated rhetoric he had
given to Amanda, Alma, and Blanche, contrasted with standard American
speech, and he made Serafina speak the broken English of a half-educated
Italian immigrant. Another reason for writing the part like this was that it

might improve his chances of getting Anna Magnani to play it: her command of English was so poor that she would have refused to play an Italian woman with fluent English. He set the action in a village on the Mississippi Gulf populated by Sicilians.

Writing to Kazan, Tennessee called the play "a comic grotesque mass to the male force." But he emphasized his ignorance of his own intentions while writing. Something inside him seemed to be struggling blindly for release and becoming frantic. "Often when I've finished, I have no idea what I've done."[35] What inevitably happened when he let go of the controls or tried not to try was that he drifted back into preoccupations that had surfaced in his earlier plays. *The Rose Tattoo* is yet another celebration of robust sexuality: he was returning to the Lawrentian theme of sexual awakening he had already developed in *You Touched Me*, *The Glass Menagerie*, and *Summer and Smoke*. The variation he now elaborates is about the reawakening of a woman who has returned to somnolence after losing the husband she adored. Serafina is a peasant who used to glory in the virility of her husband, a truck driver who claimed to be a baron and smuggled dope under his freight of bananas. But as the marriage sinks into the past tense, she becomes yet another of the Tennessee Williams characters who needs to be pressured into giving up the habit of abstinence.

Williams's original intention was to use the same actor—preferably Marlon Brando—as the husband, Rosario, and as Alvaro, another truck driver, equally impressive in his physique but in nothing else. Descended from feeble-minded peasants, Alvaro gets into every kind of trouble, including a fistfight, which he loses, but he eventually succeeds in coaxing Serafina away from the depression and degeneration that have ensued on the death of her husband and the discovery that he was unfaithful. Tennessee eventually decided that Rosario should die offstage without ever appearing: through Serafina's frenzied efforts to cope with the pain of losing him "we sense and learn more about him than would have been possible through direct observation of the living man."[36] After Rosario's death she makes him into a legend, and lives with it chastely, simultaneously imposing chastity on her nubile daughter. Like other Tennessee Williams characters who ignore their own sexuality Serafina has to undergo both punishment and conversion.

As if to compensate for cutting down on autobiographical ingredients, Williams indulges in personal allusions. Frank had been working as a truck driver in New Jersey before he moved in with Tennessee; Alvaro's surname, Mangiacavallo (which was suggested by Frank), is close to Frank's nickname, the Little Horse; while the dedication, "To Frank in return for Sicily," suggests that Tennessee was celebrating Frank's Sicilian joie de vivre. Tennessee confesses to "the desire of an artist to work in new forms, however awkwardly at first, to break down barriers of what he has done before and what others have done better before and after and to crash, perhaps fatally, into some area that the bell-harness and rope would like to forbid him."[37] When he showed *The Rose Tattoo* to Irene Selznick, she told him it was material for an opera, not a play, but Cheryl Crawford agreed to produce it.[38] One of the founders of the Group Theatre, along with Lee Strasberg and Harold Clurman, she had been working as a producer since 1938. She had also helped to found the American Repertory Theatre and been its managing director, and had often been associated with Kazan. Without disparaging *The Rose Tattoo* as commonplace, Tennessee was not altogether happy with it, believing it to be "the sketch for the best play I have written, but still not it!—and a long way short of it."[39]

In May 1950 he went with Frank to New York, where the new production was announced at a press conference, which was followed by several receptions and parties. In June they went to Paris, where they talked to Anna Magnani. Though she liked the play, she was nervous about acting in English on stage. She offered to sign up for four months on Broadway, but had too many commitments, she said, in the Italian theater to do more, and four months was too little for Cheryl Crawford. But Magnani did play the role later, in the movie. Tennessee and Frank went on from Paris to Sicily, staying in Taormina, where Tennessee went on working at the script, eager to interpolate genuine Sicilian dialect into the dialogue.

At the end of June they went to Rome, settling into an apartment on the Via Firenze, but they left for Vienna in mid-July, after the publication of *The Roman Spring of Mrs. Stone* had provoked swarms of Roman reporters and photographers into pursuing Tennessee.

Without Magnani it was hard to cast Serafina; of the other contenders for the role, the best seemed to be Maureen Stapleton. She had made her Broadway debut at twenty-one in Synge's *Playboy of the Western World*, and she was only twenty-three. Serafina has a fifteen-year-old daughter, but after Maureen Stapleton read for the part, Tennessee insisted on having her read again and again. He also helped her to get ready for an audition in which she tried to look like Serafina, with disheveled hair and a shapeless gown. She finally got the part. The young Eli Wallach was cast as Alvaro. The director was to be Daniel Mann, who had just had a success with William Inge's *Come Back, Little Sheba*.

Even after *The Rose Tattoo* opened in Chicago on 29 December, Tennessee went on revising the script. Though he had not intended to go there, the structural problems were so serious that he changed his plans, and introduced variations into the script from night to night. According to Donald Windham, Tennessee stood with Daniel Mann at the back of the orchestra counting the laughs in each scene, and "when there were not enough to make him feel 'box-office secure,'" he added new lines or new business.[40] Unsettled by the commercial failure of *Summer and Smoke* after the success of *Menagerie* and *Streetcar*, he was resorting to the kind of facile comedy that had offended him when Eddie Dowling tried to introduce it into *Menagerie*. To Donald it seemed that Tennessee had lost his integrity. "During this decade he began not only no longer to prefer his work to himself, as Gide says an artist must, but no longer to prefer his work to his box-office statements."[41] These were gratifying. After the play opened in New York at the Martin Beck Theatre on 3 February 1951, reviewers were enthusiastic, and the play won a Tony Award.

The portrait of Serafina's young daughter, Rosa, who suffers acutely from her mother's exorbitant fear of predatory boyfriends, derives partly from memories of Rose's sufferings at the hands of the overprotective Edwina, while the rose symbolism which is so recurrent in the play is a rather heavy-handed expression of Tennessee's devotion to his maimed sister. He began to visit her regularly after having her transferred to another private clinic—Stony Lodge in Ossining, New York. Cheryl Crawford, who accompanied him on several of these trips, found it touching to see them together. Twice he brought Rose across the river from Ossining to meet Carson McCullers at her home in Nyack. If Reverend Dakin had become a father substitute, McCullers was a sister substitute. Tennessee even addressed her as "Sister Woman." She greeted Rose with open arms: "Kiss me, Miss Rose." "No, thank you," said Rose, "I have halitosis."[42]

During the first half of 1951 Tennessee brought almost the whole of his family to Key West. His grandfather, his mother, and his brother stayed with him briefly at the beginning of March, and at the end of the month, his sister, accompanied by a nurse, arrived for a stay of several weeks.

In May he succumbed again to wanderlust and, traveling with Frank, made New York his first stopping point. Maureen Stapleton had endeared herself to her audiences, justifying his faith in her, and he wanted to confer with her about the play that had once been called *Battle of Angels*. It had already been through several rewrites, and would go through many more before becoming *Orpheus Descending*.

Toward the end of May he and Frank left for London, and by mid-June they were in Rome again. In early July Tennessee traveled alone to St. Tropez, sending Frank to Venice, where they would meet up again. It was here that Tennessee drafted the story "Three Players of a Summer Game." He went on working on it for ten months and eventually used it as the basis for *Cat on a Hot Tin Roof*. The summer game is croquet, and the three players are Brick Pollitt, a former athlete, tall, handsome, red-haired, and now an alcoholic; the pretty widow of a doctor; and her plump twelve-year-old daughter, Mary Louise. Becoming estranged from his wife, Margaret, and taking the doctor's widow as his mistress, Brick thinks he can cure his liquor problem "step by little step, the way that people play the game of croquet. . . . You go from wicket to wicket, and it's a game of precision—it's a game that takes concentration and precision, and that's what makes it a wonderful game for a drinker." But he slips back into his old habit and into the clutches of his domineering wife.

Tennessee was himself drinking heavily throughout 1951. In July he smashed up a Jaguar while speeding drunkenly between Rome and St. Tropez. He was shaken, but not seriously hurt, though his typewriter, flying out of the car's back seat, somehow hit him on the head. The shock left him with insomnia he could not cure with either secobarbital or liquid "calmatives."[43]

Frank's company was beginning to grate on him. "I think the reason the Horse is so nervy and temperamental is that he has nothing, but NOTHING, to do!"[44] After going with him to the Swedish premiere of *The Rose Tattoo*, visiting London in August, and going to Copenhagen in September for the Danish premiere, Tennessee kept on the move through the autumn, visiting London, Barcelona, Paris, Amsterdam, Hamburg, and Rome, partly to evade any serious confrontation with his work or his personal problems. He enjoyed Hamburg, where he waltzed to Strauss in the gay bars, cruised along the waterfront, kissed in the ruins, and had sex in the bushes, hiding with a "Herculean" blond German while a policeman stopped to smoke a cigarette less than ten yards away.[45]

Tennessee revised *The Rose Tattoo* for the London production, which was due to open in November, but when he arrived in London the original version was already in rehearsal, and he decided to abandon the revisions. After sailing back to New York in November on the *Queen Elizabeth*, he and Frank went to Key West for Thanksgiving, but Tennessee was again suffering from chest pains and attacks of breathlessness.[46] They went to New Orleans for Christmas.

9

Terminal Stretch

In the French Quarter of New Orleans street signs still give the names that the streets had when the city was under Spanish control, and the road fringing what is now the French Market was called Camino Real. This can mean either "royal road" or "real road," and Tennessee had used the title "Three Blocks on the Camino Real" for a play he drafted in New Orleans during 1946. Discouraged by Audrey Wood's reaction, he had put it away, but a few years later, calling in at the Actors Studio, he found Elia Kazan working with three actors on a scene from the play—a bizarre comic ritual in which the virginity of the Gypsy's daughter is restored at full moon. Tennessee and Kazan discussed the possibility of staging an expanded version of the play, and they afterward corresponded about this idea.

Though Tennessee was still using drugs and drinking heavily, he settled down to work on the play in Key West, and had drafted a new version by the end of January 1952. Always willing to let instinct take over from intellect when he wrote, he found that a blurring of the mind was not altogether disadvantageous: he could import a dreamlike quality into the action, and he felt oddly free. "When [the play] began to get under way I felt a new sensation of release, as if I could 'ride out' like a tenor sax taking the breaks in a Dixieland combo or a piano in a bop session." At the same time, he was deliberate in structuring the play: "In this work I have given more conscious attention to form and construction than I have in any work before. Freedom is not achieved simply by working freely."[1]

He described it in a letter as an extended poem on the romantic attitude to life.[2] As he later said, he had never come closer to making a philosophical statement about life. He believed "it is necessary to cling to romanticism, not in the sense of a weak sentimentality, but in the sense of adhering as far as you can to a gallantry, like Don Quixote's; the play is a plea for a romantic attitude toward life, which can also be interpreted as a religious attitude."[3] Don Quixote appears as a character in the play, together with Casanova, Lord Byron, Dumas's Marguerite Gautier, Proust's Baron de Charlus, and other figures from history and fiction. Williams situates his phantasmagoria in an isolated South American city where money, hope, and vitality run out quickly, while death is personified by two street cleaners who gather up the dead and stuff them into a white barrel as if corpses are a form of garbage.

Absorbed in the work, he was unexcited by the news that a Greenwich Village repertory company, the Circle in the Square, was reviving *Summer and Smoke* with a young actress, Geraldine Page, who had just played Lorca's *Yerma* for the same director, José Quintero. Tennessee did not even attend the opening performance on 24 April. But the next day Brooks Atkinson announced in the *New York Times:* "Nothing has happened in the theatre in a long time as admirable as this production." He found the analysis of character subtler and more compassionate than in *Streetcar*, and the contrasts less brutal. When Tennessee heard from Audrey Wood that the play was the surprise hit of the season, he came to New York, and, meeting José Quintero in the foyer, gave him an affectionate hug, unaware that he was leaning the point of his umbrella on the director's foot, and his weight on the umbrella.[4] Tennessee approved of the production, admiring the "witchery of [the] staging and the witchery of Geraldine Page," and the production played to full houses for twelve months.[5]

In June Tennessee left New York again to spend the summer in Europe with Frank. From Paris they traveled to Rome, where Frank spent a lot of time with a male prostitute, but they stayed till the end of September.[6] After a week in London, they sailed back to New York, settled briefly in New Orleans, and went to Key West for Christmas, taking Reverend Dakin with them.

Previewing in New Haven and Philadelphia, *Camino Real* was due to open on Broadway in the middle of March 1953. "More than any other work that I have done," he wrote, "this play has seemed to me like the construction of another world, a separate existence." The characters, he said, are mostly "archetypes of certain basic attitudes and qualities" with the mutations that would have occurred had they lived to be his contemporaries.[7] Once, when Kazan asked what the play was about, he answered: "It's the story of everyone's life after he has gone through the razzle-dazzle of his youth. Time is short, baby, it betrays us as we betray each other. Work, that's all there is! . . . There is terror and mystery on one side, honor and tenderness on the other."[8]

Williams's emphasis on the shortness of life reflects his recurring fear that he might have little time ahead of him. In the play Kilroy, a young American who has been homeless and directionless for years, used to be a champion boxer but had to quit because of his heart, which is now "as big as the head of a baby." "With something like that you don't need the Gypsy to tell you, 'Time is short, Baby—get ready to hitch on wings!'" Though he does not resemble Tennessee physically, Kilroy is given several of his characteristics, including an ineptitude that verges on the clownish and a spark of anarchy in his spirit. "Nothing wild or honest is tolerated here," Casanova warns him.

Though Kazan, to whom *Camino Real* is dedicated, regarded it as Tennessee's best play, he conceded it was "as private as a nightmare."[9] But it also makes a public statement about what we live and die for. The city represents the end of the line for romantics who have kept on the move; Tennessee had hit upon a theatrical image that could express his restlessness. Though inevitably anchored to a static set, the action depicts ceaseless journeying: the plaza belongs—so the stage direction tells us—to "a tropical seaport that bears a confusing, but somehow harmonious resemblance to such widely scattered ports as Tangiers, Havana, Vera Cruz, Casablanca, Shanghai, New Orleans." On one side of the plaza is a luxurious hotel, the Siete Mares; on the other are the flophouse, ironically called the Ritz Men Only, and the pawn shop. These would represent all the desperation and discomfort Tennessee remembered from his days of penury. Here, on the Camino Real, it is easy to run out of money and be booted from the Siete Mares to the flophouse, but it is hard to escape from the town.

The predicaments of the characters often echo or parallel Tennessee's. Charlus prefers to stay at the flophouse because he has found it hard to smuggle rough trade into the hotel, while Don Quixote, finally deserted by

Sancho Panza—Tennessee associated the name with Pancho—reflects that "new companions are not as familiar as old ones but all the same—they're old ones with only slight differences of face or figure, which may or may not be improvements."

The more sympathetic characters try to help each other—sparks of friendship fly between Kilroy and Casanova—but the emphasis is on disloyalty. Though Marguerite Gautier has found comfort in the arms of Casanova, she loses interest in him as his virility declines, and would have left him behind had she succeeded in bribing her way on to an unscheduled plane. "We have to distrust one another," she tells him, "it's our only defense against betrayal." When she fails to escape, he magnanimously forgives her for trying to desert him, and they have a brief rapprochement. "So now and then, although we've wounded each other time and again—we stretch out hands to each other in the dark that we can't escape from—we huddle together for some dim-communal comfort—and that's what passes for love on this terminal stretch of the road that used to be royal." But Marguerite betrays him again, behaving like Mrs. Stone and using some of her jewelry to buy the favors of a young man who promptly robs her. And when Kilroy seems to have won the love of Esmeralda, the Gipsy's daughter, it turns out that she and her mother are interested only in what they can get out of him.

Tennessee wanted Brando to play Kilroy, but he was in no state to do serious work: "He is living in an almost empty apartment with a pet raccoon who scrambles into your lap and tries to unbutton your fly as soon as you enter or assume a sitting position."[10] Eli Wallach was eventually given the part, and Kazan, who cast the play entirely from members of the Actors Studio, afterward admitted that the other actors were "not up to the needs of their parts. They were trained in a more realistic technique. So was I."[11]

In New York, as in New Haven and Philadelphia, reviewers were mostly hostile. Even the well-disposed Walter Kerr, writing in the *New York Times*, said it was "the worst play yet written by the best playwright of his generation."[12] Audiences were intolerant, with a noisy contingent leaving the auditorium while the play was under way, but, fortified by Nembutal and Seconal, Tennessee took his failure stoically. One night in Philadelphia, when José Quintero was standing next to him at the back of the orchestra as people were leaving early, he remarked: "Well, I don't think they are really taking the play to their hearts, would you say?"[13]

At the airport with Donald Windham,
Houston (1953)

He talked so often about wishing he could direct his own plays that when Donald Windham was offered a slot for his play *The Starless Air* at the theater Diane Arbus ran in Houston, he approached Tennessee about making his debut as a director. After a period of hedging, Tennessee accepted the challenge, and a mid-April opening was arranged. When Donald was invited to stay with him in Key West before rehearsals started, he got the impression that Tennessee still did not feel committed to the project, though Frank was apparently doing all he could to make him behave less irresponsibly.[14]

When he arrived in Houston, no hotel accommodation was available for him, and for his first night there he shared Donald's room, which had two couches in it. After being kept awake for much of the night by Tennessee's snoring, Donald saw him "open his eyes at six. Feeling around on his bedside table, he swallowed a Seconal with a whiskey chaser. Then he got up and closed the venetian blind. Back in bed he turned on his lamp, poured himself a half tumbler of whiskey, and read." Soon he went back to sleep, and after waking up at nine-thirty, said he had not slept at all.[15]

After the first reading, he announced that he had conceived "a superb idea" for the staging and needed time to work it out before Donald saw the result. Suspicious, Donald crept into the rehearsal a few days later and saw what was happening. Tennessee was improvising as he went along, adding not only business but dialogue. When Donald objected, he was accused of ingratitude and barred from rehearsals.[16]

Tennessee left before the play opened. After stopping off to visit his grandfather, who was back in Memphis planning to spend the year in a hotel, Tennessee returned to New York before leaving to spend the summer in Europe with Frank. They disembarked at Le Havre, reached Rome on 22 June, and left almost immediately for Spain, where food poisoning kept Tennessee in bed for a week. In early October, writing from Grenada to Oliver Evans, a poetry-writing teacher he had met in New Orleans, Tennessee called himself "the world's most fatiguable sightseer" and doubted whether he could muster enough energy to visit the Alhambra. But, glad to be in Europe, he felt that nothing would make him return to the United States except his grandfather.[17] After going back to Rome, he and Frank kept on the move, sometimes accompanied by Paul Bowles: from Spain they went on to Vienna, leaving to stay in Venice before returning to Rome and then going to southern Italy.

The story "Man Bring This up Road," which Tennessee wrote in Italy, reflects his fears of declining into a has-been. The central character is an American whose health is deteriorating, though he goes on pretending to be four years younger than he is. He has given up writing poetry and started making mobiles. No longer able to find patronage, he is starving when he arrives uninvited at the hillside villa of a rich septuagenarian woman who lives north of Amalfi. He begs for a job. She has been warned about him by a friend, but she finds him attractive. Unceremoniously, she takes all her clothes off, and when he fails to respond, she sends him away without feeding him. Tennessee found it easy to identify with both the desperately unsuccessful artist and the sadistic woman who would give patronage only in return for sexual favors.

Though he tried to work, Tennessee could not concentrate. After going to Tangier with Frank and Paul Bowles, he sent Audrey Wood another bulletin about his physical condition: he was suffering from hemorrhoids. He and Frank sailed back to New York at the end of October, moved into an apartment on East 58th Street, and spent $1,600 on furnishing it,[18] but they soon left for New Orleans because Oliver Evans had recommended a proctologist who could operate on Tennessee in a local clinic. After picking up Reverend Dakin, they took him with them, and stayed on after the operation till the middle of January 1954, when they moved to Key West. In letters to Brooks Atkinson and Donald Windham, Tennessee described his malaise: uncomfortable after the operation, he was more deeply upset by a feeling of uselessness—he was a wreck who could do nothing but watch movies, drink, relax on beaches. Though Frank was supportive, Tennessee had plenty of casual sex.

Tennessee had been planning to return to Key West with his grandfather again in the autumn. Staying in St. Louis, the ninety-seven-year-old man did not enjoy his summer. His daughter, he complained, gave him "four lectures a day, always winding up with a eulogy for herself." Desperate to escape, he used to sit on the porch with his suitcase, shouting at the passing cars: "ONE HUNDRED DOLLARS to anybody who will take me to the station!" But toward the end of October, a couple of days before Tennessee arrived in St. Louis, Reverend Dakin had a stroke, which partially paralyzed his left side, stopping him from going to Key West. The old man died on 14 February 1955. Busy with the rehearsals of *Cat on a Hot Tin Roof*, Tennessee did not want to break off for the funeral in Missouri, and told Maria Britneva that his grandfather would understand if he did not go. But when she said *she* would not understand, he went.[19]

Tennessee had been able to begin writing again by the spring of 1954. Working from the story "Three Players of a Summer Game," which had been started in the summer of 1951 and finished in April 1952, he developed *Cat on a Hot Tin Roof*. The differences between the story and the play show

how drastically Tennessee was capable of reworking old material. The doctor's widow and her daughter, who are both central to the story, are jettisoned, while in the story Maggie, the wife, is unsympathetic and marginal until she becomes dominant at the end, when her victory is Brick's defeat. Neither Brick's parents nor his father's cotton plantation are mentioned in the story, but both are crucial to the play. The story is mainly about the losing battle he fights against alcohol. When the play begins, that battle is already lost, but the defeat may not be irreversible, and the play ends in a victory, won mainly by Maggie, over Brick's scheming brother and sister-in-law.

The play's title derives from a saying of Cornelius's: "You're making me as nervous as a cat on a hot tin roof." Sexually frustrated and therefore nervous, Maggie is the cat. The only man she wants is the husband who refuses to sleep with her, and she knows instinctively that his alcoholism is at the root of the revulsion he now feels for her. Their relationship is built on an experience Tennessee had often had—being wanted by women he quite liked, without feeling any desire for them. The play begins with a remarkably long monologue from Maggie—there are sporadic interpolations from Brick, but all the impetus comes from her. Much of the plot's prehistory is established explicitly in this monologue. Scarcely any other modern playwright could have got away with so much preliminary speechifying, but Tennessee—partly by dint of writing so much—had developed an extraordinary technical expertise.

One feature the play has in common with *Streetcar* is that both contain long narrative speeches about past action involving love between two men, and in both plays Tennessee seems to be no less interested in this past action than in any of the onstage action. Blanche's husband killed himself after she told him that his bisexuality disgusted her; Brick's relationship with his best friend, Skipper, ended in Skipper's death, and it was Maggie who leveled against him the accusation that was to have fatal consequences. By charging him with homosexuality she goaded him into an attempt at making love to her, and, when this failed, into suicide. But the episode from the past has more relevance to the present that it does in *Streetcar*. Brick tells Maggie: "One man has one great good true thing in his life. One great good thing which is true!—I had friendship with Skipper. . . . Not love with you, Maggie, but friendship with Skipper." Commenting on the relationship between the two men, Tennessee afterwards asked the question: "Was

Brick homosexual? He probably—no, I would even say quite certainly—went no further in physical expression than clasping Skipper's hand across the space between their twin-beds in hotel-rooms and yet—his sexual nature was not innately 'normal.'"[20]

Rivalry between Blanche and Stella is paralleled in the new play by rivalry between two brothers. Big Daddy is dying of cancer, and, eager to inherit the cotton plantation, his other son, Gooper, tries to curry favor. In *Streetcar* the estate had already been sold; here it is the prize for which the brothers and their wives are contending. Brick and Maggie have no children; Gooper and Mae have five. In Brick and Maggie the values of the old South are still alive, while Gooper and Mae represent the new South. As Tennessee said, they are "the country club type."[21] This gives suprapersonal resonance to the conflict that parallels conflicts in Faulkner's work between the Compsons and the Snopeses—representatives of the old chivalry and the new opportunism.

With James Wong Howe and Burt Lancaster at filming of The Rose Tattoo

TW in Key West during the filming of
The Rose Tattoo

Tennessee went back to New York in early May 1954, but by the beginning of June he was in Rome, though not enjoying himself. Cheryl
Crawford was told that this was the worst nervous crisis of his life; teetering
on the brink of collapse, he kept himself going with alcohol, sedatives, and
stimulants. He was intending, he said, to consult a psychiatrist when he got
back to New York.

Joining him and Frank in Rome, Maria Britneva found Tennessee was
entertaining a morbid suspicion that his water was being poisoned. The

*Roses, roses all the way: Burt Lancaster and
Anna Magnani in the film of* The Rose
Tattoo

three of them traveled at the end of July to Barcelona, where he talked to
her about his anxiety. He calculated that he was using three-quarters of his
energy and creativity on fighting his fears of failure with his writing. But he
was convinced that he had "intuition and powers of sensitivity and feeling
far above his intellectual powers, and from these alone he has much to say in
the world."[22]

His fear of failure blurred into fear of death, and to alleviate his anxiety he
was drinking too much and taking too many sedatives. He also had occasional attacks of claustrophobia. One evening when he, Maria, and Frank
were in a movie theater, Tennessee suddenly had to leave and wait for the
others in a bar across the road. Afterward he described the feeling: with his
heart pounding, he felt as if he were suffocating and became so panicky that
he needed to be alone and to drink.[23]

The three of them went on to Sitges, Montserrat, and Madrid before returning to Rome, where they stayed till 22 September. When they left for
the States, they brought Anna Magnani with them. The film of *The Rose*

Tattoo was partly shot in Key West, which was used to stand in for the village on the Mississippi Gulf.

But it was harder than Tennessee had expected to get *Cat on a Hot Tin Roof* into production. Cheryl Crawford did not want to become involved, and at the beginning of 1955 Audrey Wood was negotiating with the Play-wrights Company, a management run by writers, including Elmer Rice, Maxwell Anderson, Robert Sherwood, and Robert Anderson, whose *Tea and Sympathy* had been a great success under Kazan's direction. Kazan agreed to stage *Cat on a Hot Tin Roof*, but he had reservations about the script, and when Tennessee came to New York in January, they discussed textual changes.

A character as important as Big Daddy, said Kazan, should not disappear at the end of the second act and make his presence felt in the third only through offstage groans. Kazan also felt that the long dialogue between father and son, which occupies virtually the entire second act, ought to exert a visible influence on Brick's behavior, and he wanted Maggie to be more sympathetic. Of these three suggestions, the only one Tennessee accepted gladly was the third. He had come to like Maggie better as he worked on the play, and Kazan was probably right to assume that Tennessee had himself been more important than anyone else as a model for her.

But, so far as Tennessee was concerned, the action was rooted tragically in Brick's moral paralysis, and Big Daddy had no dramatic function in the third act. Nervous, though, about losing Kazan, Tennessee gave in on all three points, producing a new third act in which a thunderstorm builds up to the reappearance of the dying man.[14] Unable to think of anything better for him to say, Tennessee makes him tell a joke about parents who take their young son to the zoo and have to answer his question when he sees an old bull elephant having an erection.

More than ever before, Tennessee was building his play out of long sequences. Most of the second act is taken up by a brilliantly structured dialogue between father and son. Big Daddy has been misled into thinking he is not dying of cancer; the climax will come when Brick tells him the truth, but before that the father wrestles manfully with the problem of his son's alcoholism, while Brick tries a variety of evasive tactics. They have never before had a real conversation, just as Tennessee felt he never had a real conversation with Cornelius until 1943, when the father talked about his alcoholism and his certainty—which Tennessee shared—that he could

A fat guy with a big cigar: Kazan talks to
Burl Ives – Big Daddy in the Broadway
production of Cat on a Hot Tin Roof

not survive much longer. Unlike Cornelius, Big Daddy is not an alcoholic, but the emotional loading of the scene depends on its autobiographical background. Had Cornelius not lurched into sudden intimacy by talking to the son he had never loved about alcoholism and dying, Tennessee would have been unable to write the second act of *Cat*. Like Cornelius, Big Daddy has two sons; unlike Tennessee, Brick has always been the favorite, and, like Cornelius, Big Daddy makes a supreme effort to break the habit of emotional evasion.

Brick's self-containment — his absorption in the past and his reluctance to communicate with anyone in the family — are basic to the first two acts, which each consist of little more than a long conversation. In both the Brick-Maggie act and the Brick-Big Daddy act there are references back to the all-important relationship with Skipper; the name may have been intended as a memorial to Kip, while the story is rooted in Tennessee's

*"I've got the guts to die, boy. Have you got
the guts to live?": Burl Ives and Paul
Newman in* Cat on a Hot Tin Roof

knowledge that Cornelius had always felt ashamed of having an effeminate
son.

Big Daddy had been suspicious of whether Brick's friendship with Skipper had been "exactly normal," and whether Skipper had wanted to live,
knowing it would have been impossible to keep up appearances of decency.
It is by revealing these suspicions that Big Daddy breaks through his son's
facade of detachment. A stage direction tells us that Brick is sweating and
breathing more rapidly. It goes on to suggest that he may have been drinking out of disgust at the mendacity that makes it necessary to keep up
appearances in this way. In a statement that seems out of place in a stage
direction, Tennessee goes on to explain: "The bird that I hope to catch in
the net of this play is not the solution of one man's psychological problem.
I'm trying to catch the true quality of experience in a group of people, that
cloudy, flickering, evanescent—fiercely charged!—interplay of live human

beings in the thundercloud of a common crisis." A play, he insists, should be a "snare for the truth of human experience."[25]

If he had misgivings about surrendering to most of Kazan's demands, they were alleviated by the play's success after it opened on 24 March 1955 at the Morosco Theatre. In the *New York Times* Brooks Atkinson declared: "It is the quintessence of life. It is the basic truth, . . . a delicately wrought exercise in human communications. . . . Mr. Williams' finest drama, it faces and speaks the truth." And in the *New York Herald-Tribune* Walter Kerr affirmed: "Mr. Williams is the man of our time who comes closest to hurling the actual blood and bone of life onto the stage; he is also the man whose prose comes closest to being an incisive natural poetry."

The play won the Pulitzer Prize, but in many ways *Cat on a Hot Tin Roof* is disappointing, both in its Broadway version and in the original version, which was used when the play was staged in London. Unquestionably Williams had developed enormous skill in manipulating the emotions of an audience. Our sympathy is irresistibly enlisted for both Brick and Maggie, partly through making us hate the scheming brother and sister-in-law, Gooper and Mae, who, intent on inheriting the plantation, try ruthlessly to endear themselves to Big Daddy and Big Mama, while discrediting Brick and Maggie. By listening through the wall, Gooper and Mae learn that Brick is stolidly rebuffing Maggie's efforts to make love, and it is partly because their hateful rivals are worsted that the audience feels so happy at the end of the play when Maggie coerces Brick into bed by threatening to cut off his supply of liquor. On one level, this provides a satisfying climax, as box-office takings attested. But it is not a satisfactory conclusion to the play's moral and emotional problems.

Williams had shown in *Camino Real* that without being either a great thinker or a great theatrical innovator, he had visions he could project excitingly in theatrical terms. Here he falls back on melodramatic storytelling of a kind well calculated to please the audience. He was emotionally involved, on a deep level, with the story of Brick and Skipper, but though he was right to leave some of the ambiguities unresolved, it is hard to believe he was incapable of digging further into the mysteries. The crucial question is skirted in the dialogue and raised only in a stage direction. Do Brick's alcoholism and his indifference to Maggie derive from disgust at the endemic mendacity that makes it impossible to come out in the open about homosexual love? This was a question of deep concern to the playwright, but he

*TW with Sam Goldwyn, Jr., and Carson
McCullers in Key West*

fails to articulate it effectively, and neither of his third acts deals adequately
with the issue raised in the second.

In April he went to Key West, taking Carson McCullers with him, and
when she left after three weeks, he reproached himself for immersing himself too deeply in his own writing to give her as much love and attention as
she needed. "I care only, very much, about the studio mornings at the
Olivetti. Perhaps in this way I can give more love to more people, at least I
sometimes hope so."[26]

In mid-June he left to spend the summer in Europe without Frank. Finding he was unable to write—"Strong coffee no longer sufficed to get the
creative juices to flow"—he moved from place to place even more restlessly
than usual, drank more, and took more Seconal, washing it down with
double martinis or with Scotch from the flask he carried around with him.[27]
The summer of 1955 was a turning point for Tennessee: from then on, as he
says, he wrote "usually under artificial stimulants, aside from the true stim-
ulant of my deep-rooted need to continue to write."[28]

TW with Gore Vidal in Key West (1956)

After seeing a bullfight in Barcelona he was so excited that he had to calm himself with a "pinkie," which he washed down with a gulp of Scotch. In a letter he wrote afterward he said he was "now half in and half out of the conscious world. It is pretty good here. All the little black dwarfettes are still scuttling about, and a few hunch-backs, and the gigolo with the great melting eyes and tiny mustache is paying flattering court, all but drinking champagne from my slipper."[29]

He stayed in Rome, and went to Stockholm for the Swedish premiere of *Cat on a Hot Tin Roof*, returning to New York in the autumn. He had agreed, though without much enthusiasm, to provide a screenplay for a movie that was first announced as "The Whip Hand" and then as "Mississippi Woman." It would end up with the title *Baby Doll*. In 1936 Tennessee had written the story[27] "Wagons Full of Cotton" and, about seven years later, had developed it into a one-act play with the same title. At the Actors Studio Kazan had worked on the play with Carroll Baker and Karl Malden, who both seemed ideal for the movie. The screenplay that was evolved for the

156

film was as remote from the original story as *Cat on a Hot Tin Roof* was from "Three Players of a Summer Game."

What survives is the main outline of the Mississippi background, with cotton gins pumping, pneumatic pipes sucking, and strands of cotton floating through the summer air. The biggest plantation belongs to a syndicate that usually gins its own cotton, but its large, well-equipped plant has been destroyed by fire, and the ginning is passed on to a man called Jake Meighan, whose equipment is more antiquated. His wife in the story is a big woman with fat arms, bulging calves, and thick ankles. The heat of the day saps her energy, making her feel too weak to fend off the advances of the plantation manager, a small man who keeps hurting her, flicking his riding crop at her, ostensibly to get rid of the flies, but there is a hint of sadism and she thinks he may hurt her in bed, though even fear fails to energize her into rebuffing him.

Felice Orlandi, Maureen Stapleton, and Myron McCormick in 27 Wagons Full of Cotton, *Playhouse Theater, New York (1955)*

In the screenplay the wife is not yet twenty. A voluptuous and simple-minded virgin, she still sucks her thumb as she sleeps in a crib in the old nursery. Her dying father gave her to the unattractive Jake Meighan on the understanding that the marriage would not be consummated until she was ready, but a deadline has since been set—her twentieth birthday. The action is of course set just before the birthday. By then she has discovered that Jake, desperate because he had lost so much business to the syndicate, had set fire to its plant. This conducts sympathy away from him while his victim, the manager of the syndicate, Silva Vaccaro—the surname is borrowed from Marion—emerges as a rival candidate for the favors of the virgin wife. In the story the syndicate manager, who remains anonymous, is perfunctorily characterized as a little man who likes big women, but in the screenplay he is a young Italian, handsome and cocky. Jake's redneck scorn for foreigners, and his recourse to words like *yellow-bellied* and *dago*, help divert the audience's sympathy from him to the Italian. Silva is resourceful enough to maneuver Baby Doll into betraying the bullying husband who orders her to say he was at home when the fire was started. Admitting he was not, she provides her evidence in writing.

Finding Tennessee unenthusiastic about the project, Kazan wrote a first draft of the script, and it was his idea to interpolate material from one of Tennessee's one-act plays, *The Unsatisfactory Supper*. In it an aunt cooks inadequate meals for a married couple, and the subplot about the aunt in *Baby Doll* is taken from the play. Without wanting to invest a lot of time or energy in the screenplay, Tennessee tried to resist what Kazan was doing. In a letter dated 23 July Tennessee said they seemed to have two different pictures in mind. What he wanted was "a grotesque folk comedy," while Kazan appeared to have set his sights on "a powerful melodrama for which there is absolutely no premise, or preparation, in mood, style, not even story-content in the work which has so far been done." Tennessee was unwilling to do any more work on the project unless he had "carte blanche as far as working out the ending and so forth."

In the end he okayed Kazan's script and promised to provide additional material, saying he would go to Benoit, Mississippi, where the film was to be shot, on condition that a swimming pool was found for him. Kazan's production manager persuaded the civic authorities to renovate a disused swimming pool, and, when he arrived, Tennessee seemed satisfied, but he soon left, saying he disliked the way people looked at him on the streets.

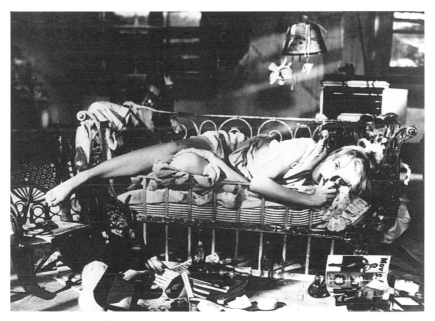

Baby Doll: *Carroll Baker in the movie*

Though he had been only seventeen and not yet a practicing homosexual when he left Mississippi, he told Kazan: "Those people chased me out of here. I left the South because of their attitude toward me. They don't approve of homosexuals, and I don't want to be insulted."[30] A few days after leaving Benoit, he sent Kazan what he most needed—an ending.

The year 1956 began with a revival of *Streetcar* at the Coconut Grove Playhouse in Miami, with the fifty-two-year-old Tallulah Bankhead playing opposite a weak Stanley as Blanche, who is meant to be about thirty. Originally, after giving up the idea that Katharine Cornell should play the part, Tennessee had wanted Tallulah, who was then forty-one, but Irene Selznick had argued that if she played it, "the moth-like side of Blanche would be demolished at once by the tiger-like side of Blanche." For Tennessee, "Blanche is a delicate tigress with her back to the wall," but he gave in.[31]

Nine years after the Broadway production he was still uncertain—or open-minded—about the way Blanche should combine toughness with fragility. In a letter written before the Miami opening, he was expecting Tallulah to give "a very exciting performance, though maybe it will not be clear that Stanley is the one that represents the brutality of the world. On the other hand, maybe her ferocity is a mask behind which something like Blanche exists and can be released in performance. One's enemy is always part of oneself."[32]

In rehearsal it was difficult for him to have dealings with Tallulah. He had expected her to think highly of Frank; instead she said: "It's very nice of you to love such a hideous person." And when he "remonstrated mildly" over a piece of business in rehearsal, she turned on him furiously, shouting: "Shut up, idiot!"[33] He retreated to Key West and returned for the opening. Disappointed with her performance, he complained that she was playing the part for vaudeville and ruining the play. Overheard by a reporter, the comment found its way into a national magazine, and he had to make public amends. The production moved on in mid-February to City Center in New York, but failed to make much impact.

10

Relentless Caper

From *The Glass Menagerie* onward, self-criticism and self-hatred had bulked large in motivating Tennessee's writing, and *Sweet Bird of Youth*, his 1956 play, contains two hostile self-portraits—one male, one female. Like Mrs. Stone, the Princess Kosmonopolis has lost her beauty and uses her money to buy sexual pleasure with younger partners. Chance Wayne, though deteriorating physically, still looks good enough to earn as a gigolo. Both he and the Princess take drugs, using alcohol as a chaser for the pills.

Tennessee's work on the play was prompted by an invitation from George Keathley, director of Studio M in Coral Gables, Miami. Asked for a new play that could be staged in April, Tennessee sent a short one-acter, *The Enemy, Time*, that he had written in 1952, basing it on the idea he had outlined at length in one of his first letters to Audrey Wood—the idea about the good-looking boy who had once seemed destined for a brilliant career but has sunk into mediocrity and alcoholism. The unproduced one-acter served as a first draft for *Sweet Bird of Youth*, which Keathley staged at Studio M on 16 April 1956.

Tennessee had long been preoccupied with the passage of time and the evanescence of youthful good looks, but of the several awkward passages in the play when characters step forward to address the audience directly, the worst occurs when Chance, about to be castrated, asks the audience for "the recognition of me in you, and the enemy, time, in us all."

161

*Geraldine Page and Paul Newman in the
movie of* Sweet Bird of Youth

The play's epigraph comes from "Legend" by Hart Crane: "Relentless caper for all those who step / The legend of their youth into the noon." When we first see Chance, who has a "ravaged young face," he is combing his "slightly thinning blond hair." Now in his late twenties, he looks older. As he remarks, "Time does it. Hardens people. Time and the world that you've lived in." But this points to one of the basic confusions in the play: the world he has inhabited is the decaying South, and it is not clear whether we are meant to blame his deterioration on that of Southern society. Tennessee comes back to this theme again and again, loading his stories and plays with generalized implications about the South, but the social and political criticism remains vague. Corruption is present mainly for the sake of atmosphere. He has little interest in pinpointing specific abuses, and unlike Amanda Wingfield and Blanche DuBois, who embody some of the old Southern values and manners, but also derive from precise observation of behavior and careful reproduction of specific rhythms and cadences, the characters in *Sweet Bird of Youth* are all close to the stereotype.

When the play opened at Studio M, Williams described it for the *New York Times* as "an examination of what is really corrupt in life."[1] The central theme is loss of innocence, but the play contains no clear analysis of how it gets lost. Certainly not, in Tennessee's opinion, through original sin. Heavenly was a beautiful girl of fifteen when Chance made love to her and photographed her in the nude, but no loss of innocence was involved in this. She has since had to undergo a hysterectomy because he infected her with a venereal disease, but we are intended not only to sympathize with her but also to agree with her when—speaking in strident rhetoric which is as simplistic as the characters' names—she blames her father, Boss Finley, a political demagogue, for Chance's physical and moral deterioration: "There was a time when you could have saved me, by letting me marry a boy that was still young and clean, but instead you drove him away. . . . So Chance went away. Tried to compete, make himself big as these big-shots you wanted to use me for a bond with. He went. He tried. The right doors wouldn't open and so he went in the wrong ones, and—Papa, you married for love, why wouldn't you let me do it, while I was alive, inside, and the boy still clean, still decent?"

Though characterized no more subtly than the villain in an average melodrama, Boss Finley is repulsive enough to make the audience want to put all the blame on him, though Chance, as an adult, was obviously responsible for his own decisions. Blessed with extraordinary physical beauty, he had found, as a young actor, that he was lacking in confidence or talent or both. He became a beach boy, a gigolo, and a prostitute. In the first act we see him with a movie actress, who had been caught unaware by the aging process. "I just wasn't young any more." Her name is Alexandra Del Lago, but she is hiding under the name Princess Kosmonopolis. She is not unlike Tallulah Bankhead in reality, but Tennessee's principal model was almost invariably himself, and he used the Princess as a mouthpiece for his chronic guilt feelings. "Monsters don't die early," she grumbles, "they hang on long. Awfully long. Their vanity's infinite, almost as infinite as their disgust with themselves."

Adding to the play in February and March 1956, Tennessee incorporated material he picked up from the press about Tallulah, who in 1951 had accused her former secretary of stealing money by forging checks. Admitting to faking the signature on checks, the woman said she had been ordered to pay for drugs, drink, and male prostitutes at times when the actress was too drunk to sign her name.[2] Tallulah claimed she had never had to pay for sex, but Tennessee, who often paid for it, conceded that in writing about the character he was also confessing his own sins. "I was Alexandra del Lago from start to finish. I've probably made every speech she made. And I meant them twice as much."[3]

Some of the play's weaknesses stem from dependence on earlier literary maps of the same territory. Faulkner had written memorably about degeneracy, materialism, and moral anarchy in the South; Fitzgerald had recognized that time passes quickly for those who chase the wrong dreams. The Princess tells Chance: "You've gone past something you couldn't afford to go past; your time, your youth, you've passed it, it's all you had and you've had it." Sometimes Tennessee uses Chance as a mouthpiece for somber reflections on the passage of time, and he often uses both characters as mouthpieces. At one point the Princess is made to say: "I've been accused of having a death wish, but I think it's life I wish for, terribly, shamelessly, on any terms whatsoever."

Though Tennessee was less skillful than usual in this play at disguising ideas and experiences he passed on to characters, the 1956 production was well received, and Kazan, who was to direct it on Broadway, came to see it in Miami.[4] Originally planned for 1957, but it did not open until 1959, at the Martin Beck Theatre, and reviewing it there, Kenneth Tynan wrote: "I suspect *Sweet Bird of Youth* will be of more interest to Mr Williams's biographers than to lovers of the theatre." From what we see of Chance, it is hard to believe in him as a producer or director, but at seventeen he won a state drama contest, and now—like the much older author—he is a drug addict.

Between his early thirties and his early forties, Tennessee had enjoyed more success than any other playwright in the history of the American theater, but he saw himself as a failure. In his own judgment he had prostituted himself artistically, compromising his integrity by changing his texts to ingratiate himself with Kazan or increase the chances of Broadway success. He did this again with *Sweet Bird of Youth*, surrendering to Kazan, who spotted the structural flaws and thought he could distract the audience from them with spectacular devices. He filled the back wall of the set with a huge television screen on which the Boss's political speech was projected.

One of the main structural weaknesses is the discontinuity between the first act and the second. In *Cat on a Hot Tin Roof* Big Daddy virtually disappears for the whole of the third act; in *Sweet Bird of Youth* the Princess disappears for most of the second. Unrealistically believing she will help him and Heavenly to a Hollywood career by sponsoring a talent competition that will be rigged for them to win, Chance goes off in pursuit of Heavenly. Tension is building around the question of whether the remnants of her love for him can survive her fear of her father's threats and her resentment about the infection that led to the hysterectomy, but though the action appears to be moving toward a climactic confrontation between Chance and Heavenly, that scene never comes, and they meet only once, staring at each other from opposite sides of the stage. The tension is shifted to the question of whether Chance will stay in the city, St. Cloud, in defiance of everything Boss Finley's henchmen are doing to scare him away. If there is some masochism in his defiance, it remains unanalyzed, except for a few hints that he wants to punish himself for being a failure. Courageously he stays on to face the gang of young men who will castrate him.

Williams and Kazan had disagreed about the sensational ending: the curtain comes down just before Chance is castrated. "From the first," Williams wrote to Kazan from Miami, "Chance did make a choice. You saw the production down here in which he decides to stay, not escape, and suffer the fate of his sweetheart. That has never been anything in my mind but the truth of the play: I departed from it, a little, experimentally, because I was afraid and thought that you would be afraid of a play about an actual physical castration, so at one point, last spring, I tried to turn it into a psychological castration. You convinced me that my first instinct had been right."[5]

The play's weaknesses are not all structural. The best of Williams's prose dialogue is more poetic than any of his verse, but in this play he depends too much on putting portentous phrases in the mouths of characters who should talk more prosaically. The Princess simply speaks for the author when she claims: "Out of the passion and torment of my existence I have created a thing that I can unveil, a sculpture, almost heroic, that I can unveil, which is true." She says Chance is "lost in the beanstalk country, the ogre's country at the top of the beanstalk, the country of the flesh-hungry, bloodthirsty ogre." Some of Williams's finest effects depend on thudding repetitions of the same word within a single sentence, but so do some of his worst.

In the spring of 1956, when he was working on the play for Keathley, his relationship with Frank was disintegrating. Once, according to Keathley,

"Tennessee turned to Frank after reading a new scene aloud and asked, 'Do you like it, Frankie?'—'No, I don't!'—'Why not?'—'I don't know, I just don't!'—'But why *not*? What's wrong with it?'—'Don't ask me, I'm not your goddamned yes-man!' And with that Frank ran into another room, packed his bags and took off for a few days."[6] One of the problems was that their partnership had been grounded on Frank's uncomplaining performance of domestic chores. As Tennessee became richer, it was easier for him to employ servants to do what Frank had done for nothing. By April, Frank, never previously a heavy drinker, was often drunk.

That Tennessee, too, had started drinking more was partly due to the warfare between them, but it also sharpened the mutual hostility. Tennessee asked Cheryl Crawford's advice on whether he should have medical and psychological treatment in New York, but instead of staying there after he left Key West, he went back to spend the summer in Rome. By the beginning of August he thought he was on the verge of a breakdown: at night he could sleep for only about an hour.[7] His reliance on drugs and alcohol increased, while his persecution complex grew worse. He was convinced that no one liked him, that his friends were all waiting impatiently for him to die.

In Venice he had met a Russian nerve specialist, Dr. Gourewitsch, who had treated Eleanor Roosevelt and Osbert Sitwell. In an unmailed letter written when he was in Miami on 7 September, Tennessee said he felt close to a crack-up, and unless his situation improved, he might fly to Zurich and ask the doctor to recommend a psychoanalyst.[8]

When Tennessee returned to New York in early September, the situation would have been comforting had he still been taking comfort from the popularity of his work. *Cat on a Hot Tin Roof* was still playing and would run for a total of 694 performances, closing at the Morosco in mid-November, just before a successful revival of *The Glass Menagerie* opened at City Center, starring Helen Hayes. Some of the reviewers, including Brooks Atkinson and John Chapman, praised this at the expense of all his subsequent plays. The year ended with yet another success when the film of *Baby Doll* opened on 18 December. In St. Patrick's Cathedral Francis Cardinal Spellman denounced the movie from the pulpit. "I exhort Catholic people from patronizing this film under pain of sin."[9] This was more helpful to the sale of tickets than any of the favorable reviews, but Tennessee was still too distraught to derive much pleasure from his success.

During the last week of September he had heard that Edwina was suffering from paranoia and had been interned in a St. Louis psychiatric ward. She had eaten nothing for days, and she was hallucinating. She thought her maid was trying to poison her, and her chauffeur to murder her. Advised that he was in no state to sustain the shock he would undergo when he saw her, Tennessee left for the Virgin Islands to recuperate before trying to help her.

He took her to Key West at the beginning of 1957, but her presence caused extra strain, exacerbating the tension with Frank. By 5 January Tennessee had made up his mind—or thought he had—to start analysis as soon as he returned to New York at the end of the month, "and then continue it in Zurich, as I am tired of living with myself as I am."[10] He believed he had been unable "to write a decent line" for the last nine months, but he had to work on *Orpheus Descending*, his rewrite of *Battle of Angels*, which was due to open at the Martin Beck Theatre in March.[11]

Most of his full-length plays had evolved into their final form either from a short story or from a one-act play or through a complex process involving both, but in no case was the evolution more complicated or protracted than with *Orpheus Descending*. In his own estimate 75 percent of the material in it was newly written, but the play's substance derived from the 1940 play *Battle of Angels*. "Nothing is more precious to anybody than the emotional record of his youth, and you will find the trail of my sleeve-worn heart in this completed play that I now call *Orpheus Descending*. On its surface it was and still is the tale of a wild-spirited boy who wanders into a conventional community of the South and creates the commotion of a fox in a chicken coop."[12] With his persistent overuse of drink and drugs, Tennessee was now living in a steadily self-destructive way, but he never created quite that furor of destructive commotion. But the play is autobiographical in a different way. He was nothing if not a professional refugee, moving endlessly from place to place, or, to use his own term, he belonged to the fugitive kind, and the play represents his most determined effort to define that kind and to justify it by suggesting that no man can keep his integrity intact if he puts down roots.

Two fugitives are introduced in the first act: Val and Carol Cutrere. In the same way that Chance Wayne had been told to stay away from St. Cloud, Carol is under orders to stay away from this small Southern town. Opposed to "the gradual massacre of the colored majority in the county," she had spent her inheritance on free clinics for blacks and protested when a black man was electrocuted for having improper relations with a white whore (an allusion to the Scottsboro case). Carol is over thirty, not pretty but with "an odd, fugitive beauty," which she exaggerates by powdering her face and lips white, outlining her eyes heavily with black pencil, and tinting her eyelids blue. Though she belongs to one of the country's most distinguished families, she is so fond of drinking, dancing, and promiscuous sex that her lifestyle is offensive to the conformist majority. Like the anticonformist Cora in "Two on a Party," Carol is modeled partly on Marion Vaccaro, who had joined Tennessee in Rome during the summer of 1956.

Val Xavier, like Chance Wayne, has the sort of good looks that women find irresistible, but now that the sweet bird of youth has flown, Val, unlike Chance, is determined to reform his life. "Heavy drinking and smoking the weed and shacking with strangers is okay for kids in their twenties but this is my thirtieth birthday and I'm all through with that route. I'm not young any more." Like Chance, he has lived a corrupt life, but we are expected to view him as an innocent; his guitar, he claims, has washed him clean when anything dirty touched him. He is disgusted, he says, with people who let themselves be bought and with buyers, but he has never been branded because he has never been caught. He compares himself to a legless bird: "Those little birds, they don't have no legs at all and they live their whole lives on the wing, and they sleep on the wind, that's how they sleep at night, they just spread their wings and go to sleep on the wind like other birds fold their wings and go to sleep on a tree. . . . —They sleep on the wind and . . . —never light on this earth but one time when they die!" (Here the effect depends partly on the repetitions of the words *wing*, *sleep*, *wind*, and *birds*; partly on the strong, simple rhythms.)

In *Orpheus Descending* many of the dramatic ingredients seem familiar because, not intending to have this script staged, Tennessee had drawn on it for ideas he could use in other scripts. Jabe Torrance owns only a dry-goods store, not a plantation, but, like Big Daddy, he is dying and is surrounded by people who try to give him the opposite impression. Like Silva Vaccaro in *Baby Doll*, Lady Torrance's father is an immigrant Italian victim of arson, and in both scripts the leading arsonist is revealed during the course of the action. The way Lady has been abandoned by her lover, David Cutrere, in favor of a society woman is reminiscent of the way Boss Finley dragged his daughter away from True Love, wanting to use her as a pawn in a marriage that would be advantageous to him, while the castration at the end of *Orpheus Descending* is startlingly similar to the castration at the end of *Sweet*

Bird of Youth. Like Chance, Val becomes a victim because he delays his departure too long, and, as the sheriff and his henchmen threaten him, the menace builds up in much the same way as it had in the previous play.

During the second act of *Orpheus Descending* Val and Lady hear the sound of wild baying: the chain-gang dogs are chasing a runaway convict. "Run boy!" says Val. "Run fast brother! If they catch you you never will run again!" But the tone changes. "Uh-huh—the dogs've got him. . . . They're tearing him to pieces!" And then a shot is fired. The death prefigures Val's. He should have kept on the wing, like the legless birds.

Trying to give the play a tragic dimension, Williams introduces references to both classical myth and Christianity. An itinerant musician with a guitar, Val is meant to resemble Orpheus, while the action coincides with Easter, and the sheriff's wife makes apocalyptic speeches about the Resurrection. At the same time, the South is portrayed as a breeding ground for all kinds of corruption, including racism, materialism, and indifference to justice. As in *The Rose Tattoo* and *Baby Doll*, the Italians, though derided as "dagos," are presented as more humane than the redneck Americans, but instead of being analyzed, the corruption is taken as much for granted as it is in *Sweet Bird of Youth*, and the characters are melodramatically divided into good guys and bad guys. Only the fugitives and the Italians (including Lady) are good, but they are idealized and sentimentalized.

Tennessee had wanted Anna Magnani to play Lady, but she again refused to commit herself for more than a couple of months, and again Maureen Stapleton got the part. The actor originally cast as Val was fired after the play opened in Philadelphia, and Cliff Robertson took over. The director was Harold Clurman, who found it difficult to handle Tennessee. When Clurman wanted to cut the prologue, which has minor characters talking in a contrived way to establish the prehistory of the plot, it was Maureen Stapleton who had to break the news to Tennessee. He gave in gracefully, but restored the prologue in the published script.

It was unusual for him to stay away from rehearsals, but this time he felt "too destroyed" to be of any help. "Of course I have been through periods somewhat like this before, when the sky cracked and fell and brained me, but this time I seem less able to struggle out of the debris." His mother's breakdown and Rose's deterioration had helped to unsettle him, but what disturbed him most was "the unaccountable collapse of my power to work, since work has always been my escape and comfort."[13]

The play opened at the Martin Beck on 21 March 1957. In the *New York Times* Brooks Atkinson welcomed it as "one of Mr. Williams's pleasantest plays. . . . But it seems to this playgoer that Mr. Williams has his story less thoroughly under control this time, and his allusive style has a less sturdy foundation."[14] Most of the other reviews were unenthusiastic, and in the *New Yorker* Wolcott Gibbs grumbled: "I don't believe that he has turned out a coherent play, or that he was quite sure of what was on his own mind."[15] The play closed after sixty-eight performances. "With *Orpheus Descending*," Tennessee told the *New York Herald-Tribune*, "I felt I was no longer acceptable to the theater public. Maybe, I thought, they'd had too much of a certain dish, and maybe they don't want to eat any more."[16]

He was already in a deep depression when he heard that his father had died at the age of seventy-seven. After quarreling with his sister, Cornelius had been living in Knoxville with a widow from Ohio. Edwina refused to attend the funeral, but Tennessee and his brother, Dakin, both went to Knoxville for it. Tennessee talked as if he no longer had any grievances against Cornelius: "I have changed my feeling about him. My father was a totally honest man. . . . He had a strong character and a sense of honor. He lived on his own terms, which were hard terms for his family but he should not be judged as he remains the mystery he is to us who live in his shadow."[17] But Donald Windham is probably right to suspect that this was no more than a show of forgiveness—that Tennessee was still unable to confront his real feelings.

Though he did his best throughout the run of *Orpheus Descending* to rally the spirits of the depressed cast, he was suffering from both his hypochondria and his persecution complex. In restaurants, according to Maureen Stapleton, whenever he heard an uncomplimentary remark, he would assume that he was the subject of the conversation.[18]

He was in the habit of pepping himself up with alcohol as he wrote, and in June 1957, after being told to cut down on drink for the sake of his liver, he found his writing less fluent: "I discovered that the Olivetti has been running mostly on gin."[19] Finally, in June, he made his long-delayed start on psychoanalysis, going five times a week to Dr. Lawrence Kubie, a Freudian who seems to have behaved in an unorthodox way, advising Tennessee to give up writing and give up his relationship with Frank. Dr. Kubie was hoping to turn his patient into a heterosexual, and Tennessee told Frank enough about the progress of the psychoanalysis to make him feel their relationship was in danger, especially when Tennessee rented a new apartment on the West Side, overlooking the George Washington Bridge. No less averse to monogamy than he had been in his thirties, he went on sleeping with Frank in the old apartment on 58th Street, but entertained friends in the new one, where Frank could not disturb them.[20]

Tennessee saw Dr. Kubie throughout the summer and fall, giving up his usual trip to Europe, and continued for the better part of a year. Later, during a period of estrangement from Frank, he described his daily routine in a letter to Paul Bowles. He was celibate and feeling no interest in sex. Nor was he interested in watching television. He was going to bed at half-past ten but, unable to sleep, reading till daybreak. He was seeing Dr. Kubie every weekday, and the doctor telephoned him Saturdays and Sundays to check on his mental and physical condition. Was he taking his pills? Was he going for a walk in the park or swimming at the Y or going to the movies? The doctor was trying—unsuccessfully—to edge him into resuming some sort of sex life.[21]

Instead of treating the sessions as confidential, Tennessee talked freely about them in a series of television interviews. Finding that he was losing patients as a result, Dr. Kubie asked Tennessee to find another analyst. He started treatment at a psychiatric clinic in Massachusetts, feeling that the sessions with Dr. Kubie had made him more honest about himself. "I came to discover a lot of unpleasant things about my character. I doubt that I have improved as a result, but at least I know they are there instead of considering myself as I used to, an unusually nice little man."[22]

11

A Bit of Shared Luck

"I think if this analysis works," Tennessee said in late 1957, "it will open some doors for me. . . . If I am no longer disturbed myself, I will deal less with disturbed people and with violent material."[1] But instead of being liberated by the analysis from his guilty obsession with Rose, he began to visit her more frequently at the clinic, Stony Lodge, and to plan a new play around her lobotomy. Having told part of her story in *The Glass Menagerie*, created a variation on the family's betrayal of her in *A Streetcar Named Desire*, and paid heavy-handed symbolic tribute to her in *The Rose Tattoo*, he returned to her story in *Suddenly Last Summer*.

Though there is no explicit mention in the play of a father's sexual assault on his daughter, Tennessee may have been resuming a topic he had broached on the couch when he implicitly raised the question of whether there had been any objective grounds for Rose's allegations. In *Suddenly Last Summer* Mrs. Venable wants brain surgery to silence a woman who is telling the truth.

The play is written as if Edwina had unilaterally condemned Rose to the operation. Mrs. Venable is explicitly warned of the dangers:

DOCTOR: Whenever you enter the brain with a foreign object . . .
MRS. VENABLE: Yes.
DOCTOR: —Even a needle-thin knife . . .
MRS. VENABLE: Yes.

DOCTOR: —In a skilled surgeon's fingers

MRS. VENABLE: Yes.

DOCTOR: —There is a good deal of risk involved in—the operation. . . .

MRS. VENABLE: You said that it pacifies them, it quiets them down, it suddenly makes them peaceful.

DOCTOR: Yes. It does that, that much we already know, but—

MRS. VENABLE: What?

DOCTOR: Well, it will be ten years before we can tell if the immediate benefits of the operation will be lasting or—passing or even if there'd still be—and this is what haunts me about it!—any possibility, afterwards, of—reconstructing a—totally sound person, it may be that the person will always be limited afterwards, relieved of acute disturbances but—*limited*, Mrs. Venable. . . .

MRS. VENABLE: Oh, but what a blessing to them, Doctor, to be just peaceful, to be just suddenly—peaceful. . . .

This sequence is theatrically suspenseful, but as an attack on Edwina it is grossly unfair: the foresight of this doctor depends on knowledge that had been accumulated after the operation. If Edwina's principal adviser was Emmett Hoctor, the surgeon who wanted to perform the lobotomy, he would have been less discouraging. The characterization of Mrs. Venable is colored by Tennessee's guilt feelings, which inflame his rage against his mother. Tennessee also knew he had benefited from the disaster. "I don't think I would have been the poet I am without that anguished familial situation."[2]

Though his father had terrified him throughout his boyhood, Tennessee had been oddly silent about this in his plays. Relationships with Pancho, Frank, and more casual lovers may have compensated in some ways for the fatherly love that had been withheld during childhood: possibly Tennessee acted out so much with his lovers that he was left with little need to complain in his plays about the lack of paternal love and the bullying. Cornelius's drunken rowdiness may be echoed in Stanley Kowalski's, but Stanley is at an early stage in the process of becoming a father, and there is no paternal aggression in either of the plays that deal directly with Rose's situation—*The Glass Menagerie* or *Suddenly Last Summer*. But the later play hints at the existence of an aggressive deity. Mrs. Venable suggests that her son, Sebastian, who had once thought of entering a Buddhist monastery, was looking for God when he took her to the Galapagos, the Enchanted Islands, which look "much as the world at large might look—after a last conflagration." On their first visit they saw the giant turtles creeping out of the sea for their annual egg-laying. Their second visit was timed for the hatching of the eggs, and they watched carnivorous birds "diving down on the hatched sea turtles, turning them over to expose their soft undersides, tearing the undersides open and rending and eating their flesh. Sebastian guessed that possibly only a hundredth of one per cent of their number would escape to the sea." He spent a whole day in the crow's nest of a schooner watching the baby turtles scuttling in panic toward the sea and being eaten alive "till it was too dark to see it, and when he came back down the rigging, he said, Well, now I've seen Him! — and he meant God. . . . He meant that God shows a savage face to people, it's all we see or hear of Him."

Images of flesh eating and cannibalism dominate the play, which is set in a junglelike garden. "There are massive tree-flowers that suggest organs of a body, torn out, still glistening with undried blood; there are harsh cries and sibilant hissings and thrashing sounds in the garden as if it were in-habited by beasts, serpents and birds, all of savage nature." In the original production the set was modeled on the magnificent two-story indoor green-house in a plantation-style house belonging to Fred and Pauline Bultman, the parents of the painter, Fritz, who had befriended Tennessee. They owned a funeral parlor, and local rumor had it that their exotic plants were watered with human blood. This may have given Tennessee one of his ideas for the play — the fictional garden which had belonged to Sebastian. He used to feed his insectivorous plants on fruit flies flown in from a Florida lab-oratory that used them for experiments in genetics. The garden provides an appropriate background for the climactic monologue in which Catherine tells the story of Sebastian's death. He fell prey to the naked, homeless, underfed boys he had been exploiting, boys who lived on the free beach in Cabeza de Lobo "like scavenger dogs." Sebastian had given orders for them to be beaten away from him, but they had chased him and, in a horrifying climax, killed and begun to eat him. The imagery in Catharine's narrative links them to the birds who swoop down on baby turtles: she hears Sebastian scream "just once before this flock of black plucked little birds that pursued him and overtook him halfway up the white hill."

This was the most ferocious theatrical image Tennessee had yet found to express the guilt he felt at eating luxuriously in cities where the natives were starving, and at paying boys to make love when they were too poverty-

Elizabeth Taylor in the movie Suddenly
Last Summer

stricken to say no. He writes as if his own predatory homosexuality had come to nauseate him. "Yes, we all use each other," says Catharine, "and that's what we think of as love."

Sebastian inherits not only Tennessee's predatory interest in boys but also his diffidence. Sebastian lived as if "nobody had any right to complain or interfere in any way whatsoever, and even though he knew that what was awful was awful, that what was wrong was wrong," he "thought it unfitting to ever take any action about anything whatsoever!" With his white suits and his habit of popping white pills because rheumatic fever has left him with a heart murmur, Sebastian resembles Williams closely. Fed up with dark boys, he feels famished for blonds. "That's how he talked about people, as if they were—items on a menu.—'That one's delicious-looking, that one is appetizing,' or 'that one is *not* appetizing'"—I think because he was really nearly half-starved from living on pills and salads." Ten years earlier, after two months in Italy, Tennessee had told Donald Windham he was tired of dark Romans and building up an appetite for northern blonds.[3]

The play tells us a lot about Tennessee's mental state while he was writing. If the two fugitives in *Orpheus Descending*, Val and Carol, are both self-portraits, so is Catharine in *Suddenly Last Summer*. The dialogue reproduces the gist of Tennessee's conversation with Dr. Kubie, who had asked why he was "so full of hate, anger, and envy." "I don't understand what hate is," Catharine declares. "How can you hate anybody and still be sane?" And she tells Dr. Cukrowicz how she had come to feel so deeply alienated from herself that she wrote in her journal as if everything were happening to someone else. "I started writing my diary in the third person, singular, such as 'She's still living this morning,' meaning that *I* was. . . . — 'WHAT'S NEXT FOR HER? GOD KNOWS!' — I couldn't go out any more."

Important though it is, the confessional element in the play is subordinate to the indictment of the mother figure. The ruthless Violet Venable is determined to stop Catharine from revealing that Sebastian had been devoured by boys who had prostituted themselves to him. The purpose of the lobotomy is to cut the story out of her brain, and Edwina, who had already sat through *The Glass Menagerie*, was invited to see another dramatization of what she had done to her daughter. Too canny to be unaware of her son's intentions, she behaved as if her skin were impervious to the sting in this one-act play. "Why don't you write a lovely, long play again, Tom?" she asked.[4]

Staged in a double bill with another one-act play, *Something Unspoken*, *Suddenly Last Summer* opened at the off-Broadway York Theatre on First Avenue on 7 January 1958 with Anne Meacham as Catharine and Hortense Alden as Mrs. Venable. The director was Herbert Machiz, who had banned Tennessee from rehearsals of the *Streetcar* revival in Florida. But this time there was a clause in the contract to stop him from repeating the ban.[5] Some of the New York critics balked at the combination of lobotomy with cannibalism in one short play. In the *New Yorker* Wolcott Gibbs objected that no other playwright could invent a story of quite such lurid perversity, while the reviewer for *Time* complained: "It matters less that noisomely misanthropic symbols keep recurring in his work than that they nowhere seem purgative." But Brooks Atkinson and Walter Kerr both reacted favorably. "No other playwright," said Atkinson, could use "ordinary words with so much grace, allusiveness, sorcery and power."[6]

The face Tennessee presented to the world in his plays was different from the face he presented to his friends in letters. Apart from his work, what mattered to him most was his sexual activity, which involved him in casual but close relationships with men he did not respect. "Remember Frank of New Orleans? The leather-jacketed ex-truck-driver who was barman at the Treasure Chest and hung out at the Rendezvous? He's tending a sidewalk hot-dog and chili stand in Miami. Ran into him a few days ago and he's much the same in appearance and manner. Promised to call me today. Gore Vidal is here, too, and we struck a bit of shared luck last night."[7]

Shared luck and casual encounters were not enough to keep Tennessee in New York. Interrupting his analysis—Dr. Kubie had taken him back—and leaving the actors to get on with performing the play, he went to Key West. He came back to New York in March and, intending toward the end of April to make a final break with Dr. Kubie, he wrote a long good-bye letter, but, delivering it by hand, he let himself be talked into resuming the analysis. He finally made the break in early June before leaving to spend the summer in Europe.[8]

In the autumn he worked on a domestic comedy, *Period of Adjustment*, saying he needed money to pay Rose's clinic fees. It is a comparatively unadventurous play, but one new feature is that he works in a reference to his father, as if he had been waiting for Cornelius to die before he could do this, though he had no compunction about inviting Edwina to plays in which she could hardly fail to recognize herself. The character of Ralph is not tailored to fit Cornelius in the same way that Amanda Wingfield and Violet Venable had been tailored to fit Edwina, but Ralph believes that "a sissy tendency in a boy's got to be nipped in the bud, otherwise the bud will blossom." He is sure he did the right thing when he "caught the little bugger playin' with a rag doll." He snatched the doll away and threw it into the fire. "I wanted a boy but I'm not sure I got one."

Ralph and his friend George were both war heroes, but their subsequent lives have been ignominious. One has married for money, the other (like Brick) has refused to confront the homosexual side of his nature. But the playwright has the power to punish them for their cowardice and reward them with connubial happiness when they behave better.

The year ended in a spate of activity. In Miami, with an assistant called Owen Philips, Tennessee was directing *Period of Adjustment* at the Coconut Grove, while in London preparations were being made for a production of *The Rose Tattoo* at the Royal Court. Maureen Stapleton, who wanted to

George Roy Hill directs the movie Period of
Adjustment

repeat her Broadway Serafina, was rejected in favor of an Italian actress, Isa
Miranda. On Christmas Eve Maureen Stapleton was deeply depressed, but
after calling her up to ask for Marlon Brando's telephone number, Tennessee took Maria Britneva, Donald, and a friend of Donald's over to her
apartment, where he pretended that no decision had yet been made about
the casting.[9]

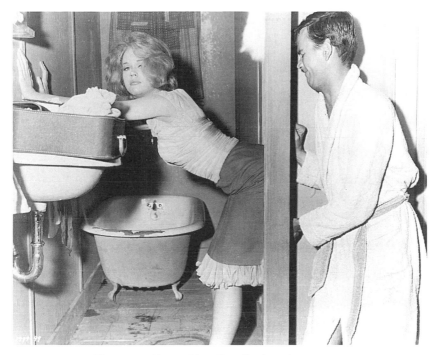

*Uncompromising position: Jane Fonda and
Robert Wagner in* Period of Adjustment

When *Period of Adjustment* opened on 29 December, Edwina came to Miami for the first night, though at home she had been complaining dementedly that a rocket from Cape Canaveral had exploded outside her window. She had combed radioactive fallout from her hair, she said, and rubbed her scorched face with cold cream. At the party in Miami after the first performance, according to the actress Barbara Baxley, Edwina "couldn't stop telling Tennessee to stand up to greet a lady, to straighten his tie, to fix his coat, to use his napkin—as if he were five years old."[10]

The new year, 1959, began with preparations for Kazan's Broadway production of *Sweet Bird of Youth*, starring Paul Newman and Geraldine Page. At the first reading by the cast, everything, according to Kazan, "fell apart." Tennessee left before the end, and Geraldine Page withdrew to her dressing room, feeling incapable of playing the part. Tennessee "doubted his own play; he wanted it withdrawn. . . . I had never seen him so timorous after a first reading, had only seen him in such a panic once before."[11] It opened on

10 March, and although the first-night audience was tremendously enthusiastic, cheering Tennessee when he joined the cast at the curtain calls, he afterward crept to his bedroom and refused to come out.

Many of the reviewers were hostile. In the *Daily News* John Chapman called Williams a "dirty-minded dramatist who has been losing hope for the human race" and had "written of moral and physical decadence as shockingly as he can." Writing in the *New Yorker*, Kenneth Tynan complained that the writing was operatic and hysterical, as if "it had long been out of touch with reality. A dust bowl, one feels, is being savagely, obsessively plowed, in defiance of the known facts about soil depletion and the need for irrigation. . . . I recognized nothing but a special, rarefied situation that had been carried to extremes of cruelty with a total disregard for probability, human relevance and the laws of dramatic structure." In the *Tulane Drama Review* Henry Popkin concluded that "Williams now seems to be in a sort of race with himself, surpassing homosexuality with cannibalism, cannibalism with castration, devising new and greater shocks in each succeeding play." But Brooks Atkinson praised *Sweet Bird of Youth* as "one of his finest dramas," and it ran for almost a year.[12]

As usual Tennessee quickly escaped from New York, heading for Miami and then Key West with Marion Vaccaro. In April, wanting to meet Fidel Castro, he flew to Havana, where Kenneth Tynan arranged a lunch with the fifty-nine-year-old Ernest Hemingway in a restaurant, the Floridita. Nervous about the confrontation, Tennessee started preparing himself at ten in the morning by drinking martinis, and he was slightly drunk when he arrived late, wearing a yachting jacket with silver buttons. "What I've always admired about your work, Mr. Hemingway," he said, "is that you care about honour among men." Asking what kind of men he had in mind, Hemingway responded: "People who have honour never talk about it."

Discussing a bullfighter, Antonio Ordonez, who was one of Hemingway's friends, Tennessee claimed to have seen his *cogidas*, the scars on his thighs. When Hemingway asked: "Do you think he would talk to us and show us his *cogidas?*" Tennessee failed to notice the irony. "Oh, I'm certain he would. As I say he's a most accessible boy."

He was equally tactless in talking about Hemingway's second wife. "They tell me she died. Did she die in great pain?"

Hemingway answered: "She died like everybody else, and after that she was dead."[13]

When Tynan said he had an appointment with Castro at two o'clock, Tennessee insisted on going with him. They were admitted to the presence during a cabinet meeting, which Castro interrupted to tell Tennessee how much he admired his plays, especially the one about the cat upon the burning roof. He hoped Mr. Williams would come to live in Cuba and write about the revolution.[14]

Later on, when Marion Vaccaro arrived in Havana, Tennessee took her to a male brothel. Together they went back to Key West, where they stayed with Frank and Tennessee worked on the play he was to call *The Night of the Iguana*, taking the title of a story he had sketched out in September 1940 when he was staying at the Hotel Costa Verde in Acapulco, after the summer season was over and before the winter season had begun. Most of his work on the story was done between April 1946 and February 1948. Giving the hotel its actual name, he describes the long south veranda with ten hammocks slung outside the screen doors of the ten bedrooms. The rooms are no more separated from one another than rooms in any other hotel, but their separateness becomes symbolic. As he said in 1961, "The drama in my plays . . . is nearly always people trying to reach each other. In *Night of the Iguana* each one has his separate cubicle but they meet on the veranda outside the cubicles, at least Hannah and Larry Shannon meet on the veranda outside their cubicles, which is of course an allegorical touch of what people must try to do."[15]

In Mexico iguanas are a delicacy, and in the story, captured by Mexican boys who work in the hotel, one is tethered to a post. Its frantic cries arouse the pity of Edith Jelkes, a pretty blonde thirty-year-old spinster, who had been an art teacher at an Episcopal girls' school in Mississippi until she had a nervous breakdown. The story describes her as having "a somewhat archaic quality of refinement," but we learn little about this quality until Edith Jelkes becomes Hannah Jelkes in the play. Edith comes from a family described with unmistakable resemblances to Tennessee's own. It is a

historical Southern family of great but now moribund vitality whose latter generations had tended to split into two antithetical types, one in which the libido was pathologically distended and another in which it would seem to be all but dried up. . . . There had been an efflorescence . . . of nervous talents and sickness, of drunkards and poets, gifted artists and sexual degenerates, together with fanatically proper and squeamish old ladies of both sexes who were condemned to live beneath the same roof with relatives whom they could only regard as monsters.

Belonging to neither of the two basic types, Edith finds it especially difficult "to cultivate any interior poise." Williams was, as so often, thinking of himself.

The only guests at the hotel are Edith and two male writers who are having an affair. Williams identified with Edith and with the older of the two men. He had often been put under embarrassing pressure by women who felt attracted to him, and his sympathy is with the writers when Edith tries to invade their privacy. Frustrated sexual desire is finding its outlet in curiosity. "You have a real gift," the older man tells her, "for vicarious experience." Made when she complains to them about the sufferings of the iguana, the comment ironically prepares the ground for the older man's unsuccessful assault on her virginity.

Williams kept going back to the story often over the period of almost two years when he was writing, but he did no more than sketch out the play he was to write twelve years later. There are brief references to a storm and to the liberation of the iguana, but he left the potential symbolism undeveloped.

In the play, which has a larger cast of characters and a wider emotional range, he involves himself more deeply, going all out to formulate his convictions about the nature of art and the forces—internal and external—that govern human life. Like *Orpheus Descending* it contains a complicated recycling of fragments from experience and earlier fiction. He draws on memories of Mexico in September 1940, of Hollywood in 1943, and of travels to Europe with his grandfather in 1928. While recycling Edith Jelkes as Hannah, he gave her qualities taken from Carson McCullers.

A year after the Second World War broke out, Acapulco had been full of pro-Nazi Germans, jubilant at the success of Hitler's blitz on London. They are not mentioned in the story, but in the play a stereotypical family of Germans is staying at the hotel. They carry around a shortwave radio and listen gleefully to news programs, and respectfully to Hitler's broadcasts. They sing Nazi marching songs.

The sensual, selfish hotel proprietor, Maxine, is modeled on Zola, the Hollywood landlady who had appeared as Olga in the story "The Mattress by the Tomato Patch" (1953), while Maxine's husband, who died shortly before the action begins, derives from Zola's husband. But neither Mexico nor Hollywood contributes as much to the play as the trip to Europe Tennessee made at seventeen with Reverend Dakin and the party of female parishioners. While his grandfather was still alive, Tennessee had felt no need to write about him—there were practical ways of expressing his affection for the old man—but here he is touchingly memorialized. The ninety-seven-year-old Jonathan Coffin gets his surname from Cornelius's great-uncle, the poet Tristram Coffin, but his character derives from Reverend Dakin. The old poet is known as Nonno, which was the name Frank Merlo had used for the old minister, whose courage and resolute cheerfulness are reproduced. Hearing that the tour guide is a clergyman, Nonno quips: "Tell him I'm too old to baptize and too young to bury but on the market for marriage to a rich widow, fat, fair and forty."

As Williams comments in a stage direction, "One can see him exchanging these pleasantries with the rocking-chair brigades of summer hotels at the turn of the century—and with professors' wives at little colleges in New England. But now it has become somewhat grotesque in a touching way, this desire to please, this playful manner, these venerable jokes." This helps to explain why Tennessee had so often wanted to travel with his grandfather and had kept inviting him to the house in Key West, while the script illuminates both sides of the banter they exchanged. When Shannon tells the old man that poets are always underpaid, the stage direction explains: "He is being fiercely, almost mockingly tender with the old man—a thing we are when the pathos of the old, the ancient, the dying is such a wound to our own (savagely beleaguered) nerves and sensibilities that this outside demand on us is beyond our collateral, our emotional reserve."

The quality of Tennessee's love for his grandfather is reflected in Hannah's tenderness toward the old poet. An unlikely couple, they have not only been traveling together but been working in partnership. Instead of being an ex-teacher, like Edith Jelkes and Blanche in *Streetcar*, Hannah is a painter who earns a precarious living from sketching tourists while the old man recites his poems. Tennessee may also have been remembering the man who was probably his first male lover—the tubercular occupant of the other attic room in the New Orleans boardinghouse had earned money by sketching in restaurants.

In the story, Edith's predatory curiosity makes little impact on the lives of the two writers, but in the play Shannon is an irresistibly attractive man with more than one female cat pursuing him across the hot tin roof, and without enough willpower to rebuff them. When he was a priest he made love to a pretty Sunday-school teacher, and as a tour guide, he has given in to a precocious sixteen-year-old, Charlotte, provoking the relentless hostil-

Ava Gardner and Richard Burton in Night of the Iguana, *the movie*

ity of her Amazonian singing teacher, Miss Fellowes, who makes sure that he loses his job with Blake Tours. Though not hostile, Maxine, who wants him as a replacement for her dead husband, is no less ruthless. Shannon would prefer to continue as a tour guide or go back to the priesthood, but, without feeling much affection for Maxine, lets himself be dragooned into staying with her.

The play is cleverly constructed around the erosion of other options. Of all the women who respond to his charm, Hannah is the only one allowed to engage the audience's sympathy. Far more tellingly than Edith, she is given "a somewhat archaic quality of refinement." This phrase could have been used to describe Amanda, Blanche, or Alma, but Hannah is more genuinely refined. Williams said he intended her "almost as a definition of what I think is most beautiful spiritually in a person and still believable."[16] Her refinement enters more subtly than any previous heroine's into her relationships. Tenderly protective toward her frail old grandfather, she is concerned and tactful when Shannon needs help, while with the tough Maxine, who recognizes her as a dangerous rival and wants to get rid of her, Hannah is scrupulously honest in admitting her poverty. It seems odd that, after writing so many plays in which sexual fulfillment is presented as a panacea, Williams should make Hannah a virgin, but she has always had valid reasons for steering clear of sexual entanglements, and the mutual attraction between her and Shannon would be less poignant if it were consummated. Their love-without-sex is the diametric opposite of the sex-without-love connection between Blanche and Stanley.

The audience is edged into wanting Shannon and Hannah to become lovers, as they nearly do, but the plot is structured to keep them apart. At the same time, both characters are self-portraits, and their relationship is a non-relationship between two people doomed to isolation. Neither can offer any sort of security to the other, for both are at the end of their tethers. On the verge of cracking up, Shannon is pursued by a ghost: "The *spook* had moved in with me. In that hot room with one bed, the width of an ironing board and about as hard, the spook was up there on it, sweating, stinking, grinning up at me. . . . He's like the Sioux Indians in the Wild West fiction, he doesn't attack before sundown, he's an after-sundown shadow." The spook sounds like the equivalent of Tennessee's blue devils. Later on Hannah tells him: "I can help you because I've been through what you are going through now. I had something like your spook. . . . I called him the blue devil. . . . I showed him that I could endure him and I made him respect my endurance." Spooks and blue devils, she says, respect "all the tricks that panicky people use to outlast and outwit their panic." The dialogue between Shannon and Hannah may sound like a dialogue between Tennessee and himself, but this is what all dramatic dialogue essentially is, and the theatrical situation is skillfully contrived to provide tension throughout their conversation. In one of their long conversations Shannon is roped into a hammock after breaking down and threatening to swim to China, meaning he would swim into the bay, where sharks and barracudas would eat him. While he is helpless in the hammock, she protects him when the Germans torment him "like an animal in a trap," but she refuses to untie him until there is no longer any danger that he might carry out his threat. He tries to pressure her, saying that all women "want to see a man in a tied-up situation." It may also be true that audiences enjoy seeing a virile man in a tied-up situation, and this is a theatrical possibility Strindberg had exploited in *The Father*. Williams had learned a great deal from Strindberg, and the sequence in *The Night of the Iguana* is highly effective, though sustained too long, and it becomes apparent that the playwright is defining his own situation.

Hannah, who resembles Tennessee in being a compulsive traveler, says: "I don't regard a home as a . . . well, as a place, a building . . . a house . . . of wood, bricks, stone. I think of a home as being a thing that two people have between them in which each can . . . well, nest—rest—live in, emotionally speaking." In traveling with Nonno, she has, as Shannon points out, built a nest in a tree that cannot stay erect for much longer, while he, as she points out, has really been traveling alone while accompanying groups of tourists and indulging in casual affairs: "You have always traveled alone except for your spook, as you call it. He's your traveling companion."

Shannon's main gesture of love to her is the act of liberating the iguana, and his longest speech to her is a rhetorical account of natives eating from a pile of excrement. His most extravagant action—in an offstage sequence—is to urinate over the luggage of the Baptist ladies after he has been forced to hand over the keys of the bus to another guide, but he is given a combination of qualities that enable him to retain the audience's sympathy. He is glamorous, vulnerable, outspoken, and honest. As a priest he could not pretend—even in the pulpit—that God was benevolent.

Look here, I said, I shouted, I'm tired of conducting services in praise and worship of a senile delinquent. . . . He's represented like a bad-tempered childish old, old, sick, peevish man—I mean like the sort of old man in a nursing home that's putting together a jigsaw puzzle and can't put it together and gets furious at it and kicks over the table. Yes, I tell you they *do* that, all our theologies do it—accuse God of being a cruel, senile delinquent, blaming the world and brutally punishing all he created for his own faults in construction.

This is reminiscent of the speeches about a vindictive God in *Suddenly Last Summer*, and is obviously a statement of Tennessee's viewpoint.

12

Betrayal and
Bereavement

After going to London in May 1959 for the premiere of *Orpheus Descending* at the Royal Court with Isa Miranda and Gary Cockrell, Tennessee and Frank returned in early June to New York, where the play was being filmed with Anna Magnani and Marlon Brando. They were finding it difficult to work together. Brando could not reciprocate her sexual interest in him, and when he mumbled his lines, she took her revenge by treating them as inaudible, and Tennessee was too nervous to intervene.

In July he drove to Pennsylvania to see the thirty-eight-year-old Diana Barrymore in *A Streetcar Named Desire*. Belonging to the famous theatrical dynasty, she had started her career brilliantly, and made six movies, only to run into difficulties as she became addicted to alcohol and drugs. "She has gone off the bottle," Tennessee reported, "and onto the happy pills and the sleepy pills, in rapid alternation." A couple of weeks previously, while scrambling some eggs, she had somehow fallen into the pan of hot fat and got second-degree burns on her bottom. "Whenever she sat down on the stage last night, she made a face like she had a throbbing hemorrhoid. Nevertheless she has the Barrymore madness and power and her last three scenes were remarkable."[1]

She had wanted to play the Princess in *Sweet Bird of Youth*, but in Tennessee's opinion she was "too much like the princess to play the princess well."[2] She was also frustrated in her hopes of marrying him: her fantasy was

Unrecognized in Sloane Square. TW before
Orpheus Descending *opened at the Royal*
Court *(1959).*

that she could rescue him from homosexuality while he rescued her from addiction. But not long after her failure in *Streetcar* she was found dead in her New York apartment.

In August he left with Frank for a trip round the world. From Japan he wrote to Brooks Atkinson complaining he had been poisoned by success.[3] In spite of all the psychoanalysis, he was more deeply disturbed than ever, and he was risking an international scandal by carrying drugs around with him.

After three months on the move he spent a month in New York, reworking his one-act play *The Night of the Iguana*, which had been staged on 2 July at the Spoleto Festival, and by the same director, Frank Corsaro, during the fall in a longer version at the Actors Studio. The manuscript of the earlier version had been only twenty-one pages; the version produced at the Actors Studio was still a one-act play, but was nearly four times as long. Tennessee went on working at it in Key West during the winter, and in January 1960 Corsaro arrived to collaborate with him. "When he was working or reworking at this play," Corsaro testifies, "he was a genius, and he was inspiring to be with. You could see his understanding of people's

With Anna Magnani on the set of
The Fugitive Kind

pain, his compassion, his gentleness, his modesty in the face of the universe. But outside the work he was becoming a travesty of himself. Those he chose to be with were such a sorry crew." He was spending time with Carson McCullers and William Inge, who were both drinking exorbitantly, with an eccentric Hungarian woman, Lilla von Saher, whom he called "the last of the crêpe-de-Chine gypsies," and with Marion Vaccaro.[4] Convinced that his luck had run out, he complained endlessly about critics and their lack of sympathy.

In June 1960 his mother and brother accepted his invitation to share a holiday with him at the Beverly Hills Hotel in Los Angeles, where Edwina enjoyed meeting Elvis Presley. Later in the month Tennessee went back to join Frank in Key West, but their relationship was steadily deteriorating. Tennessee had it in mind when writing about solitude in *The Night of the Iguana*. He felt certain he was unlovable, and his inability to believe in the reality of Frank's love for him was even harder for Frank to accept than

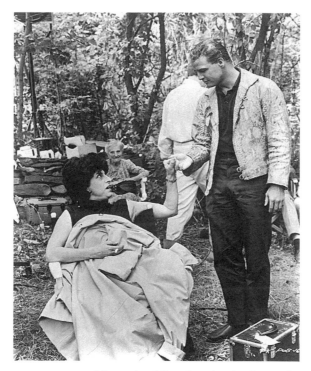

Magnani and Brando on location during the
shooting of The Fugitive Kind

Tennessee's infidelities. Taking care of his lover had been not only Frank's main pleasure in life but also his main occupation. The more unneeded and redundant he felt, the more he neglected to take care of himself.

In November *Period of Adjustment* opened in New York, directed by George Roy Hill, with James Daly, Barbara Baxley, and Robert Webber. All three actors looked too old to engage as much sympathy as was needed from the audience. The run ended after 132 performances.

Toward the end of January 1961 Tennessee left for Europe with Marion Vaccaro, and from London he wrote his last letter to Cheryl Crawford. She would have preferred to go on being both his friend and his producer, but, morbidly suspicious of people's motives for associating with him, he was liable to discard old friends without provocation, and to throw out provocations that could finish off friendships. Since 1939 Audrey Wood's help had been invaluable, but when in 1962 he published an article in *Esquire* about their relationship, she saw he was thinking of her as a "mother-image" and projecting some of his deep-seated resentments against

Edwina. The son had arrived, he wrote, at an age "when he feels humiliated by the acceptance of what he thinks is too much domination, too many decisions for him not made by himself."[5]

Rehearsals began in October for the Broadway production of *The Night of the Iguana*, directed by Frank Corsaro with a partly English cast. Margaret Leighton appeared as Hannah and Alan Webb as Nonno. Patrick O'Neal played Shannon and Bette Davis Maxine. Nervous and relying heavily on pills, Tennessee went on rewriting, unsettling the cast with new dialogue at each rehearsal. This continued throughout the tryout weeks in Rochester, Detroit, Cleveland, and Chicago, where his former champion, the reviewer Claudia Cassidy, derogated the play as bankrupt. The strain of the pre-Broadway tryout period was so intense that he intended never to undergo it again. All his future plays, he said, would be written for off Broadway.[6]

In Detroit, Tennessee was badly bitten on both ankles by his big Belgian shepherd dog, who was jealous of his relationship with Frank. One morning, while the dog was crouching like a guardian by Frank's bed, Tennessee

With Sidney Lumet (director) and Martin
Jarrow (producer) during the shooting of
The Fugitive Kind

ignored his warning growl and stepped over him to climb into bed with Frank. Later, while Frank was in the bathroom with the hotel doctor, who had come up because of Tennessee's cold, the dog jumped up on the bed and, after biting through to the bone on each ankle, went for Tennessee's throat, but Frank came out of the bathroom in time to pull him off. Though Frank then had the dog put down, he had been so attached to it that its death inflicted further damage on their relationship. Given an overdose of anti-biotics for his staphylococcic infection in both ankles, Tennessee was rushed to hospital in an ambulance, but he discharged himself when the nurses refused to give him enough Seconal to make him sleep. His ankles remained so swollen that he attended rehearsals in Cleveland and Chicago wearing bedroom slippers.[7]

The Night of the Iguana was due to open at the Royale on 28 December 1961. While it was still previewing in Chicago, Tennessee and the producer, Charles Bowden, went into a church and had a mass said for it. "I'm not a Catholic myself, but I like the Catholic mass, and by golly it opened well."[8] But reviews in New York were mixed. "Let us put down *The Night of the Iguana*," wrote Robert Brustein, "as another of his innumerable exercises in marking time." *Time*, on the other hand, praised it as "the wisest play he has ever written."[9]

After about three months Bette Davis left the cast, to be replaced by Shelley Winters. "It is hard to say which was worse, but at least La Davis drew cash and La Winters seems only to sell the upper gallery. ... La Winters has a fifth of Jack Daniel's Tennessee sour mash whiskey in her dressing-room and nips all through the show. She never enters on cue." And in a fashionable restaurant in April, Patrick O'Neal threw a table loaded with cocktails, canapés, and coffee at Audrey Wood and Frank Corsaro.[10] The production, though, went on attracting big audiences, and the play was picked as the best of the year by the New York Drama Critics' Circle.

As the relationship with Frank went on deteriorating, Tennessee thought of escaping from New York. Christopher Isherwood had invited him to California, and though Tennessee was afraid of getting on his nerves while staying in the house, he thought of basing himself at a hotel in Coronado or renting a nearby house with a pool so that they could spend time together during March. Then it began to look as if Frank would leave New York. American involvement in Vietnam was increasing, and Tennessee was pleased when he announced his intention of taking part in the "Strike for Peace" demonstrations. "It has, or appears to have, given Frank something to be seriously involved in for the first time since I have known him, which is almost fifteen years now."[11]

In *The Milk Train Doesn't Stop Here Anymore*, begun at this time, Tennessee again moved—with a lot of revision and redrafting—from a short story to a short play and finally to a full-length play. *The Night of the Iguana* was vastly superior as a play to the original story, but this cannot be said of *Milk Train*. Written in Italy during the summer of 1953, "Man Bring This up Road" is a ten-page story about a rich, self-involved woman, Flora Goforth, who offers sex but refuses food to a hungry itinerant artist. Partly because it was so short, Tennessee had been able to bring off the story without repeating too much of what he had already written about rich aging women and venal lovers. But in the play the material seems overstretched; it is also reminiscent of many earlier works, including *The Roman Spring of Mrs. Stone* and *Sweet Bird of Youth*. The characters are overexplained and the rhetoric is overblown. The rich woman, Flora Goforth, keeps her name, but the young man, formerly Jimmy Dobyne, is now called Chris Flanders.

As usual, the play is fleshed out with incidents based on recent events in Tennessee's life. The dog-bite experience gave him the idea for a pack of wolflike dogs kept on the mountainside to protect Mrs. Goforth's privacy: they maul Chris on his way up to her isolated retreat. What is more damaging to the play than the easygoing indulgence in autobiography is Tennessee's habit of using drama as a vehicle for self-accusation. Suffering from lung cancer, Frank was deteriorating rapidly, and Tennessee was taking sadistic pleasure in flaunting other lovers in front of him. Feeling qualms, he projected some of the guilt onto Flora Goforth, who enjoys tantalizing the hungry poet—indicating that he will soon be fed, and watching him squirm with impotent rage as the food fails to appear. She partially explains her misanthropic alienation by talking about the time "when I was still meeting people, before they all seemed like the same person over and over, and I got tired of the person." But the attempt at self-justification blurs into self-accusation: "Everybody who knows me knows that I am colder hearted than the gods of old Egypt!" And at another point, when she is asked whether she trusts anybody, she replies: "Nobody human, just dogs."

Except for *Camino Real*, all Williams's major plays had been realistic, though he had sometimes used such alienation effects as direct address to the audience. Wanting to stylize *Milk Train*, he introduced elements derived from Japanese Kabuki theater, adding these in the third version of the script. The reason he gave is: "I think the play will come off better the further it is removed from conventional theatre since it's been rightly described as an allegory and as a 'sophisticated fairy tale.'"[12] Two "stage assistants" are dressed in black, and, while they are rearranging the set or bringing on props, other characters treat them as if they were invisible. But they also appear in costume, playing a variety of small parts.

The play loses more than it gains from such stylistic idiosyncrasies, which indicate a lack of confidence. Williams was afraid that his kind of play was going out of fashion. He told interviewers that after relying too heavily on words and naturalism, he felt envious of such younger writers as Harold Pinter and Edward Albee, who appeared to have more freedom. In *Milk Train* the stylization clashes with the rhetoric and the emotionality. Some of the dialogue refers obliquely to his deteriorating relationship with Frank. Chris talks—not very knowingly—about the anxiety of kittens. "Their owner's house is never a sure protection, a reliable shelter. Everything going on in it is mysterious to them, and no matter how hard they try to please, how do they know if they please? . . . We're all of us living in a house we're not used to . . . a house full of—voices, noises, objects, strange shadows, light that's even stranger—We can't understand. We bark and jump around and try to—be—*pleasingly playful* in this big mysterious house but—in our hearts we're all very frightened of it." It seems that Williams— without intending to patronize Frank—was trying to empathize with his predicament as the loyal, servantlike lover of a man so superior to himself that their relationship was like that of owner and pet.

Guilt feelings about infidelity to Frank were compounded by new infidelities. While Frank was in New York, a Key West friend of his saw Tennessee hugging and kissing a painter on a sofa. Frank, who was informed, came back to Key West and—possibly under the influence of drugs—tried to strangle the painter. Tennessee called the police, and, the next day, moved out with the painter. Their affair was brief, and Tennessee was living alone in New York when he took a new lover, a good-looking young writer, Frederick Nicklaus, who had graduated from a university in Ohio and settled in New York during the fifties. When he met Tennessee, he was involved in an unhappy affair with an older writer who was aggressive when drunk and got drunk every evening. Frank's health deteriorated

With Hermione Baddeley and director
Herbert Machiz in Boston during the tryout
tour of The Milk Train Doesn't Stop
Here Anymore

steadily, but when he arrived in Manhattan, Tennessee refused to see him except in the presence of Audrey Wood.[13]

The one-act version of *Milk Train.* was to be staged at Spoleto in July 1962 with Hermione Baddeley as Mrs. Goforth. Renting a house in Tangier for four months, Tennessee took Nicklaus with him, but they had to leave after three weeks for the first rehearsal of *Milk Train*. He was nervous about Hermione Baddeley, who seemed to be drinking "even more than I do," and he had endless trouble with Nicklaus. Writing to a friend, Tennessee said he was traveling with a young poet who was "a good companion but incredibly inept at anything of a practical nature so our travels are one continual fantasy of confusions. He doesn't know how to open a door with a key, find a light switch, count change, and this morning he didn't know how to flush the toilet."[14]

At the opening night in Spoleto, Anna Magnani, who was sharing a box with Tennessee, seemed more impressed by Hermione Baddeley than by the play. A Broadway production was arranged for January 1963, to be directed by Herbert Machiz, with the same cast. Before the New York opening, the play was tried out in New Haven, Boston, and Philadelphia. In Boston, Hermione Baddeley kept her nerve when her red wig fell off shortly after her entrance. She went on dictating her memoirs, sweeping about the desk, and when she noticed the wig, she picked it up and put it on back-ward.[15]

After opening in New York on 16 January 1963, the play ran for only sixty-nine performances. Back in Key West Tennessee guiltily devoted part of his day to looking after Frank. According to Truman Capote's lover, Jack Dunphy, the cancer had started because Frank's spirit had been broken. Subordinating all his needs to Tennessee's, he had "lost himself in Tennessee's glare. He got sick on fame."[16] It is hard to be sure whether Tennessee believed he had robbed Frank of his identity. Certainly he felt remorseful, and did what he could for his dying lover, but Nicklaus was living at the house in Key West, and in the awkward ménage à trois Frank, who felt useless, mostly stayed in his room. Corsaro, who had gone there to work with Tennessee on the script for a revival of *Milk Train*, reports that while the playwright talked incessantly about Frank's illness, Frank talked about Tennessee's suicidal tendencies.[17]

When John Huston arrived in Key West to discuss the film he was going to make from *The Night of the Iguana*, Tennessee, exerting himself to be a good host, chartered a boat to take him out fishing. Nicklaus, who was un-comfortable on a boat, jumped off for a swim, but panicked and shouted for help. He was hauled aboard, and the captain watched disapprovingly while Tennessee gave Nicklaus the kiss of life.[18]

In July Tennessee took Frank and Nicklaus to Nantucket for a vacation, but Frank was weakening rapidly. Tennessee's tendency was to turn his back on illness, and for a time he lost touch with Frank, who, needing to be hospitalized, went into a charity ward. It was only when friends interceded for him that Tennessee intervened. In August Frank went into Memorial Hospital in New York, where Tennessee visited him every day, except in early September, when he left to work on the revival of *Milk Train*. It was to open in Abingdon, Virginia, before coming to Broadway. He returned to New York in time to be with Frank on the day he died, in the third week of September.[19]

It had been too easy to take Frank's presence for granted; nothing short of bereavement could have taught his lover to appreciate him fully. Writing a letter to the dead man, Tennessee said his sleep was full of dreams about suffocation, and, describing himself as too sick to know the truth, he thanked his dead friend for having told no lies. Tennessee was thinking of himself when, in *Milk Train*, he makes Chris say it is now Mrs. Goforth's habit to "go from room to room for no reason, and then . . . go back from room to room for no reason, and then . . . go *out* for no reason and come back *in* for no reason."

Tennessee did not begin to recover his sense of purpose until the autumn of 1964. "This morning," he wrote on 18 September, "for the first time in more months than I dare to remember, I woke up not wishing I hadn't."[20]

13

The Stoned Age

Talking to an interviewer in 1973, Tennessee said his professional decline had begun after *Iguana*. "I was broken as much by repeated failures in the theater as by Frank's death. Everything went wrong. My life—private and professional—and ultimately my mind broke." He could not write, he says, until he began taking shots of speed.[1] Certainly the quality of his life and work deteriorated in the early sixties, but at other times he refused to connect the change with Frank's death. When he said that all his plays after *Iguana* would be written for the off-Broadway theater, he was already signaling awareness of having exhausted a vein in his writing. It had been a remarkably rich one. Since 1944, when *The Glass Menagerie* made him famous, he had enjoyed a long run of success that could not have continued indefinitely. With his emotional insecurity and instability, and growing dependence on drugs, he did remarkably well to write so many good plays and achieve so much commercial success over such a long period.

A few days after Frank's funeral, Tennessee flew with Nicklaus to Mexico. John Huston was shooting *The Night of the Iguana* at Mismaloya, near Puerto Vallarta, with a cast that included Richard Burton, Ava Gardner, Deborah Kerr, and Sue Lyon. Huston had decided to shoot in black and white, arguing that the spectacular colors of sea, sky, jungle, flowers, birds, and beaches would distract from the story; afterward he regretted this decision.[2]

With director John Huston while The
Night of the Iguana *is being shot*

In one sequence a last-minute rewrite by Tennessee was extremely helpful. Unlike the play, the film includes a scene in which the fifteen-year-old
Charlotte comes into Shannon's hotel bedroom while he is shaving. Having
already had more than enough trouble with girls under the age of consent,
he gives reasons for not wanting to make love. Though he liked the
dialogue, Huston knew the scene was not coming to life, and when he asked
for help, Tennessee suggested the girl's abrupt entry should startle Shan-

non into knocking over the bottle of whiskey balanced on a bureau next to the shaving mirror. Explaining why he must not make love to her, he becomes so agitated that he paces about, not realizing he is cutting his feet on broken glass scattered over the floor. Impetuously, the girl kicks off her shoes and joins him, deliberately walking on the shards of glass.[3]

Before the end of October 1963 Tennessee was back in New York to work on the new production of *Milk Train*, starring Tallulah Bankhead and directed by Tony Richardson, who had taken over from Frank Corsaro. It opened on New Year's Day 1964, but even the presence of a star failed to make audiences interested in the misanthropic Mrs. Goforth, who trusts only dogs. The production closed after four performances.

Deeply depressed, Tennessee was neither going out nor answering the telephone. In March, after Nicklaus, no longer able to cope with his moods, moved out of the Key West house, Tennessee abandoned the apartment on East 65th Street and rented a penthouse on West 55th, where he lived reclusively, apart from paying daily visits to a new analyst. Thanks to all the movies made from his plays, he was better known and better off than ever before, but unhappier. Scarcely less important than his new analyst was his doctor, Max Jacobson, who treated Tennessee throughout most of the sixties. He gave his patients prescriptions for amphetamines and barbiturates as though he were a latter-day Lady Bountiful distributing alms. He taught them to give themselves intramuscular injections of a mixture he had made himself, and Tennessee carried capsules and a syringe around with him. Later the doctor was barred from practice, but Tennessee claimed to have done some of his best writing while under the influence of Dr. Jacobson's shots. "I had incredible vitality under them. And I got way ahead of myself as a writer, you know? And into another dimension. I never enjoyed writing like that."[4]

He went on drinking alcohol while taking Seconal, Nembutal, Luminal, Doriden, and phenobarbital. Suffering from insomnia, he depended on sleeping pills, and, though aware of his tendency to hypochondria, he consulted various doctors who prescribed remedies without checking on what other medicines and drugs he was currently taking.[5]

He went on swimming about twenty lengths of a pool every day despite palpitations and dizziness.[6] He also went on working regularly in the mornings, even if he afterward destroyed most of what he wrote. His next two plays were one acters that reflect his gloom. *The Mutilated* is about a friendship between two prostitutes. One has had one of her breasts removed, while the other has been serving a sentence for shoplifting. Without refusing to pity them, he portrays them as ridiculous.

The other play, *The Gnädiges Fräulein*, is courageously but unsuccessfully experimental. In *Milk Train* the deviation from realism was peripheral; in the new piece, writing under the influence of amphetamines, he made his most sustained attempt since *Camino Real* to write in a nonrealistic style. But he constructs the story around yet another return to the theme of the aging female performer who has fallen from grace. "Gnädiges Fräulein" is an untranslatably polite form of address to an unmarried woman, and the title is ironic. The eponymous heroine has sunk too low to expect politeness from anyone.

She was once a singer and cabaret artiste who performed with her lover, a Viennese dandy, in front of elite European audiences. Now, staying at a boardinghouse in a dormitory she shares with several other down-and-outers, she lives on fish she has to catch herself, battling with ferocious "cocaloony" birds—they were pelicans until the final draft. She has lost an eye in the struggle, and proceeds to lose the other during the course of the action.

The other main characters are the landlady, Molly, and the gossip columnist of the local paper, Polly. These two are like garrulous female clowns, and there is some attempt at social satire, Cocaloony Key being made to resemble Key West, but Tennessee fails to involve the audience's emotional interest in any of the characters.

The two one-act plays were scheduled for production in May 1965, but a few days before rehearsals were due to start, the producer, Charles Bowden, had still not succeeded in raising the $150,000 that was needed. "The dilemma is very hard on my nerves," Tennessee wrote, "which were already close to the point of collapse."[7] Unable to bear living alone any longer, he employed a paid companion, William Glavin. But he saw few of his friends, partly because he was, as he knew, liable to embarrass them by falling over. According to Maureen Stapleton, "the pill situation was so bad that we'd enter a restaurant and before Tenn had had even one drink, he'd fall down. After a while he was always falling down, and it wasn't alcohol—it was the pills and the shots."[8] In July he moved with Glavin to a thirty-third floor apartment on West 72nd Street.

*With Margaret Leighton before Broadway
opening of* Slapstick Tragedy

It was not until the end of 1965 that Bowden could finally go ahead with the two one-act plays, producing them under the title *Slapstick Tragedy*. They went into rehearsal in January 1966 with Margaret Leighton as the Gnädiges Fräulein and Trinket Dugan as the mutilated prostitute. Tennessee was not expecting the plays to succeed. "I don't think they'll work," he said.[9] "I must continue to dare to fail. That is my life."[10] This was realistic. One critic, Whitney Boulton, accused him of "stealing from himself." "Mr. Williams is turning old ground and reworking old characters."[11] Harold Clurman was less unsympathetic. He wrote that the slapstick of *The Mutilated* "consists of deliberate bitchery." He found *The Gnädiges Fräulein* more interesting, though he could not bring himself to smile at it. "I was too conscious that its author was in pain."[12]

Tennessee's pain did not distract him from what was going on in Vietnam. The war provoked one of his rare political statements. In an insert prepared for the program he denounced it as "incredibly cruel": "believe me, nothing that will be won out of this war will be worth the life of a single man who died in it."[13]

He was working at the beginning of 1966 on a movie treatment of *Milk Train*. Though Audrey Wood was no longer allowed to befriend him, she still looked after him well financially. The film deal brought him $150,000 for the rights and for writing the screenplay, plus $20,000 as coproducer. But nothing could save him from the depression that he dramatized in *I Can't Imagine Tomorrow*, a dialogue in which the two characters, a woman and a man, are given no other names than One and Two. Dividing his sense of isolation between them, Williams depicted two depressed characters, neither of whom has any contact except with the other. Neither can look forward to anything but death, and they pass the time by watching television and playing games. In one of these they write down whatever comes into their heads. Two reads out a sentence One has written: "Time lives in the world with us and has a big broom and is sweeping us out of the way, whether we face it or not."

Williams developed the idea in *The Two-Character Play*, making the two characters into brother and sister. The play, as he confessed on the title page, was written "from the state of lunacy. . . . It is the story of the last six or seven years of the 1960s. The play is about disorientation. These people are as lost as I am. They are two sides of one person." The brother and sister are members of a touring company. They arrive in a theater to find that all the other actors have defected. With only part of the set, they try to put on a play which overlaps with their own lives.

Williams's plays had pushed his own life onto the stage, sometimes interwoven with his sister's. Throughout his adult life he had been aware of having a strongly feminine side to his nature and had felt in danger of disintegrating. With none of his lovers had he achieved such an intense rapport as he had in adolescence with Rose, and, having lost her, he interiorized his image of her, viewing her as part of himself. Sometimes this identification took bizarre forms. A journalist friend, Dotson Rader, recalls a number of evenings when he helped Tennessee to pick up young men in bars. On some of these evenings, Tennessee, wearing a wig, would sit in the darkest part of the bar saying he was Rose. If recognized, he would deny that he was Tennessee Williams: "I'm Miss Rose. My brother Tom died many years ago."[14] *The Two-Character Play* can be read as an attempt to do for himself what neither of his psychoanalysts had been able to do for him. He was trying to recover the goodness, the innocence, the purity he had lost, and he still tended to identify the loss with the loss of Rose. At one stage, according to

Glavin, he spoke about getting himself admitted to Stony Lodge as a patient to be reunited with her. His thinking on this subject was extremely confused, and the confusion seeps into his late plays. After the premiere of *The Two-Character Play* one critic wrote: "It would need a psychoanalyst—and preferably Tennessee Williams's own—to offer a rational interpretation of the enigmas that litter the stage like pieces of an elaborate jigsaw."[15]

To some extent his writing was therapeutic, but he also regarded it as a justification for raising the potency of the sedatives he took to steady his nerves after an excited stint of working and to get enough sleep overnight to feel capable of working in the morning. He was using Doriden, a hypnotic drug usually prescribed in doses of 250 milligrams once or twice daily; by 1966 his daily intake was four or five grams. It induced hallucinations, slurred his speech, and made him walk unsteadily, exacerbating both his persecution complex and his irritability. At the same time, it increased his need for stimulants. Like so many addicts, he was trapped in a spiral of increasing need. The permissive Dr. Jacobson supplied him with prescriptions, and whenever he needed extra supplies, several other doctors were glad to oblige.

At the beginning of 1967 he went to the Virgin Islands with Glavin and worked on the screenplay for *Milk Train* and on a new play based on his story "The Kingdom of Earth," which had been started in 1942 and published in 1954. It was written in the first person from the viewpoint of a crude farm worker called Chicken, born illegitimate. Dying of tuberculosis, his more sensitive half brother, Lot, who owns the farm they work, has just married a busty, simpleminded girl. Nervous he will be cheated of the farm he had expected to inherit on his half brother's death, Chicken appropriates the girl. Though fairly brutal, the story is straightforward, economical, and effective; like "Man Bring This up Road," it loses much of its force when dramatized by a writer who could not stop himself from vulgarizing his material as he introduced unnecessary complications. In the play Myrtle is a showgirl no longer able to get jobs, while Lot is a transvestite, who eventually dies in his mother's white dress, and the farm is liable to be flooded so rapidly that they may not even escape with their lives. The flood—and perhaps some elements in the original story—derive from D. H. Lawrence's "The Virgin and the Gipsy." Williams's story never overstresses the contrast between the two half brothers, and they never seem stereotypes, but in the play they are as schematically and as self-consciously

Lynn Redgrave and James Coburn star in
Last of the Mobile Hot Shots (Blood Kin
in Europe), film version of Kingdom of
Earth *(1970)*

contrasted as the spiritual Alma and the sensual John in *Summer and Smoke*.
Reading the story, no one would have been reminded by Lot of Alma or
Blanche DuBois, but the play makes him take a place in the long line of Tennessee Williams characters who try vainly to plant elegance and refinement
in soil that is too coarse.

In the summer of 1967, hearing that the producer David Merrick had
read the one-act version of *Kingdom of Earth* in *Esquire* and wanted to stage a
full-length version, Tennessee was uncertain whether he had enough
strength to do the work. In July he and Glavin were in Spain, where the
main source of friction was Tennessee's paranoid suspicion that Glavin was
stealing or hiding his drugs. Tennessee insisted on coming back to New
York for new supplies, but they left again for Rome, where he met Joseph
Losey, who was directing the movie version of *Milk Train*, starring Richard
Burton, Elizabeth Taylor, and Noël Coward, and they met again in Sardi-
nia, where the movie was being shot. According to Losey, Tennessee was
capable only of drinking, swimming, and sleeping. "He was clearly in no
condition to do any rewriting for us. He left me to cut the script as best I
could."[16]

*With Richard Burton and Elizabeth Taylor
during the filming of* Boom! *(film version
of* The Milk Train Doesn't Stop Here
Anymore*)*

Tennessee and Glavin went back to New York in late August, but after hearing that Carson McCullers was dying, they left for Key West. She died on 29 September. Early in December Tennessee went to London with Audrey Wood for the world premiere of *The Two-Character Play* at the Hampstead Theatre Club. In the hotel he kept repeating "I want to die," to which she retorted: "I'm terribly sorry, you may want to die, my friend, but God is not ready for you. God is not strong enough to take you."[17] This gave him the idea for a speech he added to the one-act play *I Can't Imagine Tomorrow* before it was premiered on television in 1970. Partially derived from the story of the gatekeeper in Kafka's *The Trial*, the speech contains a story about a little man who is refused entry to the house of death by a guard who tells him he is too early. He must go back down the mountain and return in twenty years.

Kingdom of Earth opened during February 1968 in Philadelphia, directed by José Quintero, who described Tennessee as "very nervous": "His nerves would provoke this laugh that was like a hyena's—sometimes at the worst possible moments. He would be riding the action of the play, and would become more and more nervous as it developed. When the action neared the crisis he would let out one of his laughs, and, of course, it was most disconcerting."[18] Tennessee was incapable of disguising his state of mind, and this helped to demoralize the actors. The production, which opened on 27 March, had a Broadway run of less than a month.

His behavior became increasingly unpredictable, and in June he told Glavin they must give up their apartment on West 72nd Street. After they had moved into the St. Moritz Hotel on Central Park South, Tennessee launched a loud verbal onslaught against Glavin in a Third Avenue restaurant on 22 June, accusing him of theft and disloyalty. While the humiliated Glavin was waiting for him outside the restaurant, Tennessee asked for paper and wrote to Dakin, saying that if he suddenly met a violent death, it should not be mistaken for suicide. "I am not happy, it is true, in a net of con men." Finding no one in the apartment, and unable to contact his brother, Dakin told the police Tennessee was missing, and the news found its way into the *New York Times*.[19]

While Tennessee was in London during the summer of 1968, Maria Britneva arranged for him to see the nerve specialist who had looked after her mother. In the waiting room Tennessee was "running up and down the room like a lion in a cage," and to stop him from bursting into the doctor's examining room Maria had to sit with the back of her chair against the door.[20]

At the beginning of 1969, alerted by Audrey Wood to the precariousness of his brother's life, Dakin arrived in Key West. Tennessee could neither talk coherently nor walk without stumbling. His vision was blurred and he was sleeping for periods of up to twenty-four hours. Dakin, who had been converted to Catholicism while doing his military service, had no difficulty in persuading Tennessee to meet a priest, and a Jesuit from a Key West church, Father Joseph LeRoy, paid several visits to the house. On 10 January, five days after Dakin's first meeting with the priest, Tennessee, who had already been baptized into the Episcopal church, was baptized in the Church of St. Mary Star of the Sea, and later in the month he flew to Rome, where he met Pedro Arrupe, head of the Jesuits. Later on Tennessee said he had never taken his conversion seriously. He found the church's rituals beautiful, and its doctrines ridiculous.

In February, ill with flu, he spent almost a week in a Miami hospital. After being discharged in time for the New York rehearsals of his one act play *In the Bar of a Tokyo Hotel*, he took an overdose of sleeping pills before a party given by Maureen Stapleton, but he told her when he arrived, and she immediately gave him mustard diluted in hot water, which made him throw up the pills.

The one-act play *In the Bar of a Tokyo Hotel* was scheduled for an April opening at the Eastside Playhouse, directed by Herbert Machiz, and when Machiz was fired, Tennessee took over as director. According to Anne Meacham, who played the leading part, "He stumbled a lot that April during rehearsals," but was mostly lucid when directing her and Donald Madden, who was playing opposite her. Glavin confirms that he was "sensitive and beautiful and encouraging with them," though it seemed almost miraculous that he could regain so much of his self-control.[21] He actually enjoyed taking the actors into his confidence about the agonizing uncertainty behind the play. In the same way that he had tried, while writing it, to validate the life behind his art, he tried while directing it to dramatize his experience in a way that would be helpful to the actors. The play, he told them, was about the particularly humiliating doom of the artist. He has made, at the beginning of his career, an almost total commitment of himself to his work. As Mark truthfully says, the intensity of the work, the unremitting challenges and demands it makes to him and of him (in most cases daily), leaves so little of him after working hours that simple, comfortable being is impossible for him. As death approaches he "hasn't the comfort of feeling with any conviction that any of his work has had any essential value."[22] Tennessee's life had been devoid neither of adventure nor sensual pleasure. Though he had worked extremely hard, there had been nothing ascetic or self-denying about his vocation, but in his drugged and confused state, he felt as if he had let his writing sap his capacity for living.

The first night was postponed several times, and there were twenty-two previews before the play opened on 11 May. The consensus of reviews was strongly unfavorable. In the *New York Times* Clive Barnes wrote: "Mr. Williams has perhaps never been over-reluctant to show the world his wounds—but in this new play he seems to be doing nothing else. The play repelled me with its self-pity as much as it fascinated me with the author's occasional resurgences of skill. . . . But the philosophic content of the play . . . is a cotton puffball of commonplace."[23]

Afterward Tennessee went to St. Louis, but it was harder than ever for him to carry on a conversation with his mother, who was now eighty-four, and he made up his mind to visit Japan for a production of *Streetcar* at the

Bungakuza Theatre. Glavin was ill, but Anne Meacham volunteered to accompany Tennessee, who was in no state to travel alone. They arrived in Tokyo on 21 June, but it was hard for her to cope with his moods and demands. It was illegal to import drugs, and at the hotel, where he was injecting himself with amphetamines, as well as taking both Seconal and Doriden, she was nervous the police would be called in. She arranged for them to be moved to a rented house, where he overtaxed her patience, accusing her of stealing drugs and syringes.

By mid-July he was back in New York, and soon left for Key West with Glavin. More restless than ever, Tennessee wanted to keep on the move. By the end of the month they were in a San Francisco hotel, where he talked about his intention of moving into Stony Lodge with Rose. Glavin was sufficiently alarmed about his condition to contact Dakin, who arrived but could do nothing to help. Feeling persecuted by fellow guests at the hotel, Tennessee behaved so badly that he and Glavin were asked to leave. In mid-August they returned to New York.

In September they went briefly to New Orleans, where they met Pancho, who had settled into steady respectability, and they went on to Key West. According to a local journalist, Tennessee was paranoid in his fear that enemies were planning to break into the house and kill him. One day he had an accident at home when builders were constructing a new kitchen for him and the electric stove was in the patio. Stumbling around with a pan he wanted to heat on the stove, he somehow sat down on it, getting third-degree burns on his bottom. A friend telephoned Dakin, who seized the opportunity of persuading his hypochondriacal brother he should go into Barnes Hospital in St. Louis. Interned in the mental ward, he was treated like a prisoner and, abruptly deprived of drugs, he suffered chronic withdrawal symptoms and—according to him—two heart attacks. He never forgave Dakin, although, according to Maureen Stapleton, the intervention had saved Tennessee's life.[24] By the beginning of December he was back in Key West, looking healthier and claiming he was taking only one drink a day plus a few pills.

14

Everyone Else
Is an Audience

By the beginning of 1970 Truman Capote had already written the scurrilous portrait of Tennessee that appears in the unfinished novel *Answered Prayers*. The book was published posthumously in 1986, but excerpts, including the passage about Tennessee, appeared in *Esquire* during 1975 and 1976. Though Tennessee's name is never mentioned, Mr. Wallace is described as having been "the most acclaimed American playwright" and having deteriorated into "a chunky, paunchy, booze-puffed runt with a play moustache glued above laconic lips." He wears horn-rimmed glasses, carries pencils in his vest pocket, accumulates trembling lengths of ash on his cigar, and drinks undiluted Scotch from a glass stained with toothpaste.

The narrator, Jones, who is in his mid-thirties, works for an agency that provides "service"—meaning call girls and boys. When, visiting Wallace's hotel, he is sexually assaulted by the playwright's black English bulldog, Mr. Wallace indulgently pulls it away, talking "in a voice jingling with gin-slurred giggles." For the past two days he has been in no state to walk his dog. There are piles of dog shit and puddles of piss in the hotel room, which is littered with "messy laundry." Speaking with a strong Southern accent in a "way-down-yonder voice mushy as sweet potato pie," the writer tries to use his charm on the younger man, saying he is like a Dostoevsky character. "You're one of his people. Insulted and injured. Me too; that's why I feel safe with you."

Naked in the double bed, Jones is uncertain, when he feels his navel signed with hot ash, whether the pain was inflicted deliberately. Mr. Wallace says he is liable to die suddenly. "And if I do, it won't be a natural death. . . . Promise me you'll write to *The Times* and tell them it was murder." In any case, he says, he is dying of cancer. Jones inquires what kind of cancer, and the answer is: "Blood. Throat. Lungs. Tongue. Stomach. Brain. Asshole." It started seven years ago, he says, when the critics turned against him. "They're killing me out of envy and ignorance. And without shame or remorse."

"Here's a dumpy little guy," Jones decides, "with a dramatic mind, who, like one of his own adrift heroines, seeks attention and sympathy by serving up half-believed lies to total strangers. Strangers because he has no friends, and he has no friends because the only people he pities are his own characters and himself—everyone else is an audience."[1] Himself an ex-friend—and no other enemies are more dangerous than ex-friends—Capote was writing with merciless accuracy, aiming his satirical darts at Tennessee's most repulsive traits and exposing the squalid messiness of his daily life in luxury hotels. Mr. Wallace is a man who has lost control over his own daily routine and, having nothing else to live for, uses his wealth to indulge his persecution complex, his egocentricity, his self-pity, and his streak of cruelty.

The prodigious energy that had once been channeled into writing was being wastefully and self-destructively diffused. When Tennessee told Gore Vidal he had slept through the sixties, Vidal, whose nickname for him was "Bird," reassured him that he had not missed a thing. "But if you missed the sixties, Bird, God knows what you're going to do with the seventies."[2] At the beginning of the new decade, the fifty-eight-year-old playwright—unlike Wallace—did have one purpose in life. He was determined to overcome the critics' resistance and make the comeback that had eluded him during the sixties. Success must still be within reach. "I know it will happen again," he said.[3]

He gave many—too many—self-indulgent and uninhibited interviews, checking himself only occasionally to say he was talking too intimately. In one of these he admitted to having been "around the bend," and situated his conversion to Catholicism in his period of madness, though he claimed to believe in God. "Every time I have a play opening I will go into a room alone and kneel down and pray, and sometimes it's just a bathroom and I'll kneel down by the bathtub." Sometimes he would kneel down in a church, but would always choose a time when the church was empty.[4]

By mid-March 1970 he was taking better care of himself, rationing himself to occasional glasses of wine and a single daily glass of hard liquor, taken before dinner. "A person with my tension has to have something to keep him in his skin but must avoid things that may blow him out of his skull." He was swimming regularly and still taking no pills, except for an antidepressant, Sinequan, that was prescribed by his New York doctor.[5]

He still hated being alone and still needed plenty of sex, but little emotion was involved in casual liaisons: he was attracted to his lovers by their looks and youth, while they responded to his fame and money. He was still neurotically suspicious, and, unable to trust Glavin, Tennessee fired him. The ensuing succession of paid companions caused a great deal of trouble. He paid them two or three hundred dollars a week, and, when he fired them, he often had to continue the payment. The first of them to be dismissed, Harry O'Lowe, was paid three hundred dollars a week to stay out of Key West.[6]

In September a mysterious lump developed under Tennessee's left nipple, "so that the left side of my torso, from the waist up, is rather like a nymphette's."[7] His doctors advised him not to make the trip he was planning to the Far East with his friend Oliver Evans, but he refused to be deterred. In Bangkok, where he stayed at the Oriental Hotel in a suite once occupied by Noël Coward, he dissolved some opium in his tea, and within half an hour found he could not stand up. He went on vomiting all day. Later he and Evans moved to the Amarin Hotel, where he reported that "practically the whole staff is hustling. All in all, this is just about the most decadent place I have ever been and I mean including Tangiers." They went on to Hong Kong, and sailed back on the *President Wilson*, leaving on 10 December and putting in at Honolulu on Christmas Eve. Back in Key West he felt ill. In mid-January 1971 he reported that he was "coughing all night like Frankie" and feeling indifferent to whether he lived or died.[8]

When George Keathley offered to stage *Out Cry*, the revised version of *The Two-Character Play*, in Chicago, Tennessee, after moving into a hotel there, slipped back into his twenty-four-hour dependence on drugs. He had gone on using Sinequan, but had been washing it down with a fairly strong martini,[9] and by July, when he quarreled with Audrey Wood, he was also injecting himself with Ritalin (the brand name for methylphenidate hydrochloride) and using 100 milligrams of Nembutal when he needed to sleep.

In the dressing room of the leading lady, Eileen Herlie, Keathley enraged Tennessee after a preview by suggesting an alteration to a line of dialogue, and when Audrey Wood intervened, trying to persuade Tennessee to consider the suggestion, he rounded on her. According to Maria Britneva, who was there, "He shouted abuse and screamed hysterically at her; he accused her of stifling his work and wanting him not to succeed. He said that she wanted him to die and that he was going to outlive her. And then he fired her. Audrey was extremely dignified but seemed to crumple physically." Maria tried to stop the flow of abuse, "but he was like a madman."[10] As Audrey walked out of the dressing room, she heard him say: "That bitch! I'm glad I'm through with her!"[11] Later in the year she saw him approaching in a New York restaurant. She held out her hand, but myopically uncertain who he was, withdrew it. Rejected, he stalked off, and they never spoke again, though he stayed with the agency. She arranged for a younger agent, Bill Barnes, to look after him, and there would soon be work for Barnes to do.

In rewriting *The Two-Character Play* Tennessee had been more compulsive and persistent than with any play since *Night of the Iguana*. When he changed the title of *The Two-Character Play* to *Out Cry*, he explained: "It fits so perfectly. I had to *cry out*, and I did. It's the only possible title. . . . It's a history of what I went through in the Sixties transmuted into the predicament of a brother and a sister. . . . I think *Out Cry* is my most beautiful play since *Streetcar*, and I've never stopped working on it."[12] *Out Cry* opened on 8 July, and the reviewer in the *Chicago Tribune*, William Leonard, summed it up by taking a phrase from the dialogue—"ponderously symbolic undrama."[13]

After leaving Chicago Tennessee felt unsettled. He left for Paris to see *Sweet Bird of Youth*, translated by Françoise Sagan with Edwige Feuillère as Alexandra del Lago. Sagan had reserved a room for him in a hotel overlooking the Père Lachaise cemetery, but, taking this to be an unsavory joke about his imminent death, he insisted on moving to another hotel.[14]

By the end of November he had been to Key West, New Orleans, and Houston, where *Camino Real* was revived at the Alley Theatre, but he arrived drunk at the opening night and, according to one of the actors, was "practically carried backstage."[15] In an attempt to stop himself from shut-

The house at 1014 Dumaine Street, New Orleans

tling about so much from place to place he bought a house in the French Quarter of New Orleans. Located at 1014 Dumaine Street, it still had slave quarters in the back garden. The house was divided into two apartments, and he rented one out, installing a housekeeper to manage both. He kept the upper apartment, which had a beautiful balcony, for himself. There were three rooms, plus a kitchen and a bathroom. There was a patio with a fish pond and a small swimming pool, which was never used, being in need of repair.[16]

After the failure of *Out Cry* he set his hopes on the expanded version of another one-act play, *Confessional*, which he called *Small Craft Warnings*.

The phrase occurs on the second page of his memoirs. During his first infatuation with the theater, he says, he had known other young artists, but each had disregarded "the small craft warnings in the face of which we were continually sailing . . . each with his crew of one, himself that crew and its captain. We were sailing along in our separate small crafts but we were in sight of each other and sometimes in touch, I mean like huddling in the same inlet of the rocky, storm-ridden shoreline, and this gave us a warm sense of community." Though he said it would be his last play, he believed that "a remnant of life" could save him from "a sinking into shadow and eclipse of so much of everything that has made my life meaningful to me."[17] One character, Quentin, is used as a mouthpiece for a confessional speech:

There's a coarseness, a deadening coarseness, in the experience of most homosexuals. The experiences are quick, and hard, and brutal, and the pattern of them is practically unchanging. Their act of love is like the jabbing of a hypodermic needle to which they're addicted but which is more and more empty of real interest and surprise. This lack of variation and surprise in their . . . "love life" . . . spreads into other areas of . . . "sensibility?" . . . Yes, once, quite a long while ago, I was often startled by the sense of being alive, of being *myself, living!* Present on earth, in the flesh, yes, for some completely mysterious reason, a single, separate, intensely conscious being, *myself: living!*

He has lost his capacity for being surprised, and so had Tennessee. "Quentin's long speech," he said, "was the very *heart* of my life."[18]

Since watching the failure of what he had claimed to be his most beautiful play since *Streetcar*, it was harder to be ambitious. Again and again he settled for premieres in obscure theaters. That he was unhappy with the venue of *Small Craft Warnings* is clear from an April 1972 letter to the producers: "I know it's no use suggesting that the show be transferred to a theater further uptown or in a section less associated in the public mind with the hazards of the ghetto."[19] But as he had said in a 1971 letter, what mattered to him most was the feeling that he was still active in the theater, "and just staying active is sufficient for my purposes. I don't need more than the assurance that I am not prematurely counted out as an active playwright.—Like swimming and love, it's all that keeps me going."[20]

Small Craft Warnings was scheduled to open on 2 April 1972 at the Truck and Warehouse Theatre, directed by William Hunt. The cast included a transvestite actor, Candy Darling, who introduced Tennessee to Paul Morrissey, a friend of Andy Warhol's. When Hunt withdrew from the production after a quarrel, Tennessee took charge of rehearsals until Richard Altman arrived to replace Hunt. The production was successful enough to move uptown to the New Theater, where it opened on 6 June, and Clive Barnes wrote in the *New York Times*: "I suspect it may survive better than some of the much-touted productions of his salad years."[21]

In the opening performances Tennessee made his debut as an actor, playing the drunken doctor. The original actor had been allowed to leave town for four days' work on a movie, and, hearing that the stage manager was going to stand in for him, Tennessee decided to play the part himself. "I guess I have to admit that I am a ham and that I loved it." After the curtain came down he took part in a question-and-answer session with the audience.[22]

After five performances, the actor returned to his role, but later left again, and the stage manager took over. He was, according to Tennessee, "a nice Mississippi fag but with such a lisp that he sounds like a river boat's coming into the landing." Seizing the chance to enjoy himself and to boost business at the box office, Tennessee again stepped in. Partly because of the Ritalin he was injecting into himself, he was an unreliable performer, fluffing lines and self-indulgently deviating from the script to express his anger. One night he threw a glass and his spectacles into the audience. "Luckily a friend seated in the front row retrieved the glasses." In another fit of rage he sidetracked into an attack on the management, making the doctor say: "A synonym for a manager in the theatre . . . is a con-man — and all playwrights are shits with their back to the wall."[23] The other actors were appalled and embarrassed at each of his ad-libs, and he behaved especially badly just before the play closed to make way for a Noël Coward revue. When the doctor, returning from performing an abortion, was asked how it had gone, Tennessee answered: "Not as bad as it will go at the New Theater next week if they bring in Nelly Coward."[24]

In August he accepted an invitation to be an honorary juror at the Venice Film Festival. According to Morrissey, who was in Venice with Tennessee and afterward invited him to Montauk, he "simply could not be left alone for any period of time that summer or in the fall, back in New York. He depended entirely on others for advice — not only about his plays, but about all the practical details of everyday life."[25] As Tennessee knew, though, people who seemed to like him often had ulterior motives for seeking out his company. "Age bothers me only in this area; at my age, one never knows whether one is being used as an easy mark or if there is a true response."[26] But in New York he became sexually involved with a young writer, Robert Carroll, who had grown up in an impoverished home, the ninth child of a Virginia coal miner, and had fought in Vietnam.[27]

Unable either to embark on a major new project or to give up the habit of writing every day, Tennessee worked on his memoirs and kept making changes to *Out Cry*. The memoirs had been commissioned by Doubleday, and he saw an opportunity to make "a cool million." It was enjoyable to put his recollections together, hitting out at people who had—in his view—let him down, and at the end of July he said he was "knocking out" an average of sixteen pages a day.[28] Nor was it only in letters to friends that he talked disparagingly about the book he was writing. "I want to admit to you," he tells the reader, "that I undertook this memoir for mercenary reasons," and, disingenuously, he claims that this is "the first piece of work, in the line of writing, that I have undertaken for material profit."[29]

He wrote carelessly, depending on his unreliable memory instead of consulting newspaper files, letters, documents, and other people's memories of the same events. The only research he apparently did was to reread interviews he had given. This made him slip inadvertently into the same superficiality and sensationalism that had annoyed him on his first reading of the interviews. He had often complained that journalists had taken advantage of him, though he talked in such an unguarded way that they could take advantage merely by selecting from what he had said. Now, by selecting from their selections, he gave his literary imprimatur to both his own verbal exaggerations and the journalists' distortions.

He also writes maliciously about some of his most devoted and most vulnerable friends, such as Jo Healy, who could hardly fail to recognize herself in the portrait of Miss Nameless, an "Irish biddy, deep in her cups and mean as a rattler." She begins "to show her bitch colors" at a party when he and a friend make fun of her. "Of course, when the evening was over, I began to feel a bit sorry for Nameless. She is so tough in her loneliness, her spinsterhood, and her archaic 'principles,' which are as hypocritical as 'principles' of her vintage could possibly be." Much later, after she had read this, Jo Healy wrote to a friend: "This sadness has been the only situation in my entire life when I have felt so shamed and defiled that I have been unable to discuss it with any member of my family or close friends."[30]

One of the main incentives for revising *Out Cry* was that Paul Scofield had expressed interest in playing Felice, the brother. At first Tennessee did his utmost to make the British actor commit himself, but instead of persisting, he gave in to an opportunistic argument from his new agent, Bill Barnes: why not give the part to his client Michael York, who had just played the Christopher Isherwood part in the movie *Cabaret?* When an agent represents both playwrights and actors, he is constantly under temptation to put packages together in this way, but if the fifty-year-old Scofield was the right age for the part, it was obvious that the thirty-year-old York was too young, and, unlike Maureen Stapleton, he was not an actor who could convincingly play older parts.[31] He grew a beard, but this did not help, and he shaved it off after the first preview in New York on 28 February 1973.

Peter Glenville directed, with Cara Duff-MacCormick as the sister, Clare. Rehearsals began in New York in the middle of December 1972. On 5 January 1973, when the play had its first run-through, Tennessee was shocked that Michael York and Cara Duff-MacCormick touched each other so much. His relationship with Rose, he told them, had been much less physical, but by the end of the rehearsal period he was willing to accept the touching and the kissing. The play contains a number of abusive references to the audiences. It was obvious to Peter Glenville that several of these passages might provoke hostile reactions, and before the pre-Broadway tour opened on 18 January at the Shubert Theater in New Haven, he cut several of these, including "Do they seem human? . . . No." But he kept: "It sounds like a house of furious unfed apes." In Philadelphia, at the matinee on 27 January, someone applauded the dangerous line "Perhaps the audience demanded their money back."

At the end of the evening performance on 1 February, when a member of the audience said he must be mad to have come, Tennessee retorted: "Yes, you are. Go look at yourself in the mirror." But in general there was little hostility from the audience, and after the subscription-based matinees for students there was a symposium at which they were invited to question Tennessee and the two actors about the play. Tennessee explained that he had written it at a time when he did not know where he was, and that Felice and Clare represented conflicting elements in his own ego, masculine and feminine, positive and negative, active and passive.[32]

After the play was staged in Washington at the Kennedy Center on 5 February, newspaper reviewers—unlike the critics who reviewed it on television—were friendly, and business at the box office improved, averaging $45,000 a week. The play opened on Broadway on 1 March. In his *New York Times* review Clive Barnes called it a "very brave and very difficult play." Some people, he said, would scoff, while others would find it stimulating.[33] The scoffers prevailed, and the production closed after only twelve performances.

Tennessee was having such an unhappy time in the theater that he decided to write a play for television. *Stopped Rocking* (originally titled *A Second Epiphany*) was written for Maureen Stapleton, and he willingly made revisions when producers and broadcasting executives asked for them, but the project was abandoned.

The house in New Orleans failed to cure his restlessness. He flew to Los Angeles for a "silver anniversary" production of *Streetcar*, and, with Robert Carroll as his traveling companion, booked a flight to Honolulu and a passage on a cargo-passenger ship to Hong Kong, leaving on 28 March. He liked the idea of a sea voyage, but not the reality. The passengers, he complained, were "all over eighty—crones, my dear," the food was foul—a scalding curry as the main course at each meal, "served by detestable East Indians. We have been virtually immured in our cubby-hole cabin." They disembarked at Yokohama, stayed one night, and flew to Hong Kong, where they took rooms at the President Hotel, making plans about how to continue their travels. Carroll, who was working on a novel called *Old Children*, was in favor of finding a cottage where they could both write. He could finish his novel while Tennessee worked on his memoirs. So long as the cottage had a swimming pool, Tennessee said, he was quite agreeable, and, after flying to Bangkok, they spent a day looking at small houses in Pattaya, but Tennessee disliked everything they viewed. "I can't settle down even for a month in a steaming hot hell-hole like Pattaya in the hottest season of the year in an ugly bungalow." They were at such different stages of their lives and careers that their needs were probably incompatible: the life-style Carroll wanted was one Tennessee could no longer bear. He accused Carroll of finding him intolerable. "I find you repulsive," Carroll answered, and Tennessee retorted: "Not as repulsive as you'll be a year from now."[34]

They left Thailand in mid-April, flying to Istanbul, where they had a double bedroom overlooking the Bosphorus—"sea fog but ships and birds faintly visible through it." Next they flew to Rome, which Tennessee still loved, "despite the sadness of the change that I find there lately: the suffocating traffic, the noise, the strikes, the up-tightness of the Romans."[35]

When they got back to the States, they agreed to separate. Carroll would fly to San Francisco, and Tennessee, who wanted to be in New York for the opening of a new *Streetcar* with Rosemary Harris as Blanche, would afterward go on alone to Key West. Believing the liaison was ending, he felt both unhappy and relieved. "You'll doubt my word for this," he wrote to Maria Britneva, who was now married to Lord St. Just, "but it was the only one since Frank that I cared about." Maria had never liked Carroll, whom she nicknamed the Enfant Terrible. She had expected the affair to bring Tennessee more pain than pleasure.

At the end of April 1973, hearing Edwina was ill, Tennessee went to St. Louis. She was refusing to eat—"probably thinks the food's poisoned: begs me to take her to the south of France. She puts up a wonderful front. Very brave."[36] He stayed with her for a week before returning to Key West and going on to New York, where he stayed at the Elysée Hotel. He called it the Hotel Easy Lay and took to staying there regularly: a large suite on the twelfth floor was permanently reserved for him. He was invited to Moscow for a world congress of writers. Bill Barnes thought he should take a house on Long Island for the summer. His own inclination was to take a cure in Aix-en-Provence.

But when Carroll reappeared in New York, the affair resumed, though he went on alternating between "great sweetness . . . and down-right beastliness of behavior which makes it all but impossible for me to go out with him in public. He goes out of his way to be rude to everyone." But Tennessee, willing to put up with any amount of bad behavior, and wanting Carroll to go on holiday with him again, gave him the choice between Tangier and Positano. He chose Positano, but said, after they arrived, that he hated the place, and he took every opportunity to humiliate Tennessee. When they were invited to the villa where Franco Zeffirelli was staying, Carroll lay back chain-smoking and ignoring everyone. On other occasions he told people that he was Tennessee's "hired companion," and boasted about his past as a street hustler in New York. By the end of May Tennessee was thinking of sending him back to New York. Instead, he rented a large apartment in the Palazzo Murat, and they moved in on 31 May. The day before they moved, Carroll kept threatening to kill himself and Tennessee said: "Oh, you mustn't do that, it would please too many people."

In June Tennessee made a serious attempt to get rid of him, giving him money and a ticket to New York. Another good-looking young companion,

Tom Field, arrived from England, but Carroll, wanting to embarrass Tennessee, stayed in Positano.[37]

In July Tennessee took Field to Tangier for two weeks and saw Paul Bowles, who was withdrawn and untalkative. Tennessee put this down to the kef Bowles was smoking. Unlike Carroll, Field did not throw tantrums, but he turned out to be almost equally unsatisfactory as a companion: he kept saying how much he missed his mother and his roommates. He was in poor health. He had undergone an operation the previous year for what may have been Hodgkin's disease, a malignant condition in the lymph nodes, which protect the body from infection, and he was now vulnerable to any passing virus. When Tennessee paid over a thousand dollars to rent a villa on the New Mountain, it looked as though Field would be too ill to help him manage it or even to drive the rented car.[38]

In Tangier Tennessee worked on a new stage play, *The Red Devil Battery Sign*, which was written on the assumption that he could establish a correspondence between his personal crisis and the political situation. All fiction depends to some extent on notching private preoccupations into a narrative that has a public relevance. Though they came directly from his family experience, the relationships in *The Glass Menagerie* seemed to have a bearing on everyone else's family experience, and in all his best plays Williams had succeeded in creating a resonance that involved the audience's emotions. To carry on writing for the theater, he needed to believe this gift had not deserted him, but his late plays seem self-indulgent because he was no longer capable of grafting the confessional elements onto characters and stories that came vigorously to life.

The Red Devil Battery Sign was a promising title. As he knew, his paranoid hysteria derived largely from his use of drugs, especially Seconal, which was often called "red devil," while a battery with the same name was advertised with a flashing neon sign. Though there was a genuine connection between the collapse of American optimism in the fifties and the desperation he shared with so many of his friends, and though in *Streetcar* interpolating street life into the action had helped to give the desperation of the characters a social dimension, the characters and the plot of *The Red Devil Battery Sign* are too weak to bear such a heavy loading. The Woman Downtown is yet another reincarnation of the faded aristocratic belle, while the rhetoric is dangerously inflated.

Tennessee went on to London and, after returning to New York, consulted several doctors, who prescribed medication for cardiac palpitations, high blood pressure, high cholesterol, and anxiety. Returning to rest in Key West, he wrote a story, "Completed," about a twenty-year-old girl whose life is already completed.

He was wondering whether he should bring Rose to live with him. He visited her regularly in Ossining, at Stony Lodge, and often brought her to New York for a few days, looking after her affectionately, though she waved to strangers, explaining that as queen of England she must acknowledge all her children. And when Tennessee took her out to dinner with a television producer who, trying to be friendly, said that his sister had the same name, Rose, she retorted that her name was Evelyn Develyn Dakin.[39]

According to Dotson Rader, who often saw him with Rose at this period, she would often behave like a naughty child, demanding a chocolate sundae before she ate anything else when he took her out to dinner in a restaurant, and refusing to go to bed at her usual bedtime—eight o'clock in the evening. Tennessee always behaved like an indulgent parent, never losing his temper with her and, in her absence, explaining to other people that she behaved badly because it was the only way she could assert power.

At the end of September he went to Beverly Hills for the California preview of *Summer and Smoke* in a new production which was bound for Broadway. It starred Eva Marie Saint, who had played opposite Brando in *On the Waterfront*. Afterward Tennessee withdrew to Key West for a couple of weeks, but he was soon on the move again, accepting an invitation to give a reading at the University of Texas in Austin, where a big collection of his manuscripts and letters had been lodged in the archive. About five thousand students turned up to hear him read. After going back to New York he went to Providence, Rhode Island, for a tryout of *Vieux Carré*. David Merrick, who had bought *Red Devil Battery Sign*, wanted Elia Kazan to direct it, but Tennessee, not wanting to resume their old partnership, would have preferred a younger director, Milton Katselas, who had revived *The Rose Tattoo* in 1966 at City Center and *Camino Real* at Lincoln Center in 1970.

Tennessee was intending to invite both Edwina and Dakin to Key West for Christmas, but changed his mind, and during a checkup in a clinic, he was advised to cut down on the amount of traveling he did. Ignoring the admonition, he flew to Los Angeles with his new boyfriend, whom Maria had nicknamed Hop, Skip, and a Limp "because he walked like Lord Byron." There they celebrated Christmas with friends, went on to spend a

In London's Embankment Gardens with
Claire Bloom before she starred in the 1974
West End production of Streetcar

quiet week at Puerto Vallarta in Mexico, and flew back to New Orleans, where Tennessee had had red wall-to-wall carpeting installed in the front room of the apartment. A letter from Rose was waiting for him; it said that his son, a splendid creature, had come to dinner.[40]

By the end of January 1974 Robert Carroll was back in Tennessee's life. They traveled together to New York, where it had always seemed easier to keep him under control. But his moods were as bad as ever, and on 4 February he destroyed nearly all his possessions, including clothes and a camera worth eight hundred dollars. Tennessee, who thought highly of Carroll's novel, *Old Children*, locked manuscripts away to keep them safe.[41]

In March Tennessee went to London for the first night of *Streetcar*, which was being revived in a production starring Claire Bloom. The director was Edwin Sherin, a former actor who had been directing since the end of the fifties. Tennessee had recently seen and admired his Broadway production of John Hopkins's *Find Your Way Home*. Maria St. Just threw a stylish party, and Tennessee stayed with her and Lord St. Just at their country home, Wilbury Park, near Stonehenge. He went on to Aix-en-Provence, and, quite incapable of cutting down on travel, thought of flying to Casablanca and going on to Marrakech.[42]

In the same way that he had once gone on revising stories after they were published, he went back again and again to plays that had been staged. Anne Meacham raised the money for a new production of *The Gnädiges Fräulein*, which Tennessee reworked for her under the title *The Latter Days of a Celebrated Soubrette*, but it ran for only one performance, on 16 May 1974, at the Central Arts Cabaret Theatre in New York. And on 17 June, when a revised version of *Out Cry* was staged off-Broadway, by the Thirteenth Street Repertory Company, audiences were small and unimpressed.

In July *Cat on a Hot Tin Roof* was revived in Stratford, Connecticut, by the American Shakespeare Theatre with Elizabeth Ashley as Maggie and Keir Dullea as Brick. The production moved on to Broadway in September 1974 at the ANTA Theatre, where it was a critical and commercial success, and Maria St. Just, who was in New York, saw Tennessee a lot. According to the producer Charles Bowden and his wife, Paula, Maria brought "a family feeling, a continuity" into Tennessee's life, which became more social. She would telephone friends and invite them to his suite at the Elysée, promising to cook dinner. She and Tennessee would then go shopping, and in grocery stores he tried to restrain her from spending too much, while at the dinner party, by constantly pouring the wine from his glass into the aspidistra, she tried to stop him from drinking too much.[43]

At the beginning of 1975 he was making plans with two film producers for a television special he had written under the title *Stopped Rocking*. He still wanted Maureen Stapleton to star in it, and he was hoping to get either Burt Lancaster or Max von Sydow to play opposite her. Edwin Sherin, who had been engaged to direct *The Red Devil Battery Sign*, was hoping to start rehearsals in the spring. He wanted Claire Bloom to play the Woman Downtown, and her producer husband, Hillard Elkins, was now involved with Merrick in presenting the play. They both wanted Anthony Quinn to play the male lead, King Del Rey, but, though he was interested, he kept postponing the date at which he would be available to start rehearsing.[44]

In February Tennessee was given the key to the City of New York. At the ceremony Rose, who was sitting next to him on the dais, behaved impeccably. Afterward he withdrew to Mexico but came back to work on the script of *The Red Devil Battery Sign* with Sherin, who went to stay at the Key

West house. According to him, Tennessee seemed "terribly shy and re-jected, as if hesitant about reaching out to any director." He was anxious about his health and was surrounded by hangers-on, "a loud and boisterous crew who weren't really worthy of him." He was getting up at five in the morning to work for three or four hours before they breakfasted by the pool. He swam after working with Sherin on the script, and slept after lunch. When Edwina, now in her ninetieth year, flew out to stay at the house, Tennessee said he neither liked her nor felt comfortable with her.[45]

The production was scheduled to open on Broadway in mid-August, after previewing in Boston and running in Washington for four weeks. Re-hearsals should have begun on 14 May, but Quinn again procrastinated, saying he would not be free until 2 June, which would have meant sacrificing the week in Boston. In fact, rehearsals began on 12 May, and when David Merrick put in an appearance at the theater, Tennessee said: "As I live and breathe, it's Mr. Broadway!" He riposted: "I thought you said you'd be dead before we went into rehearsal." Tennessee's answer was: "Never listen to a dying duck in a thunderstorm. I'm going to outlive you." The play was to open in Boston at the Shubert Theatre on Monday 18 June. Maria St. Just, who was invited to see the final rehearsal and the first night, thought Quinn was "brilliant," but Claire Bloom was almost inaudible, and there was serious discussion about replacing her with Faye Dunaway, who was having dinner with Tennessee in a restaurant when Claire Bloom embarrassed them by arriving with her agent.[46]

A public preview was held on Saturday, 16 June. The theater was full, but before the curtain went up, Sherin, at the insistence of Anthony Quinn, appeared on stage to tell the audience that it was going to see a "working rehearsal" and that if any of them would prefer to come back later in the run as Quinn's guests, they would be welcome. But no one took up the offer.[47]

The play opened two days later, but the review in the *Boston Globe* could hardly have been more vicious. Calling the play "dreadful," the critic, Kevin Kelly, complained about vacuity and a "lurking pomposity" in Tennessee's "ever-darkening vision." "The real clue to this vacuity may be found in the desperation of the play's plotting. . . . The voltage in the symbolism wouldn't light a penlight. . . . When the diversion of the music and the scenery lets up, there are performances and my-oh-my what a mess!"[48] Merrick closed the production after ten days.

The disgruntled Quinn was determined to bring the play to New York, even if he had to finance it himself, and he said so on television, but he wanted to take over as director, as well, using an assistant. According to Bill Barnes, Merrick was still interested and two other top producers wanted the play, but Tennessee was skeptical. Quinn was also keen to make a movie of the play, and wanted Tennessee to write a screenplay. Worrying about his age, Quinn said he would look too old for the part unless he played it within the next few months. Tennessee, who wanted to work simultaneously on the screenplay and the revision of the play for the stage, said Quinn should make the film as soon as possible but not release it until the play had completed its Broadway run.[49]

It was a busy and gratifying autumn for Tennessee. *Summer and Smoke* was revived off-Broadway on 16 September at Roundabout Stage One. Sherin directed *Sweet Bird of Youth* with Irene Worth and Christopher Walken, and the production, which opened during October at the Kennedy Center in Washington, transferred to Broadway, where it ran till the spring. When the *Memoirs* were published, the book was a best-seller, and Tennessee was aware of having become a cause célèbre. At a promotional signing session one afternoon in a Doubleday bookstore, he broke the shop's record by signing over eight hundred copies.[50] And a week before Christmas, *The Glass Menagerie*, which had been revived at the Brooks Atkinson Theatre during May, returned to the Circle in the Square with Maureen Stapleton as Amanda.

All through this busy autumn Tennessee's life was liable to be disrupted by new crises in his turbulent relationship with Robert Carroll. Tennessee wanted to pay him off, but he was demanding a hundred thousand dollars, and in October, when Tennessee gave him only a thousand, he reappeared in Key West. In December, when Maria St. Just was playing in a production of *The Red Devil Battery Sign* at the English Theatre in Vienna, Tennessee promised her to come without Carroll. Though he did arrive in Vienna alone, Carroll appeared a few days later, and one evening, when the three of them were in a taxi, he said Tennessee could no longer write. Maria told the mortified playwright to get out of the cab with her and spend the night at the boardinghouse where the actors were staying. Shouting abuse at both of them and trying to hit Tennessee, Carroll pursued them into the building, where Keith Baxter, the actor who was playing Quinn's part, bundled them into the elevator.[51]

The relationship survived, of course, as it had survived so many other quarrels, but when Tennessee took Carroll to San Francisco, where his new play *This Is (An Entertainment)* was due to open on 16 January 1976 at the Geary Theatre, staged by the American Conservatory Theatre, he was unable to keep Carroll off the streets, which were "crawling with hustlers which he finds irresistible as drugs and he doesn't bother to use the protectives such as 'Sanitube.'"[52] The disease he caught was passed on to Tennessee at the same time as he was having to cope with the failure of the play.

Like *The Red Devil Battery Sign, This Is (An Entertainment)* suggests American society is disintegrating, but the idea justifies neither the fragmentation of the structure nor the inconsistency of the style. The main character is a lecherous countess who cuckolds her husband, a munitions manufacturer, and reacts to every new contingency by saying "This is." The play had been written too carelessly, if not too quickly, and when the critic Ruby Cohn asked Tennessee how his plays germinated, his answer was that they grew off the empty sheet of paper that faced him every morning in his typewriter. "He is such a grand old man," she concluded, "that I suppose no one will tell him when a play simply stinks."[53]

15

Q u a r r e l s o m e   L o v e r

"Although I feel well physically," Tennessee told an interviewer in May 1976, when he was on his way to the film festival at Cannes, "I know that I'm approaching the end of my life and thank God that I'm not scared."[1] In fact he was to survive for nearly seven years, but though he continued his routine of getting up every day before dawn to write, he could not wean himself off drugs, and his behavior often created embarrassment.

He had agreed to act as honorary president of the jury at Cannes, but he arrived with his bulldog and refused to go anywhere without her, which stopped him from attending the party held in his honor on the first night. He also refused to sit in the jury box at the movie theater: it made him nervous, he said. To avoid journalists, he tried to go in and out of buildings through side doors, but since most of these were locked, he usually drew more attention to himself. Maria St. Just had agreed to join him in Cannes, her only condition being that Carroll—who was now on speed—did not come. Because of the dog, she and Tennessee moved to the Hôtel du Cap, which had a garden, and Maria helped housebreak the dog.[2]

In June or July he had another major quarrel with Carroll in Key West, and left for California with a former friend of Andy Warhol's, a hustler who had switched to a career as a photographer. When he argued that photography would supersede both painting and literature, Tennessee's response was: "Thank God Renoir and Van Gogh didn't have a Kodak!" After the photographer had started an affair with "another young rip-off artist" and had locked the dog in a cupboard for several hours, he was dismissed with a ticket to New York, but he left for the airport in a car Tennessee had rented, and it disappeared. Tennessee soon found another secretary-companion, Dick Ellis, who had ambitions as a poet.[3]

In October 1976, going back to San Francisco, Tennessee took a room at the El Cortez Hotel, where he had stayed during rehearsals of *This Is*, but he was asked to leave after embarrassing some of the other guests by making a scene in the lobby. Generally his behavior went on deteriorating, according to the producer Gloria Hope Sher. After seeing Sherin's revival of *Eccentricities of a Nightingale* in Buffalo she presented the play at the Morosco Theatre in New York, where it opened on 23 November. "He loved everyone in the play," she said, "and everything connected with it, and his laugh filled the theatre. . . . But he didn't seem to be eating much. . . . He only picked at food. The wine saw him through any social occasion. And the minute he had one sip of red wine, his personality changed completely. He became very aggressive, caustic to waiters, unpleasant to be with. A maitre d' once had to ask him to calm down." The red wine quarreled with the drugs he was taking. But he needed company. "He was frightened to be alone," she went on, "and anyone who extended a helping hand would be confided in." He was even more dependent on the kindness of strangers than he had been in the forties, and in her copy of the program for *Eccentricities of a Nightingale* he wrote: "Stay in my life, Gloria, to keep me alive."[4]

Nobody was more set on staying in his life than Carroll, who rejoined him before the play opened. But when Tennessee announced his intention of flying off to the Virgin Islands, Carroll refused to go. Still on speed, he was afraid he might be unable to obtain supplies in the Caribbean. Never at a loss to find willing companions, Tennessee left with another young writer.[5]

He came back to New York in time to be initiated as a life member of the American Academy of Arts and Letters at a ceremony on 3 December, and he was planning a trip to England. In February 1977 he helped to prepare a production of *Vieux Carré*, which was due to play in Boston and New Haven before opening on Broadway in April at the St. James's Theatre. Explicitly and rather verbosely autobiographical, the script was based on his 1938 experiences in the boardinghouse on Toulouse Street. Sylvia Sidney, who played the landlady, Mrs. Wire, reports: "We were nervous and he was sad.

. . . He was frightened of getting old, terrified that he was no longer attractive, that his figure wasn't good anymore, that he couldn't attract young men except with his money."[6] His nervousness helped to demoralize the cast, and he antagonized the critics by making repeated public attacks on them. After a postponement due to complications over the set, the play opened in New York on 11 May, but the reviews were mostly hostile and only five performances were given.

Tennessee and Carroll had been living together again since February, and in Key West, whenever Tennessee was away, Carroll was letting criminals and drug dealers sleep at the house. But in April the police launched a major antidrug operation, and the addicts who had been smoking had to make do with pills. Almost going berserk, Carroll threatened to kill himself, but he got through the crisis with the aid of the Valium that Tennessee gave him at four-hour intervals.[7]

In June, when Tennessee went to London for the production of *The Red Devil Battery Sign* at the Roundhouse, he could barely walk. According to the producer, Gene Persson, from the American Conservatory Theatre in San Francisco, "He was staggering, he was unable to arrange the practical details of everyday life, money appeared and disappeared strangely." It also failed to appear when he was expecting it: he complained afterward that Persson had cheated him.[8]

Needing to recuperate, Tennessee withdrew to Key West, where Carroll was still in residence. His behavior improved whenever he ran out of speed, and sometimes he even cooked for Tennessee. One evening, when they were in Washington, eating in a restaurant, another friend of Tennessee's, a young man who worked for a psychiatric clinic, frightened Carroll by telephoning the clinic and saying he had an emergency case—a patient needing immediate admission.[9] Himself addicted both to Carroll and to drugs, Tennessee could hardly be intolerant of the young man's addiction, but he did resent Carroll's suspicious absences late at night, his cruelty to the dog, his inconsiderate way of inviting uncouth young friends to the house, and his narcissistic self-involvement. If a letter arrived for Tennessee from someone Carroll knew, he would immediately ask what it said about him. Neither of them trusted the other. Whenever Tennessee gave Carroll letters to mail, he felt uncertain whether they would arrive, and if Carroll lost one of his headbands, he suspected Tennessee of confiscating it.

Some of the tiffs were no worse than the ones Tennessee used to have with Pancho and Frank, but he never felt as emotionally committed to Carroll as he had to them. Complaining about the boy in his letters to Maria, he invariably used one or other of her unflattering nicknames for him—the Twerp or the Enfant Terrible. And though Tennessee hated traveling alone, Carroll's company was more of a liability than an asset. Invited to Australia, Tennessee had been offered a round-trip passage to Sydney, plus expenses, and Carroll wanted to go with him, but he could not be trusted not to cause trouble, and Tennessee had other reasons for hesitating about whether to make the journey. He was suffering from hypertension, and a cataract was forming on his right eye—the one that had previously given him no trouble. He was told the cataract would develop only slowly, but, always apprehensive about any new symptom, he felt sure his eyesight was deteriorating from day to day.[10]

As always, work gave him a sense of security, and he still had plenty to do. He was making the *Baby Doll* screenplay into a stage play called *Tiger Tail*. He was still working on *The Red Devil Battery Sign*, rewriting the ending to please Keith Baxter, who was going to play the leading part in London, and he was rewriting a one-act play that dated from 1975, *Creve Coeur*. He had high hopes of *Tiger Tail*, which was tried out in Atlanta during January 1978 at the Alliance Theatre, directed by Harry Rasky, but the production was not transferred to New York. Tennessee did better with *Creve Coeur*, which was premiered in June 1978 as part of an American extension of the Spoleto Festival in Charleston, South Carolina. At a formal reception on the first night, Tennessee appeared in shorts, sneakers, and a Panama hat. Reviews were favorable enough to warrant a transfer to New York, where the title was changed to *A Lovely Sunday for Creve Coeur*. The play opened on 10 January 1979 at the Hudson Guild, an off-Broadway theater, where it had thirty-six performances.

In August 1978 Tennessee went to London, where *Vieux Carré* was being produced in the West End. Sylvia Miles played the landlady, Mrs. Wire, with Karl Johnson as the young writer and Richard Kane as the dying painter. The director was Keith Hack. Reviews were generally unfavorable, and Tennessee, who was staying with Maria at Wilbury Park, was deeply depressed, feeling he had little time or strength left.[11]

At the beginning of 1979 violence invaded his life in Key West. On 5 January his gardener was found dead in bed. He had been shot, and there was a pile of Tennessee's manuscripts under the bed. During the next ten days Tennessee's house was burgled twice, with only six days between the two raids. And at the end of the month the sixty-seven-year-old writer was mugged in Duval Street, though he was not badly hurt. He was soon working again. He went back to *The Milk Train Doesn't Stop Here Anymore*, revising it for the English Theatre in Vienna under the title *Goforth!* The intention was that Sylvia Miles would play the lead and that the production would transfer to London, but in the end the new version was never staged in Vienna.

He was also working on *Clothes for a Summer Hotel*, a play he had written in 1975 about Scott and Zelda Fitzgerald. This aroused the interest of the producer Roger Stevens and the director José Quintero, who met him in Washington during July 1979 to discuss it.

Though it was hard for him to make major changes in his routine, he tried to stabilize his domestic life in the autumn of 1978 by renting a new apartment at Manhattan Plaza, a complex on West 42nd and 43rd Streets. At the same time he transferred to a new agent at International Creative Management, Mitch Douglas. Finding he was spending more time in his suite at the Elysée Hotel than in his new apartment, he soon gave up the apartment. But he did succeed, after seven years of turbulent intimacy, in ending his relationship with Carroll, who was sent back to Boone County, Virginia, and paid $150 a month to stay away. Though much less money than he had been demanding, this was enough to keep him at a distance, and Tennessee employed a new secretary, Jay Leo Colt.

In November 1979 Rose was going to be seventy, and her brother continued his efforts to make life less unpleasant for her. He often brought her to New York, taking her to restaurants and cutting up her meat for her. After he acquired a second house in Key West, a two-story gray clapboard building on Van Phister Street, he arranged for her to live there with a cousin of theirs, Stella Adams, as her companion. Over a year went by before she had to be recommitted to Stony Lodge.

The year ended better for Tennessee than it had begun. During December, in the presence of President Carter, Ella Fitzgerald, Henry Fonda, Aaron Copland, Martha Graham, and Tennessee were honored at the Kennedy Center for their contribution to the arts. Deeply moved, Ella Fitzgerald began to cry. Tennessee lent her his handkerchief and misinterpreted the mascara stains when he got it back. "Look," he whispered, "even her tears are black."

He was snoozing, and Maria, who was accompanying him, had no shoes on when the First Lady, Rosalynn Carter, came to their box. They were taken to meet the president, who congratulated Tennessee.[12]

His play about Scott and Zelda Fitzgerald, *Clothes for a Summer Hotel*, was due to open on Broadway at the Cort Theatre in March 1980, directed by Quintero with Geraldine Page as Zelda. Scott was played by Kenneth Haigh, the English actor who had appeared as Jimmy Porter in the original production of John Osborne's *Look Back in Anger* (1956). *Clothes for a Summer Hotel* was already in rehearsal when, at the end of January, the Tennessee Williams Performing Arts Center at the Florida Keys Community College in Key West was inaugurated with a production of a one-act play he had written in 1969, *Will Mr. Merriwether Return from Memphis?*

On its way to New York, *Clothes for a Summer Hotel* was unfavorably reviewed in Chicago, and though it was snowing on the morning the notices appeared, José Quintero found Tennessee sitting on the steps of the Art Institute. He said: "I'm waiting for them to open because I know they will have a swimming-pool, because this is a place for artists where I can catch my breath to go on living."[13] The play opened in New York on 26 March, Tennessee's sixty-ninth birthday. The mayor of New York, Edward Koch, proclaimed the day Tennessee Williams Day, but this did not stop the critics from savaging the play, which closed on 16 April, shortly before Tennessee was called to the White House, where the president pinned the Medal of Freedom to his chest.

It is doubtful whether his mother could take any pride in the honor. Since 1975 she had been verging on insanity, and her last years had been spent in a nursing home. She died in June 1980 at the age of ninety-five. Tennessee was staying with an artist friend, Vassilis Voglis, on Long Island, and when Dakin called with the news at three in the morning, Voglis did his best to make Tennessee come to the telephone, but he just rolled over in bed: "It's probably the news that my mother has died. . . . Tell them to call me in the morning."[14]

He spent some of the month in Europe, working on a new play, *The Everlasting Ticket*, and traveling with a friend, Henry Faulkner, another artist, but one with less dignity than Voglis. In Taormina, where they stayed at the San Domenico Palace Hotel, Faulkner lurched along the Corso, singing in an unsteady falsetto and stopping boys to make crude sexual proposals. It was useless for Tennessee to pretend that they were not together, and at the hotel they shared a room for the first three nights. After being kept awake by persistent coughing and groaning, Tennessee gave Faulkner five hundred dollars and made him move out. He got himself a studio and spoke of spending the whole summer there, but Tennessee did not want to stay for more than a week.[15]

After flying back to the United States he met Gregory Mosher, who ran the Goodman Theatre in Chicago and offered to stage three of Tennessee's one-act plays. They settled on *A Perfect Analysis Given by a Parrot*, *The Frosted Glass Coffin*, and *Some Problems for the Moose Lodge*. These were grouped together under the title *Tennessee Laughs*.

In the autumn he accepted an invitation to be Distinguished Writer in Residence at the University of British Columbia in Vancouver. He was offered a salary of two thousand dollars a week, but was required to lecture—sometimes twice in one day—on various aspects of theater. To give him more incentive to accept the offer, the university authorities followed a suggestion from his new agent, Mitch Douglas, and arranged for a new production of *The Red Devil Battery Sign* to go into rehearsal. The director had detailed discussions with Tennessee about the script, which was cut down to four-fifths of its former length.[16]

Arriving in Vancouver during October, and settling into the twenty-seventh floor of a high-rise hotel, he had a view of the mountainous little islands along the Pacific coast and the harbor, which was full of big freighters and small sailing boats. He decided that after Venice, Vancouver was the most beautiful city he had ever seen, but he became so nervous about the play in rehearsal and about his teaching commitments that he fled to San Francisco. After resting a couple of days, he went back, and his hosts, fearful of losing him again, treated him more deferentially and more considerately, introducing him to young people likely to give him a good time.[17]

Generally, though, it had become harder to carry on any professional dealings with him: he was no longer keeping appointments or opening his mail, and he was more prone to paranoid suspicions, accusing friends and colleagues of stealing money and forging checks. After *The Red Devil Battery Sign* had opened in Vancouver on 18 October, he left for Chicago, where the triple bill had its premiere on 8 November. Of the three plays the one that appealed most to Mosher and his director, Gary Tucker, was *Some Problems for the Moose Lodge*, which they offered to stage as a full-length play if Tennessee was interested in doing more work on it.

Peg Murray and Scott Jaeck in A House
Not Meant to Stand *at the Goodman
Theatre, Chicago (1982)*

He expanded it into *A House Not Meant to Stand*, intending the derelict
house to represent the state of society, but most of his energy went into
depicting a quarrelsome and unstable family modeled on his own. The
central characters are named Bella and Cornelius, after his aunt Belle and
his father. Though he is a drunken loudmouth, like the real Cornelius, Cornelius McCorkle also has political ambitions, modeled partly on their
paternal grandfather's and partly on those of Dakin, who had been running,
unsuccessfully, for the Senate.[18] Tennessee also works in a pessimistic reference to his addiction and his dwindling appetite for life: "When a man's got
to live off pills in the quantity and at the price, with only temporary relief at
best, why I say it's time to quit hangin' on, it's time for a man to let go."
Early in 1981 he told Mosher it might be nice to be dead without having to
go through the business of dying.

Staged by the Belgian director André Ernotte, the play was due to open
in the studio theater at the Goodman on 1 April. Tennessee attended rehearsals, but only in the mornings. He rewrote energetically, tailoring the
roles to fit the actors, but his stamina was dwindling. On 26 March a party

*TW celebrating his seventieth birthday with
Vassilis Voglis and Jane Smith*

was held at the Goodman for his seventieth birthday. Many stars and former friends were invited, but none of the stars came, and only a few close friends, including Vassilis Voglis. After the play had been staged in the studio theater, it needed more work, and Tennessee's revised version was staged again, by the same director with the same cast, in the main theater of the Goodman just over a year later, opening on 27 April 1982. *Time* hailed it as his best play for ten years, but, reviewing it in the *Chicago Tribune*, Richard Christiansen complained that there were "great lengths of ranting repetition alternating with disconnected, unprepared, unfulfilled moments. And the stinging fury of Williams's poetry, which hits with brutal force in some of the enraged monologues, is mixed with cheap laughs."[19] The play ran till the end of May.

The discontinuity between one moment and the next reflected the abruptness of Tennessee's mood changes. In excesses of bitter pessimism he had wanted to cancel the production; in bursts of gaiety he would laugh and want to dance. Half-aware he was being absurd when he accused people of conspiring against him, he tried to make his paranoia into a joke. He said Mitch Douglas had been negotiating with the airlines to induce a heart attack by putting him on a depressurized plane, and he threatened to expose the crimes of his enemies unless they used a hit man to silence him.

The last new play to be staged during his life was *Something Cloudy, Something Clear*, which was produced in New York by the Jean Cocteau Repertory at the Bouwerie Theatre, opening on 24 August 1981. A memory play set in the dunes of Provincetown during the summer of 1940, it affectionately resuscitates Kip, Frank, and Tallulah Bankhead. As usual, Tennessee did a lot of rewriting during rehearsal, and he tried to insist on canceling the production. As the director, Eve Adamson, put it, "he was really trying to sabotage his own play, to harm himself before the critics got a chance to harm him."[20]

In the *Village Voice* Michael Feingold suggested: "Perhaps the play is something in the way of an elegy memorial for and an apology to Kip, in which Williams pictures himself for once not as the poet pining for a doomed love, but the unscrupulous, horny bastard on the make; in effect the playwright as stinker. . . . Only the minor characters are signs that Williams is still capable of more than alternately wallowing in sentiment and kicking himself for the falseness of his wallow."[21]

In the autumn, when he and Harold Pinter were given Common Wealth Awards of eleven thousand dollars each, Tennessee's advice to the younger writer was: "Harold, take care of your health. I could have done a lot more if I had taken care of my health."[22]

On 2 December a gala was organized in his honor at Lincoln Center, but it was canceled because most of the tickets remained unsold.

In February 1982 the mayor of New York presented him with the city's medallion of honor, and at a party the following evening he saw his old friend Truman Capote. When Tennessee asked him when he thought they would meet again, the answer was: "In Paradise."

In July Tennessee traveled to Taormina with his friend Jane Smith and a young film director, Peter Hoffman, who was interested in making two of his stories into a screenplay. Staying once again at the San Domenico Palace Hotel, he still wrote every morning, but, suffering from arthritic pains in his right shoulder, he was treated with cortisone shots and took powerful painkillers which made it impossible for him to write for more than short periods. He felt too frail to go on, as they had planned, to Russia, where they could have spent the million dollars which had accumulated in royalties that he had to spend inside the country.

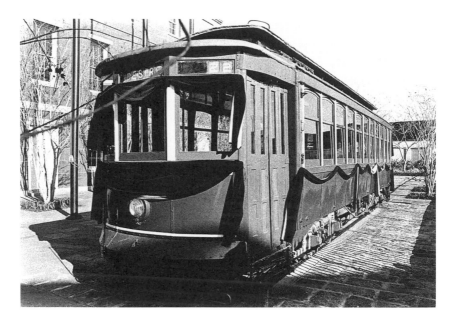

New Orleans streetcar in mourning for
TW's death, March 1983

At the end of September Hoffman went to stay with him in Key West to work on the screenplay. Refusing to eat and living on wine, coffee, and Seconal, Tennessee was incapable of settling down to work. At the beginning of October, he told Hoffman they would go to Asia together, but they got no farther than New York.

In November Tennessee made his last public appearance at the 92nd Street Y in New York. His speech was slurred, and he started his talk by saying he had almost forgotten to turn up. On Christmas Eve, thanks to the intervention of neighbors in Key West, he was taken to the hospital, where he was found to be dehydrated, and the drugs had to be flushed out of him.

He had planned to spend Christmas with Maria at Wilbury Park but canceled the arrangement, though she offered to fly out and travel back to England with him. He telephoned her, though, from New Orleans, saying he would come to London the next day. They spent a week together, and though Tennessee seemed withdrawn, he was untypically and punctiliously early for every appointment, "as though he didn't want to miss a second of any contact." One morning he called her saying he was leaving for Rome, and inviting her to his hotel for breakfast. She offered to travel with him, but he wanted to be alone, and after a final glass of red wine with him at the airport, she kissed his hand.[23]

He had seldom been willing to travel alone, but in February 1983 he went back, on his own, to the San Domenico in Taormina, where the waiters could not persuade him to take any interest in food. Back in New York in his suite at the Elysée, he had little contact with any of his friends.

When Jane Smith saw him on 24 February, he struck her as seeming different, like a stranger. He had an odd look in his eyes, and his voice sounded as if it were "coming from somewhere different."[24]

In the evening, retiring to his suite in the hotel with a bottle of wine, he drank in bed, also taking a variety of drugs, including cocaine. To spoon two Seconal tablets into his mouth he used the cap from a bottle of eyedrops, and somehow got it stuck in his throat.

Or at least, this is what seems to have happened. There was an autopsy, and the pathologist, Dr. Michael Baden, later made a public statement expressing puzzlement over the position of the bottle cap, which was not found in the dead man's larynx, but in his mouth. According to Dakin, for whom bleeding and bruising to the face and body are conclusive proof of violence, Tennessee was murdered by a hired killer. In July 1993, Dakin asked the New York police to reopen their investigation, naming the two people who, according to him, had hired the killer.[25]

There are reasons for being cautious about Dakin's allegations. Though he eventually received a hundred thousand dollars after challenging his brother's will in court, he had been left only twenty-five thousand dollars and that was not due to be paid until Rose died. No one could have been surprised that Tennessee left most of his estate to Rose, but it was surprising that at his funeral his remains were displayed in an open casket, and that instead of being cremated and having his ashes scattered over the Gulf of Mexico, as he had wished, he was buried in the family plot at St. Louis, a city he had always hated.

Appendix: Analysis of Recycling

Plays are often recycled as movies, but much of the reworking Tennessee Williams did was more complicated. He often developed short stories into plays, and one-act plays into full-length plays. Once he made a play out of a movie that had been based on two one-act plays, one of which had derived from a story. This table provides a guide—necessarily incomplete—to interrelationships among his stories, plays, and films.

Battle of Angels, *Orpheus Descending*, and *The Fugitive Kind*

Play *Battle of Angels* written 1939; staged at the Wilbur Theatre, Boston, 30 December 1940.

Play *Orpheus Descending* finished 1957; staged at the Martin Beck Theatre, New York, 21 March 1957.

Movie *The Fugitive Kind* (screenplay: Tennessee Williams) released 1960.

"Portrait of a Girl in Glass" and *The Glass Menagerie*

Story "Portrait of a Girl in Glass" written 1941–43; published 1948.

Screenplay "The Gentleman Caller" written 1943.

One-act play *The Glass Menagerie* written 1943.

Appendix

Seven-scene play *The Glass Menagerie* written 1943–44; staged at the Civic Theatre, Chicago, 26 December 1944, and at the Playhouse Theatre, New York, 31 March 1945.

Movie *The Glass Menagerie* released 1950.

Summer and Smoke and *Eccentricities of a Nightingale*

Play *Summer and Smoke* written 1945–47; staged at the Gulf Oil Playhouse, Dallas, 8 July 1947, at the Music Box Theatre, New York, 6 October 1948, and at the Circle in the Square, New York, 24 April 1952.

Movie *Summer and Smoke* released 1961.

Play *Eccentricities of a Nightingale* may have been written 1951, although Donald Windham believes it was a first version of *Summer and Smoke* rather than a re-vision; staged at the Tappan Zee Playhouse, Nyack, New York, 25 June 1964, and at the Morosco Theatre, New York, 23 November 1976.

The Enemy, Time and *Sweet Bird of Youth*

One-act play *The Enemy, Time* written 1952; published 1959.

Play *Sweet Bird of Youth* written 1956; staged at Studio M, Miami, 16 April 1956; revised and staged at the Martin Beck Theatre, New York, 10 March 1959.

Movie *Sweet Bird of Youth* released 1962.

"Three Players of a Summer Game" and *Cat on a Hot Tin Roof*

Story "Three Players of a Summer Game" written 1951; revised 1952; published 1952.

One-act play *Three Players of a Summer Game* written 1954; staged at the White Barn Theatre, Westport, Connecticut, 19 July 1955

Three-act play *Cat on a Hot Tin Roof* written 1953–55; third act revised 1955; staged at the Morosco Theatre, New York, 25 March 1955; original three-act version staged at the Comedy Theatre, London, 30 January 1958.

Movie *Cat on a Hot Tin Roof* released 1958.

Period of Adjustment

Three-act play *Period of Adjustment* written 1957–58; staged at the Coconut Grove Playhouse, Miami, 29 December 1958; revised version staged at the Helen Hayes Theatre, New York, 10 November 1960.

Movie *Period of Adjustment* (screenplay: Isobel Lennart) released 1962.

"27 Wagons Full of Cotton", *The Unsatisfactory Supper, Baby Doll,* and *Tiger Tail*

Story "27 Wagons Full of Cotton" written 1935; published 1936.

One-act play *27 Wagons Full of Cotton* written before 1946; staged at Tulane University, New Orleans, 18 January 1955, and at the Playhouse Theatre, New York, 19 April 1955.

Unrelated one-act play *The Unsatisfactory Supper, or The Long Stay Cut Short* written before 1945; published 1945; staged in London, 1971.

Movie *Baby Doll* (screenplay: Tennessee Williams and Elia Kazan) released 1956.

Play *Tiger Tail* written 1978; staged at the Alliance Theatre, Atlanta, in the winter of 1978.

The Night of the Iguana

Story "The Night of the Iguana" begun 1940; written 1946–48; published 1948.

One-act play *The Night of the Iguana* staged in Spoleto, Italy, 2 July 1959.

Three-act play *The Night of the Iguana* staged at the Royale Theatre, New York, 29 December 1961.

Movie *The Night of the Iguana* released 1964.

"Man Bring This up Road," *The Milk Train Doesn't Stop Here Anymore, Goforth!* and *Boom!*

Story "Man Bring This up Road" written 1953; published 1959.

One-act play *The Milk Train Doesn't Stop Here Anymore* written 1959–62; staged in Spoleto, Italy, 11 July 1962.

Six-scene play *The Milk Train Doesn't Stop Here Anymore* written 1962–63; staged at the Morosco Theatre, New York, 16 January 1963.

Play *Goforth!* written 1979, never staged.

Movie *Boom!* released 1968.

The Gnädiges Fräulein and *The Latter Days of a Celebrated Soubrette*

One-act play *The Gnädiges Fräulein* staged as part of a double bill, *Slapstick Tragedy,* at the Longacre Theatre, New York, 22 February 1966.

Play *The Latter Days of a Celebrated Soubrette* staged at the Central Arts Cabaret Theatre, New York, 16 May 1974.

Appendix

The Two-Character Play and *Out Cry*

One-act play *The Two Character Play* staged at the Hampstead Theatre Club, London, 12 December 1967.

One-act play *Out Cry* staged at the Ivanhoe Theatre, Chicago, 8 July 1971; revised version staged at the Lyceum Theatre, New York, 1 March 1973.

"The Kingdom of Earth," *Kingdom of Earth, Kingdom of Earth (The Seven Descents of Myrtle), Last of the Mobile Hot Shots (Blood Kin)*

Story "The Kingdom of Earth" begun 1942; published 1954.

One-act play *Kingdom of Earth* written 1966; published 1967.

Two-act play *Kingdom of Earth (The Seven Descents of Myrtle)* written 1966–67; staged at the Ethel Barrymore Theatre, New York, 27 March 1968.

Two act play *Kingdom of Earth* revised after 1968; staged at McCarter Theatre, Princeton, New Jersey, 6 March 1975.

Movie *Last of the Mobile Hot Shots* released 1970; entitled *Blood Kin* for European release.

Confessional and *Small Craft Warnings*

One-act play *Confessional* written 1967; staged at the Maine Theatre Arts Festival, Bar Harbor, Maine, summer 1971.

Two-act play *Small Craft Warnings* staged at the Truck and Warehouse Theatre, New York, 2 April 1972.

Chronology

1880   Cornelius Coffin Williams born

1885   Edwina Dakin born

1895   Her father, Walter Edwin Dakin, ordained as a minister

1906   Edwina meets Cornelius

1907   June: they marry, and honeymoon in Gulfport, Mississippi, where he has been appointed manager of three telephone exchanges

1909   Edwina runs away from Cornelius, returning to her parents in Columbus, Mississippi, where he visits her on weekends. 17 November: their first child, Rose Isobel, born.

1911   After losing his job with the telephone company, Cornelius works as a shoe salesman. 26 March: their second child, Thomas Lanier, born.

1913   The family moves to Nashville, Tennessee, and in

1915   to Clarksdale in western Mississippi

1916   Tom's diphtheria develops into Bright's Disease according to the diagnoses of the local doctor. Tom is left paralyzed and unable to use his legs for about two years.

1918   Tom and Rose are separated from their grandparents, moving with their parents to St. Louis, where Cornelius is given an office job

1919   A third child, Dakin, is born 21 February

1920   Tom's friendship with Hazel Kramer begins

1921   Edwina has a miscarriage

1923   Tom starts at Ben Blewett Junior High School

1924   Ghost story in school magazine

1925   Essay on factory fumes in school yearbook. Moves to Soldan High School, where he writes movie reviews for the school newspaper.

1927   Moves to University City High School and wins third prize ($5) from the magazine *Smart Set* for his answer to the question "Can a good wife be a good sport?"

1928 His story "The Vengeance of Nitocris" is published in magazine *Weird Tales*. Tom sails to Europe with Reverend Dakin and a party of female parishioners. In Paris he has what he called a "nearly psychotic crisis."

1929 Attends University of Missouri at Columbia

1930 Earns money during summer vacation by selling *Pictorial Review*. Falls in love with a boy during the autumn term, but the relationship remains unconsummated.

1931 Cornelius punishes him for low grades by making him work through the summer vacation in a clerical job. Back at the university in the autumn, he enters the School of Journalism.

1932 Cornelius withdraws him from the college, and he studies shorthand and typing in night classes, doing menial work during the day for the International Shoe Company

1933 Writes verse and stories. "Stella for Star," his twenty-third submission to the magazine *Story*, wins him $10 when awarded first prize in the Winifred Irwin competition.

1934 June: begins ten months of working in a warehouse for the shoe company

1935 Spring: has what he claims is a heart attack, and recuperates at his grandparents' home in Memphis, where he writes a one-act play, *Cairo! Shanghai! Bombay!* which is staged by amateurs on 12 July. Autumn: attends Washington University in St. Louis and writes plays for an amateur group, the Mummers.

1936 His story "27 Wagons Full of Cotton" is published in *Manuscript*.

1937 *Candles to the Sun* staged in St. Louis. Takes a play-writing course at University of Iowa. Lobotomy performed on Rose. Tom has what was probably his only heterosexual affair.

1938 Graduates with a degree in English literature. Goes to Chicago and in December to New Orleans, where he gets a series of part-time jobs.

1939 Moves to an attic apartment at 722 Toulouse Street in the old French Quarter, and it may have been here that he has his first homosexual affair. Sends out scripts under the name Tennessee. February: subtracting three years from his age, he enters some of his plays in a contest organized by the Group Theatre. Travels to California, wanting to try his luck as a Hollywood scriptwriter. A cataract is forming on his left eye. He takes odd jobs on poultry farms. Gets job at a shoe store in Culver City. Is awarded a prize of $100 by the Group Theatre, and his plays are sent to the agent Audrey Wood. Travels to Taos in New Mexico, where he visits Frieda Lawrence, and returns to St. Louis, where he works on his play *Battle of Angels*. September: first meeting with Audrey Wood in New York. Stays for several weeks before returning to St. Louis. Awarded a Rockefeller Foundation grant of $1,000.

1940 January: moves back to New York, where he lives in a YMCA. Meets
Donald Windham and joins a play-writing seminar run by John Gassner at
the New School for Social Research, where students put on his one-act play
The Long Goodbye in April. Classified 4F, he is exempt from war service.
Leaves New York for spells in Memphis and in Provincetown, on Cape
Cod, where he has an affair with Kip Kiernan. September: stays in
Acapulco at the Hotel Costa Verde. Returns to St. Louis before going back
to New York. 30 December: *Battle of Angels* is staged by the Theatre Guild
in Boston, but

1941 its run ends 11 January. February: stays in Key West. Stays in St. Louis but
keeps on the move throughout the spring and summer, returning to New
Orleans in September. Leaves in early November but returns in mid-
December. He starts the story "Portrait of a Girl in Glass," which will be
developed into *The Glass Menagerie*.

1942 Returns to New York, staying with various friends and lovers while doing
odd jobs, including one at the Beggar's Bar in Greenwich Village.
Collaborates with Donald Windham on dramatizing D. H. Lawrence's
story "You Touched Me." June: stays in Georgia with Paul Bigelow and
friends. August: goes to Jacksonville and works for the War Department
operating a teletype machine on the night shift. Late November: returns to
New York, doing another series of odd jobs, including stints as elevator
operator in a hotel, bellhop, and usher in a movie theater.

1943 Spring: returns to St. Louis. April: Audrey Wood secures for him a six-
month contract with M-G-M as a scriptwriter. May: he rents rooms on
Ocean Avenue, Santa Monica, and, while working on a script for Lana
Turner, develops "Portrait of a Girl in Glass" into a screenplay, "The
Gentleman Caller." October: loses his Hollywood job. 13 October: *You
Touched Me* opens in Cleveland. Christmas: Returns to St. Louis, where his
grandmother is dying.

1944 6 January: grandmother dies. January: writes the story "Oriflamme."
March: goes to New York. April: awarded $1,000 by the American
Academy of Arts and Letters, he leaves for Provincetown, where he works
on *The Glass Menagerie* (a reworking of "The Gentleman Caller"). 26
December: it opens in Chicago.

1945 January or February: starts work on *A Streetcar Named Desire*. 31 March:
The Glass Menagerie opens in New York. April: leaves for Mexico, where he
stays at a guest house near Guadalajara, working on *A Streetcar Named
Desire*. September: returns to New York. 25 September: *You Touched Me*
opens in New York. December: leaves for New Orleans.

1946 January or February: starts living with Pancho Rodrigues y Gonzalez.

April: returns to St. Louis. May: suffering from abdominal pain, he is examined in Wichita, Kansas, and goes on to Taos. Summer: after a brief stay in New York, vacations with Pancho on Nantucket. Beginning of friendship with Carson McCullers. He works on *Summer and Smoke*. September: suffering from gastric pains, he returns to New York for tests. October: settles with Pancho into an apartment in New Orleans, where he continues working on *Summer and Smoke*, as well as drafting *Camino Real*. December: Reverend Dakin comes to stay and

1947   January: travels with TW and Pancho to Key West. March: sends script of *A Streetcar Named Desire* to Audrey Wood. June: leaves with Pancho for Provincetown, where they rent a cottage. He meets Frank Merlo. 8 July: *Summer and Smoke* opens at the Gulf Oil Playhouse, Dallas, Texas. 3 December: *A Streetcar Named Desire* opens in New York. It wins the New York Drama Critics' Circle Award and the Pulitzer Prize.

1948   January: escapes to Paris. February: moves on to Naples, Calabria, Sicily, and Rome. Summer: pays his first visit to London, where John Gielgud is preparing a production of *The Glass Menagerie*. August: travels back to New York on the *Queen Mary*. 6 October: *Summer and Smoke* opens in New York. October: Frank Merlo moves in with him. He arranges for Rose to be moved into a private clinic. November: he and Frank leave for Tangier, going on to Fez and Casablanca.

1949   January: they drive along the Riviera to Rome. April: TW goes to London, where *A Streetcar Named Desire* is about to open. September: goes to New York. Winter: rents a cottage in Key West and works on *The Rose Tattoo*.

1950   June: with Frank in Paris. They go on to Rome and to Vienna in July. *The Roman Spring of Mrs. Stone* is published and the film of *The Glass Menagerie* is released. December: *The Rose Tattoo* opens in Chicago and

1951   3 February: in New York. It wins a Tony award. March: his grandfather, mother, and brother come to stay with him in Key West. May: goes with Frank to New York and then London. June: they go to Rome. July: TW goes to Saint Tropez before joining Frank in Venice, where he drafts the story "Three Players of a Summer Game." August: goes with Frank to London. Autumn: goes to Denmark, Germany, Sweden, Spain, France, Holland, and Italy. November: back to New York on the *Queen Elizabeth* to spend Thanksgiving in Key West and Christmas in New Orleans. The film of *A Streetcar Named Desire* is released and

1952   wins the New York Film Critics' Circle Award. January: rewrites *Camino Real*. 24 April: *Summer and Smoke* revived in New York. June–September: in Paris and then Rome with Frank. October: after a week in London they return to New York but leave in November for New Orleans taking

Reverend Dakin with them to Key West for Christmas.

1953   19 March: *Camino Real* opens in New York. Spring: works on *Cat on a Hot Tin Roof*. April: directs *The Starless Air* by Donald Windham in Houston. Returns to New York. June–October: in Rome, Spain, Vienna, Venice, and southern Italy. 27 October: back in New York, where he leases a furnished apartment. December: in New Orleans, where he undergoes surgery.

1954   January: goes with Frank Merlo and grandfather to Key West. Spring: works on *Cat on a Hot Tin Roof*. May: in New York. "An Evening at the 92nd Street Y" with Carson McCullers. June–September: in Rome with Frank Merlo. October: starts filming *The Rose Tattoo* in Key West.

1955   14 February: death of Reverend Dakin. 24 March: *Cat on a Hot Tin Roof* opens in New York, where it runs for 694 performances, winning the Pulitzer Prize, and the Drama Critics' Circle and Donaldson awards. April: to Key West with Carson McCullers, who stays for three weeks. Summer: in Europe without Frank Merlo, moving restlessly from place to place, unable to write. Becomes more dependent on drugs. Autumn: back in New York, he works on screenplay for *Baby Doll*.

1956   January: revival of *Streetcar* in Miami with Tallulah Bankhead. February: the production transfers to New York. 16 April: *Sweet Bird of Youth* premieres in Miami. Spring: relationship with Frank Merlo deteriorating. Summer: in Rome, verging on a nervous breakdown. September: back in New York. Learns that his mother has been committed to a psychiatric ward but leaves for the Virgin Islands before trying to help her.

1957   January: takes his mother to Key West, where he works on *Orpheus Descending*. 21 March: it opens in New York. May: Cornelius dies at seventy-seven. June: Tennessee starts psychoanalysis with Dr. Lawrence Kubie.

1958   7 January: *Garden District* (*Suddenly Last Summer* and *Something Unspoken*) opens off-Broadway and (16 September) in London. 30 January: *Cat on a Hot Tin Roof* opens in London. The film of *Cat on a Hot Tin Roof* is released. Early June: breaks off analysis with Dr. Kubie and leaves for Europe. Autumn: works on *Period of Adjustment*. 29 December: it opens in Miami.

1959   15 January: *The Rose Tattoo* opens in London. 10 March: *Sweet Bird of Youth* opens in New York. April: goes to Cuba, where he meets Ernest Hemingway and Fidel Castro. 14 April: *I Rise in Flame, Cried the Phoenix* opens in New York. May: goes to London for British premiere of *Orpheus Descending*. 2 July: one-act version of *The Night of the Iguana* staged at the Spoleto Festival, directed by Frank Corsaro. August: leaves with Frank for three months of traveling.

1960   January: Corsaro arrives in Key West to work on *The Night of the Iguana* with TW. June: his mother and brother vacation with him in Los Angeles. 10 November: *Period of Adjustment* opens in New York. *Fugitive Kind* (the movie of *Orpheus Descending*) is released.

1961   January: leaves for Europe with Marion Vaccaro. 28 December: *The Night of the Iguana* opens in New York.

1962   April: *The Night of the Iguana* wins the New York Drama Critics' Circle Award. 11 July: *The Milk Train Doesn't Stop Here Anymore* opens at the Spoleto Festival.

1963   16 January: *The Milk Train Doesn't Stop Here Anymore* opens in New York. July: vacation in Nantucket with Frank and Frederick Nicklaus. August: Frank goes into hospital. September: Frank dies. September—October: in Mexico where John Huston is filming *The Night of the Iguana*. Tennessee returns to New York.

1964   1 January: revival of *Milk Train* opens on Broadway, but closes after four performances. March: Nicklaus moves out of Key West house. The film of *The Night of the Iguana* is released.

1965   July: moves with a paid companion, William Glavin, into an apartment on West 72nd Street.

1966   23 February: *Slapstick Tragedy* opens in New York

1967   January: goes to Virgin Islands with Glavin and works on screenplay for *Milk Train*. July: they go to Spain. August: they return to New York. 29 September: Carson McCullers dies. December: goes to London for the world premiere of *The Two-Character Play* at the Hampstead Theatre Club.

1968   February: *Kingdom of Earth* opens in Philadelphia, and 27 March: on Broadway. June: abandons the apartment on West 72nd Street, moving with Glavin into the St. Moritz Hotel on Central Park South.

1969   January: Dakin arrives in Key West and organizes TW's conversion to Catholicism. He is baptized on 10 January. February: in a Miami hospital with flu. After discharging himself he takes an overdose of sleeping pills. 11 May: *In the Bar of a Tokyo Hotel* opens in New York. 21 June: he arrives in Tokyo for a production of *Streetcar*. July: returns to New York but leaves for Key West and then San Francisco. Mid-August: after being asked to leave the San Francisco hotel, returns to New York. September: goes to New Orleans November: Dakin has him committed to the mental ward of a St. Louis hospital. December: back in Key West.

1971   July: revival of *The Two Character Play* under the title *Out Cry* in Chicago, where he quarrels with Audrey Wood.

1972   April: *Small Craft Warnings* opens at the Truck and Warehouse Theatre and transfers to the New Theatre on 6 June. August: juror, Venice Film Festival.

1973   1 March: New York premiere of *Out Cry*. 28 March: leaves with Robert
       Carroll for Yokohama, Hong Kong, and Thailand. May: they go to Italy.
       July: TW spends two weeks in Tangier with Tom Field, where TW works
       on *The Red Devil Battery Sign*.

1974   March: to London for new production of *Streetcar*. May: *The Latter Days of
       a Celebrated Soubrette*, a reworking of *The Gnädiges Fräulein*, opens and
       closes after one off-Broadway performance. June: *Out Cry* produced
       unsuccessfully off-Broadway. July: revival of Cat *on a Hot Tin Roof* in
       Stratford, Connecticut, and in September, on Broadway.

1975   May: *The Glass Menagerie* revived at the Brooks Atkinson Theatre. Spring:
       Edwin Sherin goes to Key West to work with TW on *The Red Devil Battery
       Sign*, which Sherin will direct. June: it opens disastrously in Boston. 16
       September: revival of *Summer and Smoke* in New York. October: revival of
       Sweet Bird of Youth opens in Washington and transfers to Broadway.
       Revival of *The Glass Menagerie* at Circle in the Square. 16 December:
       Summer and Smoke revived at the Circle in the Square.

1976   16 January: *This Is (An Entertainment)* staged by the American
       Conservatory Theatre in San Francisco. May: president of the jury at
       Cannes. October: ejected from a hotel in San Francisco. December:
       initiated as life member of the American Academy of Arts and Letters.

1977   April: *Vieux Carré* staged on Broadway. June: in London for *The Red Devil
       Battery Sign*, which opens at the Roundhouse.

1978   January: *Tiger Tail*, a stage version of *Baby Doll*, tried out unsuccessfully in
       Atlanta. June: *Creve Coeur* staged in Charleston. August: goes to London
       for West End production of *Vieux Carré*. Autumn: leases a new apartment
       at Manhattan Plaza; employs a new secretary, Jay Leo Colt; and transfers to
       a new agent at International Creative Management, Mitch Douglas.

1979   10 January: *Creve Coeur* opens in New York at the Hudson Guild Theatre.
       December: honored at the Kennedy Center by President Carter.

1980   26 March: *Clothes for a Summer Hotel* opens at the Cort Theatre. June:
       Edwina dies at the age of ninety-five. Autumn: accepts an invitation to be
       Distinguished Writer in Residence at the University of British Columbia in
       Vancouver.

1981   24 August: *Something Cloudy, Something Clear* staged at the Bouwerie
       Theatre, New York.

1982   27 April: *A House Not Meant to Stand* opens in Chicago at the Goodman
       Theatre. July: holiday in Taormina.

1983   24 February: dies in New York.

Notes

Abbreviations

Con   *Conversations with Tennessee Williams*
CS   *The Collected Stories of Tennessee Williams*
DW   *Tennessee Williams' Letters to Donald Windham, 1940–1965*
EDW   Edwina Dakin Williams, *Remember Me to Tom*
LF   Donald Windham, *Lost Friendships*
Mem   Tennessee Williams, *Memoirs*
NYT   *New York Times*
Sp   Donald Spoto, *The Kindness of Strangers*
StJ   *Five O'Clock Angel: Letters of Tennessee Williams to Maria St. Just*
WIL   Tennessee Williams, *Where I Live*

Prologue

1 Sexton, "Flee on Your Donkey," *Live or Die* (Boston: 1966), 4.
2 *DW*, 91.
3 Ibid., 249.
4 Ibid., 169.
5 *Mem*, 131.
6 Kenneth Tynan, *Curtains* (London: 1961), 268.
7 *DW*, v–vi.
8 Kazan, *Life*, 494–95.
9 *DW*, vi–vii.

10 Elia Kazan, quoted in Sp, 179.
11 *CS*, xxiii.
12 Letter to Paul Bigelow, 15 July 1940.
13 Gore Vidal, introduction to *CS*, xx.
14 *DW*, v.
15 Kazan, *Life*, 335.
16 Tennessee Williams in *NYT*, 8 March 1959. Reprinted as the foreword to *Sweet Bird of Youth, Collected Theatre*, 4:5.
17 Ibid., 4:7.

18 *Con*, 231.

19 Vidal, "Selected Memories," 138.

20 EDW, 23–24.

21 Note for "The Accent of a Coming Foot" in a manuscript of early writings, *Pieces of My Youth*, reprinted in *CS*, 571.

22 Sp, 44–45.

Chapter 1: Where You Hang Your Hopes

1 Tennessee Williams, "Facts about Me," in *WIL*, 58.

2 Dakin Williams, quoted in Sp, 12.

3 Tennessee Williams, quoted in EDW, 26.

4 *Mem*, 12.

5 EDW, 25.

6 Tennessee Williams, quoted in EDW, 26.

7 Tennessee Williams, quoted in "The Life and Ideas of Tennessee Williams," *PM*, 6 May 1945.

8 Tennessee Williams, quoted in EDW, 26.

9 *Con*, 87, 327.

10 *Mem*, 11.

11 Tennessee Williams, quoted in EDW, 19.

12 EDW, 15, 21.

13 Ibid., 23–24.

14 *Con*, 17.

15 *Mem*, 11–12.

16 EDW, 24.

17 Ibid., 29.

18 Tennessee Williams, quoted in EDW, 30.

19 Dakin Williams, quoted in Sp, 17.

20 Sp, 17.

21 Tennessee Williams, "Grand," in *CS*.

22 Letter to Lucy Freeman, September 1962.

23 Tennessee Williams, "The Rainbow." Manuscript with drawings. Butler Library at Columbia University.

24 Sp, 19.

25 Tennessee Williams in *NYT*, 8 March 1959. Reprinted as foreword to *Sweet Bird of Youth, Collected Theatre*, 4:3.

26 *Mem*, 17.

27 Williams in *NYT*, 8 March 1959, *Collected Theatre*, 4:3.

28 Ibid., 4:4.

29 Sp, 23.

30 *Mem*, 16.

31 Ibid., 15.

32 *Con*, 230.

33 *Mem*, 18.

34 Dakin Williams, quoted in Sp, 18–19.

35 *Mem*, 19–20.

36 Ibid., 20.

37 Ibid., 21–23.

38 Sp, 30.

Chapter 2: Columbia and Washington

1 *Mem*, 24–25.

2 Letter to Walter Dakin, 29 November.

3 *Mem*, 25–26.

4 The *Missourian*, 12 April 1930.

5 *Mem*, 28.

6 *Mem*, 120.

7 Ibid., 29.

8 *Con*, 231.

9 *Mem*, 31–33; Elmer Lower, quoted in Sp, 35–37.

10 Sp, 35–37.

11 *Con*, 257.

12 Tennessee Williams, quoted in Gilbert Maxwell, *Williams and Friends*, 24.

13 Sp, 36–37.

14 EDW, 62.

15 *Mem*, 36; EDW, 63; Sp, 41.

16 *Con*, 114.

17 EDW, 68.

18 Dakin Williams, in Williams and Mead, *Tennessee Williams*, 63.

19 EDW, 64–65.

20 *Con*, 10.

21 Sp, 20.

22 Dakin Williams, quoted in Sp, 43.

23 Letter to Dakin Williams, 25 June 1935.

24 EDW, 72.

Chapter 3: Student Playwright

1 William Jay Smith, *Army Brat* (New York: 1982), 190.

2 *Mem*, 122.

3 Smith, in *New York Post*, 25 April 1958.

4 Smith, *Army Brat*, 193.

5 Letter to his grandparents, 6 August 1936, quoted in EDW, 83.

6 *St. Louis News-Times*, 19 October 1936.

7 Tennessee Williams, "Something Wild . . . ," in *WIL*, 9–10.

8 Willard Holland, quoted in Sp, 56.

9 Williams, "Something Wild," 12.

10 *Mem*, 125; EDW, 85.

11 E. C. Mabie, quoted in Tennessee Williams, "The Past, the Present, and the Perhaps." Article in *NYT* reprinted as foreword to *Orpheus Descending, Collected Theatre*, 3:221.

12 EDW, 97.

13 *St. Louis Star-Times*, 1 December 1937.

14 *Mem*, 42–43.

15 Ibid., 43.

16 Ibid., 45–46.

17 *Con*, 229–31 (quote, 231).

18 *Mem*, 49.

19 *Con*, 327.

20 EDW, 85.

21 Williams and Mead, *Tennessee Williams*, 64; Sp, 278–79; EDW, 85.

22 *Con*, 327; EDW, 84.

23 EDW, 86.

24 *Con*, 162.

25 EDW, 84.

26 Ibid., 89–90.

27 Ibid., 92.

28 *LF*, 223.

29 *Mem*, 48; EDW, 98.

Chapter 4: Exit Tom, Enter Tennessee

1 Tennessee Williams, interview with Eric Paulsen, quoted in Holditch, *Last Frontier*.

2 Tennessee Williams, interview with Dick Cavett, 1974, quoted in Holditch, *Last Frontier*.

3 Ibid.

4 Tennessee Williams, "In Memory of an Aristocrat" and "The Angel in the Alcove" both in *CS*.

5 EDW, 102.

6 Letter to Walter Dakin, n.d.; EDW, 101–02.

7 *Con*, 231.

8 Tennessee Williams, quoted in Tischler, *Rebellious Puritan*, 61.

9 Tischler, *Rebellious Puritan*, 62; *LF*, 172.

10 *StJ*, 240; letter to Anne Bretzfelder and "B. J.," n.d.

11 *StJ*, 240.

12 Letter to Audrey Wood, n.d.

13 Letter to Audrey Wood, 5 May 1939.

14 Letter to Audrey Wood, 30 July 1939.

15 Letters to Audrey Wood, 29 and 16 July 1939.

16 *StJ*, 241.

17 Ibid., 242.

18 Letter to Walter Dakin, 2 October 1939.

19 Smith, *Army Brat*, 91.

20 Letter to Audrey Wood, 11 November 1939; letter to Audrey Wood, n.d.

21 Letters to Audrey Wood, 30 November and December 1939.

22 Letter to Walter Dakin, 19 January 1940.

23 EDW, 110.

24 *Con*, 261.

25 *LF*, 173.

26 Ibid., 172.

27 Letter to Anne Bretzfelder, 7 March 1940.

28 *DW*, 3; Windham, *Footnote to a Friendship* (Verona: 1983), 110.

29 *LF*, 172.

30 Ibid., 178.

31 *DW*, 13.

32 Ibid., 6.

33 Fragment of a letter dated 8 July 1940; *DW*, 9–11.

34 *LF*, 180, 222–23.

Chapter 5: You Old Bitch!

1 Letter to Joe Hazan, 3 September 1940; *DW*, 17.

2 *DW*, 13.

3 *Mem*, 58–59.

4 Ibid.; *DW*, 15.

5 Margaret Webster, *Don't Put Your Daughter on the Stage* (New York: 1972), 69.

6 EDW, 119; letter to Paul Bigelow, 18 December 1941.

7 *LF*, 181.

8 EDW, 122.

9 Alexander Williams, review of *Battle of Angels*, *Boston Herald*, 30 December 1940; Elliot Norton, review of *Battle of Angels*, *Boston Post*, 30 December 1940.

10 William Jay Smith, quoted in *Dictionary of Literary Biography. Documentary Series* (Detroit: 1984).

11 *DW*, 110.

12 Fritz Bultman, quoted in Sp, 88.

13 Postcard to Audrey Wood, 8 February 1941.

14 *Con*, 232.

15 Letter to Jo Healy, n.d.

16 *Mem*, 64.

17 *DW*, 20.

18 Letters to Audrey Wood, 27 February and 10 March 1941.

19 Letter to Audrey Wood, mid-March 1941.

20 Letters to Audrey Wood, 11 and 18 April 1941 and undated.

21 Letter to Paul Bigelow, 28 July 1941.

22 Letter to Audrey Wood, 27 October 1941; Holditch, *Last Frontier*, 14–15.

23 Letter to Paul Bigelow, 18 December 1941.

24 Letter to Audrey Wood, 25 September 1941.

25 Letter to Paul Bigelow, 25 September 1941.

26 Letter to Audrey Wood, 3 November 1941; letter to Paul Bigelow, November 1941.

27 *Mem*, 71.

28 *LF*, 182; telephone conversation with Jean Bultman, 1 November 1991; *StJ*, 236.

29 *StJ*, 237; *LF*, 182–83.

30 *StJ*, 237; letter to Mary Hunter, 1 August 1942.

31 Letter to Paul Bigelow, 31 August 1942; letter to Audrey Wood, received 4 September 1942.

32 Letter to Andrew Lyndon, 1943.

33 *DW*, 55.

34 Letter to Audrey Wood, received 30 July 1942.

35 *DW*, 56.

36 Ibid., 59, 61, 58.

Chapter 6: Hollywood Worm

1 Letter to Audrey Wood, received 23 May 1943.

2 *Mem*, 76.

3 Letters to Audrey Wood, received 23 May and 2 June 1943.

4 Letter to Paul Bigelow, 23 May 1943.

5 *DW*, 63.

6 Ibid., 105.

7 Letter to Paul Bigelow, 23 May 1943.

8 *DW*, 66; letter to Audrey Wood, received 15 June 1943.

9 Christopher Isherwood, *My Guru and His Disciple* (New York: 1980), 135–36.

10 *Mem*, 78; Christopher Isherwood, quoted in Sp, 98.

11 *DW*, 71.

12 *Mem*, 78

13 Ibid.

14 *DW*, 85.

15 Letters to Audrey Wood, 21 October, 2 August, and July 1943.

16 *DW*, 84, 100.

17 Ibid., 101.

18 Ibid., 112–13.

19 Ibid., 118–19.

20 Ibid., 126.

21 *CS*, x.

22 *DW*, 126, 128.

23 Ibid., 130–31.

24 *LF*, 223.

25 *DW*, 148.

26 EDW, 145.

27 *Mem*, 82.

28 EDW, 146; *DW*, 160; *Mem*, 82 (quote).

29 *DW*, 156.

30 *Mem*, 81; Tennessee Williams, quoted in Marguerite Courtney, *Laurette* (New York: 1955), 396.

31 *LF*, 176.

32 EDW, 148–49.

33 *DW*, 159–60.

34 *Con*, 330.

35 Letter to Audrey Wood, 23 March 1945.

36 *DW*, 157.

37 Randolph Echols, quoted in Sp, 114.

38 Quoted in EDW, 151–52.

39 Arthur Miller in *TV Guide*, 3 March 1984.

40 Tennessee Williams, "On a Streetcar Named Success," *WIL*, 16–17.

Chapter 7: Desire and Cemeteries

1 Mike Steen, *A Look at Tennessee Williams*, 151.

2 Tennessee Williams, "On a Streetcar Named Success," *WIL*, 18.

3 *LF*, 228.

4 Williams, "Streetcar Named Success, 18.

5 *LF*, 230.

6 Sp, 118.

7 *DW*, 178.

8 Letter to Audrey Wood, 15 January 1946.

9 *Mem*, 99.

10 Ibid.

11 Sp, 122–24.

12 *Mem*, 100–101.

13 Letter to Audrey Wood, 15 January 1946.

14 *Mem*, 106.

15 Ibid., 106–07.

16 Sp, 128.

17 *Mem*, 109.

18 *Con*, 228.

19 Ibid.

20 *Mem*, 109.

21 Ibid.

22 Tennessee Williams, press release from Liebling-Wood agency, 1947, quoted in Sp, 129.

23 *DW*, 306.

24 Elia Kazan, quoted in Sp, 140.

25 *Con*, 43.

26 Tennessee Williams, quoted in Gilbert Maxwell, *Williams and Friends*, 132.

27 *Mem*, 111.

28 Elia Kazan, "Notebook for *A Streetcar Named Desire*," in Toby Cole and Helen Krich Chinoy, eds., *Directing the Play: A Sourcebook of Stagecraft* (London: n.d.), 307.

29 Elia Kazan, quoted in Michel Ciment, *Kazan on Kazan* (London: 1973), 71.

30 *Mem*, 132–33.

31 Ibid., 133–34.

32 Kazan, *Life*, 341–42.

33 *Con*, 337.

34 *Mem*, 131–32.

35 Elia Kazan, quoted in Sp, 136.

36 *Mem*, 137.

Chapter 8: Roman Spring

1 *DW*, 201–02.

2 Ibid., 206.

3 Letter to Cheryl Crawford, 14 July 1950.

4 Letter to Jo Healy, n.d.

5 *DW*, 207–08.

6 *Mem*, 141.

7 Letter to Oliver Evans, 31 January 1948.

8 *DW*, 216.

9 Harold Acton, *Memoirs of an Aesthete* (New York: 1970), 2:213.

10 Gore Vidal, *Matters of Fact and Fiction* (New York: 1978), 132.

11 Letter to Audrey Wood, received 16 June 1948.

12 *DW*, 220–21.

13 Letter to Audrey Wood, received 16 June 1948.

14 *DW*, 223.

15 *StJ*, 5.

16 Ibid., 4.

17 *Mem*, 150.

18 *DW*, 225.

19 Brooks Atkinson, review of *Summer and Smoke*, *NYT*, 7 October 1948; John Gassner, review of *Summer and Smoke*, *Forum* 110 (December 1948).

20 *DW*, 225, 226.

21 Letter to Brooks Atkinson, n.d.

22 Christopher Isherwood, quoted in Sp, 153.

23 *StJ*, 16, 19, 16.

24 Letter to Paul Bigelow, 1 July 1948.

25 Letter to Audrey Wood, 5 December 1948.

26 *Mem*, 161.

27 *DW*, 234, 235–37.

28 Ibid., 241.

29 Bernard Braden, conversation with the author, 3 December 1991.

30 *StJ*, 26.

31 *Con*, 159.

32 *StJ*, 30.

33 *LF*, 248.

34 Draft of unpublished article, Austin, Texas.

35 Letter to Elia Kazan, n.d.

36 Tennessee Williams, "The Meaning of *The Rose Tattoo*," *WIL*, 56.

37 Ibid.

38 *Mem*, 161.

39 Letter to Cheryl Crawford and Audrey Wood, 16 August 1950.

40 Donald Windham, *Footnote to a Friendship*, 59–60.

41 *LF*, 63.

42 Sp, 172–73.

43 *StJ*, 43–44.

44 Ibid., 44.

45 Letter to Oliver Evans, 8 May 1952.

46 *StJ*, 68.

Chapter 9: Terminal Stretch

1 Tennessee Williams, "Foreword to *Camino Real*," *WIL*, 64, 65.

2 Letter to Cheryl Crawford, February 1952.

3 *Con*, 67.

4 José Quintero, "The Imprint He Left," *Performing Arts*, August 1983.

5 *Mem*, 201.

6 *StJ*, 57.

7 Williams, "Foreword to *Camino Real*," *WIL*, 63.

8 Kazan, *Life*, 496–97.

9 Kazan, reported in *StJ*, 71; Kazan, *Life*, 494.

10 Letter to Peter Glenville, n.d.

11 Kazan, *Life*, 498.

12 Walter Kerr, review of *Camino Real*, *NYT*, 20 March 1953.

13 Quintero, "The Imprint He Left."

14 *LF*, 248–49.

15 Ibid., 249–50.

16 Ibid., 250–51.

17 Letter to Oliver Evans, 7 October 1953.

18 Letter to Oliver Evans, November 1953.

19 *StJ*, 103, 102, 107.

20 Ibid., 110.

21 *Con*, 46.

22 *StJ*, 95.

23 Ibid., 97.

24 Tennessee Williams, "Note of Explanation," *Cat on a Hot Tin Roof*, *Collected Theatre*, 3:167–68.

25 Brooks Atkinson, review of *Cat on a Hot Tin Roof*, *NYT*, 25 March 1955; Walter Kerr, review of *Cat on a Hot Tin Roof*, *New York Herald-Tribune*, 25 March 1955.

26 *StJ*, 113.

27 *Mem*, 169; Sp, 201.

28 *Mem*, 171.

29 *StJ*, 121.

30 Kazan, *A Life*, 562; Tennessee Williams, quoted in Ciment, *Kazan on Kazan*, 75.

31 Williams, "T. Williams's View of T. Bankhead," *WIL*, 152, 153.

32 *StJ*, 131.

33 Ibid.

Chapter 10: Relentless Caper

1 *NYT*, 17 April 1956.

2 *Time*, 5 October 1983.

3 *Con*, 159.

4 *StJ*, 133.

5 Letter to Kazan, 29 December 1968.

6 Sp, 205.

7 Letter to Cheryl Crawford, 3 August 1956.

8 *StJ*, 138.

9 Francis Cardinal Spellman, quoted in Sp, 210.

10 *DW*, 292.

11 *StJ*, 139–41.

12 Tennessee Williams, "The Past, The Present and the Perhaps." Article in *NYT* reprinted as foreword to *Orpheus Descending, Complete Theatre*, 3:220.

13 *StJ*, 141.

14 Brooks Atkinson, review of *Orpheus Descending*, *NYT*, 22 March 1957.

15 Wolcott Gibbs, review of *Orpheus Descending*, *New Yorker*, 30 March 1957.

16 Tennessee Williams in *New York Herald-Tribune*, May 1957.

17 Tennessee Williams in *New York Post*, 4 May 1957.

18 Sp, 215.

19 *StJ*, 147.

20 *Con*, 169 and 245, and *StJ*, 149.

21 Letter to Paul Bowles, n.d.

22 *StJ*, 144; letter to Oliver Evans, November 1958.

Chapter 11: A Bit of Shared Luck

1 *Con*, 50.

2 Ibid., 260.

3 *DW*, 215.

4 Edwina Dakin Williams, quoted by Anne Meacham in Sp, 220.

5 *StJ*, 151.

6 Wolcott Gibbs, review of *Suddenly Last Summer*, *New Yorker*, 18 January 1958; review of *Suddenly Last Summer*, *Time*, 20 January 1958; Brooks Atkinson, review of *Suddenly Last Summer*, *NYT*, 9 January 1958.

7 Letter to Oliver Evans, n.d.

8 *StJ*, 151–52.

9 *LF*, 68.

10 Letter to Kazan, 29 December 1958; Barbara Baxley, quoted in Sp, 229.

11 Kazan, *Life*, 545.

12 John Chapman, review of *Sweet Bird of Youth*, *New York Daily News*, 11 March 1959; Kenneth Tynan, review of *Sweet Bird of Youth*, *New Yorker*, reprinted in *Curtains*, 306; Henry Popkin, review of *Sweet Bird of Youth*, *Tulane Drama Review* (March 1960); Brooks Atkinson, review of *Sweet Bird of Youth*, *NYT*, 11 March 1959.

13 Kenneth Tynan, *Right and Left* (London: 1967), 333–36.

14 Ibid.

15 *Con*, 86.
16 Ibid., 83.

Chapter 12: Betrayal and Bereavement

1 *StJ*, 161–62.
2 *Mem*, 177.
3 *New York World Telegram and Sun*, 11 March 1959.
4 Frank Corsaro, quoted in Sp, 240; Tennessee Williams, quoted in ibid.
5 Tennessee Williams in *Esquire*, December 1962.
6 *Con*, 101.
7 *Mem*, 181–82.
8 *Con*, 109.
9 Robert Brustein, review of *The Night of the Iguana*, *New Republic*, 22 January 1962; review of *The Night of the Iguana*, *Time*, 5 January 1962.
10 *StJ*, 180.
11 Letters to Andreas Brown, 19 and 25 February 1962.
12 Tennessee Williams, "Author's Notes," *The Milk Train Doesn't Stop Here Anymore*, Collected Theatre, 5:3.
13 *Mem*, 184–89.
14 Letter to Andreas Brown, 2 July, 1962.
15 *Mem*, 195–97.
16 Jack Dunphy, quoted in Gerald Clarke, *Capote: A Biography* (London: 1988), 247.
17 Sp, 257.
18 John Huston, *An Open Book* (New York: 1980), 308.
19 Dotson Rader, speaking at the Tennessee Williams Festival, New Orleans, 1993; Sp, 258–59.
20 Letter to Paul Bowles, 18 September 1964.

Chapter 13: The Stoned Age

1 *Con*, 235, 343.
2 John Huston, *Open Book*, 309.
3 Ibid., 310–11.
4 *StJ*, 187; *Con*, 303.
5 Kenneth Holditch, conversation with the author.
6 Letter to Oliver Evans, 27 April 1966.
7 *Con*, 108; *DW*, 316.
8 Maureen Stapleton, quoted in Sp, 264.
9 *Con*, 120.
10 Tennessee Williams, quoted in Sp, 265.
11 Whitney Boulton, review of *Slapstick Tragedy*, *New York Morning Telegraph*, 24 February 1966.
12 Harold Clurman, review of *Slapstick Tragedy*, *The Nation*, 14 March 1966.
13 *Con*, 128.
14 Dotson Rader, speaking at the Tennessee Williams Festival, New Orleans, 1993.
15 Herbert Kretzmer, review of *The Two-Character Play*, *London Daily Express*, 13 December 1967.
16 Joseph Losey, quoted in Sp, 270.
17 Audrey Wood, *Represented by Audrey Wood* (New York: 1981), 192.
18 José Quintero, *If You Don't Dance They Beat You* (Boston: 1974), 4.
19 *NYT*, 29 June 1968.
20 *StJ*, 196.
21 Sp, 277.
22 Ibid., 278.
23 Clive Barnes, review of *In the Bar of a Tokyo Hotel*, *NYT*, 12 May 1969.
24 Sp, 284–85.

Chapter 14: Everyone Else Is an Audience

1 Truman Capote, *Answered Prayers*
  (London: 1988), 59–65.
2 Vidal, *Matters of Fact and Fiction*,
  134–35.
3 Tennessee Williams to David
  Gregory, quoted in Sp, 292.
4 *Con*, 140–41.
5 *StJ*, 200–202.
6 Ibid., 200.
7 Ibid., 208.
8 Ibid., 213, 216 (quote), 221, 222
  (quote).
9 Ibid., 234.
10 Ibid., 231.
11 Wood, *Represented By*, 200.
12 *Con*, 239.
13 William Leonard, review of *Out Cry*,
  Chicago Tribune, 9 July 1971.
14 *StJ*, 245.
15 Ray Stricklin, "Memories of
  Tennessee," *Drama-Logue*, 9–15
  June 1983.
16 *StJ*, 251–55.
17 Notes for published script of
  London edition of *Small Craft
  Warnings*.
18 *Con*, 228.
19 Letter to Marco De Maria, William
  Orton, and Robert Currie, 27 April
  1972, reprinted in London edition of
  Small Craft Warnings.
20 Letter to Bill Barnes, 17 October
  1971, reprinted in London edition of
  Small Craft Warnings.
21 Clive Barnes, review of *Small Craft
  Warnings*, *NYT*, 7 June 1972.
22 *StJ*, 263.
23 Ibid., 270.

24 *Con*, 227.
25 Paul Morrissey, quoted in Sp, 303.
26 *Con*, 232.
27 *StJ*, 292.
28 Ibid., 270.
29 *Mem*, xviii.
30 *LF*, 109–10.
31 *StJ*, 264.
32 Michael York, "Tennessee Williams
  in Rehearsal," in Sheridan Morley,
  ed., *Theatre 73* (London: 1973).
33 Clive Barnes, review of *Out Cry*,
  NYT, 2 March 1973.
34 *StJ*, 286–88.
35 Ibid., 288.
36 Ibid., 291.
37 Ibid., 290–98.
38 Ibid., 298.
39 Sp, 309; *StJ*, 299.
40 *StJ*, 306.
41 Ibid., 309.
42 Ibid., 310.
43 Ibid., 317–18.
44 Ibid., 323.
45 Edwin Sherin, quoted in Sp, 310.
46 *StJ*, 326.
47 *Boston Globe*, 18 June 1976.
48 Kevin Kelly, review of *The Red Devil
  Battery Sign*, *Boston Globe*, 19 June
  1975.
49 *StJ*, 327–28.
50 Ibid., 331.
51 Ibid., 332.
52 Ibid., 335.
53 Ruby Cohn in *Educational Theatre
  Journal* (October 1976).

Chapter 15: Quarrelsome Lover

1 Tennessee Williams in *Interview*, June 1976.

2 *StJ*, 342–46.

3 Ibid., 351–52.

4 Sp, 318.

5 *StJ*, 353.

6 Sylvia Sidney, quoted in Sp, 324.

7 *StJ*, 357–58.

8 Gene Persson, quoted in Sp, 320; *StJ*, 360.

9 *StJ*, 359.

10 Ibid., 360–68.

11 Ibid., 367.

12 Ibid., 376.

13 Tennessee Williams, quoted in David Galligan, "Director José Quintero: Recollections of a Friendship," *The Advocate*, 15 September 1983.

14 Tennessee Williams, quoted in Sp, 346.

15 *StJ*, 379–85.

16 Ibid., 381–82.

17 Ibid.

18 Williams and Mead, *Tennessee Williams*, 332.

19 Richard Christiansen, review of *A House Not Meant to Stand*, *Chicago Tribune*, 28 April 1982.

20 Eve Adamson, quoted in Sp, 355.

21 Michael Feingold, review of *Something Cloudy, Something Clear*, *Village Voice*, 16 September 1981.

22 Tennessee Williams, quoted in Sp, 356.

23 *StJ*, 392.

24 Jane Smith, conversation with the author, 12 November 1991.

25 Geordie Grieg, "Death at the Easy Lay: was it a literary murder?" *Sunday Times*, 24 July 1993.

Select Bibliography

Works by Tennessee Williams

Androgyne, Mon Amour: Selected Poems. New York: 1977.

Baby Doll and *Tiger Tail*. New York: 1991.

Collected Stories. Introduction by Gore Vidal. New York: 1985.

Conversations with Tennessee Williams, edited by Albert J. Devlin. Jackson, Miss.: 1986.

Five O'Clock Angel: Letters of Tennessee Williams to Maria St. Just, 1948 – 1982, with a commentary by Maria St. Just. New York: 1990.

In the Winter of Cities: Poems. New York: New Directions, 1964.

Memoirs. Garden City, N. Y.: 1975.

Moise and the World of Reason. New York: 1975.

Out Cry. New York: 1969.

The Roman Spring of Mrs. Stone. New York: 1950.

Small Craft Warnings. London: 1973.

Stopped Rocking and Other Screenplays. Introduction by Richard Gilman. New York: 1984.

Tennessee Williams' Letters to Donald Windham 1940 – 1965, edited by Donald Windham. New York: 1977.

The Theatre of Tennessee Williams. New York: 1971 – 92.
 vol 1: *Battle of Angels; The Glass Menagerie; A Streetcar Named Desire*
 vol 2: *The Eccentricities of a Nightingale; Summer and Smoke; The Rose Tattoo; Camino Real*
 vol 3: *Cat on a Hot Tin Roof; Orpheus Descending; Suddenly Last Summer*

262

vol 4: *Sweet Bird of Youth; Period of Adjustment; The Night of the Iguana*

vol 5:*The Milk Train Doesn't Stop Here Anymore; Kingdom of Earth (The Seven Descents of Myrtle); Small Craft Warnings; The Two Character Play*

vol 6: *This Property Is Condemned; The Purification; The Last of the Solid Gold Watches; Auto-da-Fe; The Strangest Kind of Romance; 27 Wagons Full of Cotton; The Lady of Larkspur Lotion; Hello from Bertha; Portrait of a Madonna; Lord Byron's Love Letter; The Long Goodbye; Talk to Me Like the Rain and Let Me Listen; Something Unspoken*

vol 7: *In the Bar of a Tokyo Hotel; I Rise in Flame, Cried the Phoenix; The Mutilated; I Can't Imagine Tomorrow; Confessional; The Frosted Glass Coffin; The Gnädiges Fräulein; A Perfect Analysis Given by a Parrot; Lifeboat Drill; Now the Cats with Jewelled Claws; This Is the Peaceable Kingdom, or Good Luck God*

vol 8: *Vieux Carré; A Lovely Sunday for Creve Coeur; Clothes for a Summer Hotel; The Red Devil Battery Sign*

Where I Live: Selected Essays, edited by Christine R. Day and Bob Woods. New York: 1978.

You Touched Me! A Romantic Comedy in Three Acts (with Donald Windham). London: 1947.

About Tennessee Williams

Arnott, Catherine M. *File on Tennessee Williams*. London and New York: 1985.

Bigsby, C. W. E. *A Critical Introduction to Twentieth-Century American Drama*. Vol 2: *Williams/Miller/Albee*. Cambridge: 1984.

Boxill, Roger. *Tennessee Williams*. London: 1987.

Holditch, W. Kenneth. *The Last Frontier of Bohemia: Tennessee Williams in New Orleans*. Privately reprinted from *The Southern Quarterly*.

Kazan, Elia. *A Life*. New York: 1988.

Leavitt, Richard F. *The World of Tennessee Williams*. New York and London: 1978.

Maxwell, Gilbert. *Tennessee Williams and Friends: An Informal Biography*. Cleveland, Ohio: 1965.

Nelson, Benjamin. *Tennessee Williams: His Life and Work*. London: 1961.

Spoto, Donald. *The Kindness of Strangers: The Life of Tennessee Williams*. Boston: 1985.

Steen, Mike. *A Look at Tennessee Williams*. New York: 1969.

Tharpe, Jac, ed. *Tennessee Williams: A Tribute*. Jackson, Miss.: 1977.

Tischler, Nancy M. *Tennessee Williams: Rebellious Puritan*. New York: 1961.

Vidal, Gore. "Selected Memories of the Glorious Bird and an Earlier Self," in *Matters of Fact and Fiction*. New York: 1978.

Williams, Dakin, and Shepherd Mead. *Tennessee Williams: An Intimate Biography*. New York: 1983.

Williams, Edwina Dakin (with Lucy Freeman). *Remember Me to Tom*. New York: 1963.

Windham, Donald. *Lost Friendships: A Memoir of Truman Capote, Tennessee Williams, and Others*. New York: 1987.

Wood, Audrey (with Max Wilk). *Represented by Audrey Wood*. New York: 1981.

Index

Index